The Ambassadors

ALSO BY JONATHAN WRIGHT

God's Soldiers

Jonathan Wright

THE AMBASSADORS

From Ancient Greece to Renaissance Europe,
the Men Who Introduced the World to Itself

HARCOURT, INC.

Orlando   Austin   New York   San Diego   Toronto   London

Requests for permission to make copies of any part of the work
should be submitted online at www.harcourt.com/contact or
mailed to the following address: Permissions Department, Harcourt, Inc.,
6277 Sea Harbor Drive, Orlando, Florida 32887-6777.

www.HarcourtBooks.com

First published in the UK by Harper Press.

Library of Congress Cataloging-in-Publication Data
Wright, Jonathan, 1969–
The ambassadors: from ancient Greece to Renaissance Europe,
the men who introduced the world to itself/Jonathan Wright.—1st ed.
p. cm.
I. Ambassadors—History—To 1500.   2. Ambassadors—History—16th century.
I. Title.
JZ1418.W75   2006
327.209—dc22   2005033185
ISBN-13: 978-0-15-101111-7   ISBN-10: 0-15-101111-7

Text set in Centaur MT
Designed by Lauren Rille

Printed in the United States of America

First U.S. edition
K J I H G F E D C B A

In memory of my father,

William Noel Wright

CONTENTS

The Middle Centuries

Medieval

Renaissance

INTRODUCTION

IRKSOME AS THEY WERE, the misadventures of Iosip Grigor'ye-vich Nepea did not really bear comparison with the very worst moments in the chaotic history of diplomacy. Nepea, the ambassador of Tsar Ivan IV to the English court of Mary Tudor, was not slain by an Iroquois hatchet (which is what happened to a French envoy in North America in 1646); nor was his cap nailed to his head (the fate of Turkish ambassadors to Vlad the Impaler in the fifteenth century). Nonetheless, his sea voyage from Russia in 1556 was riddled with bad fortune.

"Contrary winds and extreme tempests of weather" separated the ships in his convoy soon after their departure from the port of St. Nicholas. One crashed into rocks off the Scandinavian coast, while another was forced to put ashore and winter in Norway. His own ship drifted ever northward, and on November 7, 1556, it was smashed to pieces at Pitsligo Bay in Aberdeenshire. The ambassador survived but he was given a boorish reception by the local Scottish inhabitants. His entire cargo "was by the rude and ravenous people of the country thereunto adjoining, rifled [and] spoiled." When news of the disaster reached the English court, two men, Lawrence Hussie and George Gilpin, were charged with locating the ambassador and escorting him to London.

They found Nepea in Edinburgh on December the 20th and immediately arranged for heralds to be sent to the site of the shipwreck. It was hoped that they might persuade the locals to return the plundered goods, but they met with little success. A great deal of wax was turned in, but there was no trace of the falcon, the jewels, or the "twenty entire sables, exceeding beautiful, with teeth, ears and claws" which Nepea had intended to present to the queen.

The ambassador travelled south, and late in February 1557 he approached the English capital. Finally, after months of hardship, a moment of pageantry more befitting his ambassadorial rank was in prospect. A London draper, John Dimmock, witnessed the spectacle of Nepea's entry into the city. Twelve miles outside the city walls, Dimmock remembered, the ambassador was greeted by eighty eminent merchants, all sporting gold chains. With their liveried servants in tow, they escorted Nepea to a house four miles farther down the London road and showered him with gifts of gold, velvet, and silk.

The next morning, after taking in a local fox hunt, he was led into town. He was greeted by Viscount Montague, "diverse lusty knights, esquires, gentlemen and yeomen," and another delegation of merchants who presented him with a "footcloth of Orient crimson velvet, enriched with gold laces." They proffered a horse, which Nepea duly mounted and rode to Smithfield, where he was received by the mayor and his aldermen, all dressed in scarlet. With "people running plentifully on all sides," they rode together toward the ambassador's well-appointed lodgings in Fenchurch Street.

There were many visitors to these "richly hanged and decked" rooms over the next three months. Bishops and government ministers called for "secret talks and conferences," and London society was regularly to be seen "feasting and banqueting him right friendly." Nepea was shown "the most notable and commendable sights" in the capital, from St. Paul's, to the Guildhall, to the Tower of London, and on March 25th was finally granted an audience with Queen Mary and her husband, Philip II of Spain, at Westminster. After meeting with the lord chancellor and the lord privy seal, Nepea presented their majesties with the few sables he had managed to salvage from the shipwreck, and, through English and Spanish translators, conveyed greetings from his master, Ivan IV.

After enjoying a "notable supper garnished with music" arranged by the city's merchants on April 28th, Nepea began to prepare for his homeward journey. On May 3rd, "after many embracements and diverse farewells, not without expressing of tears," he set sail aboard the *Primrose Admiral,* headed for Gravesend. He carried with him "certain letters tenderly conceived" from the king and queen, and a fine haul of gifts: for himself, a gold chain and some gilt flagons; for the tsar, scarlet, violet, and azure cloth, and a male and female lion. Of inestimably greater value were the tales he took home and the impression he left behind.[1]

Throughout history, ambassadors would be in the vanguard of cultural discovery, and Nepea's visit to London was a defining moment in England's relationship with Russia. He was an extraordinarily unusual visitor, and it is unlikely that many, if any, of the people who lined the streets of London on that day in February 1557 had so much as seen a Russian before. There had been a time when the kingdom of Rus, centered on the old capital of Kiev, had enjoyed thriving cultural, economic, and dynastic links with Europe. However, with the Mongol invasions of the thirteenth century (a catastrophe to which we will return), sustained, meaningful contact between Russia and the West had been all but lost.

Then, in 1480, Tsar Ivan III pronounced Muscovy's independence from its now much-weakened Mongol overlords, secured a prestigious marriage to the daughter of the Byzantine emperor, and set about expanding his kingdom's territories. Novgorod was taken in 1478, Pskov in 1510, and the city of Smolensk was seized from Lithuania four years later. From the end of the fifteenth century Russian envoys began appearing regularly in Europe, and Italian architects travelled east to ply their trade, but England was slow to emulate such encounters.

Finally, in the early 1550s, the English adventurers Hugh Willoughby and Richard Chancellor began the search for a northwest land route, via Russia, to the riches of Asia. With an eye to seeking out new markets for English cloth, a group of aristocrats and merchants funded an expedition in 1553, with Chancellor serving as the voyage's pilot general. His ship was separated from the rest of the convoy and arrived at the Baltic port of St. Nicholas towards the end of August. He travelled south and after a few weeks reached the tsar's court in Moscow. Ivan was asked if he would allow Englishmen to "go and come . . . to frequent free marts with all sorts of merchandise, and upon the same to have wares for their return." The tsar agreed, and in 1555, after Chancellor's return to England, Queen Mary granted a royal charter to the Muscovy Company.[2]

That May, Chancellor once more embarked for Moscow, carrying letters of trading privilege for the tsar's signature. His companion on his homeward journey was none other than Iosip Nepea. When the ambassador's ship crashed into the rocks in Pitsligo Bay, Chancellor perished trying to save the lives of Nepea and his entourage. Consolidating economic ties was the very purpose of Nepea's embassy to London. But there was far more to be gained, cultivated, and experienced from the exertions of ambassadors than commercial aggrandizement. They would also furnish that most precious of ambassadorial commodities: observations and descriptions of places that few, if any, of their countrymen were ever likely to visit.

Over the course of millennia, from the cuneiform civilizations of the ancient Near East to the empires of the modern era, it has been the ambassadors who have allowed the world to meet itself. They would embark on missions of faith and trade, of politics and love, but wherever they journeyed they would as likely as not report back on everything—the moralities and the myths, the plants and the animals, the fashions and the foods—they encountered.

In the two hundred years after Nepea's embassy, dozens of ambassadors would shuttle back and forth between the two countries. One of them, Giles Fletcher, began his embassy to Moscow in 1588. His "cosmographical description" of the country was unsurpassed in its breadth and detail for almost two centuries. Fletcher painstakingly catalogued the humdrum—"the length and breadth of the country...the names of the shires," the rivers and lakes. He noted the times when different plants were sown, offered a digest of Russian history, itemized the country's chief exports (furs, tallow, honey, iron, and salt), and commented on Russian costume and diet (a penchant for apples, peas, cherries, and cucumbers). It is difficult for us to appreciate just how revelatory the accurate reporting of such basic information was to Tudor England.

Fletcher, like so many future visitors, was perhaps most taken by Russia's changeable climate. In winter, he recounted, people were wary of holding a pewter dish lest their fingers freeze against it. The sight of frozen corpses in sleds was commonplace, and many unlucky people "lose their noses, the tips of their ears, and the balls of their cheeks." In especially hard winters "the bears and wolves issue by troops out of the woods, driven by hunger, and enter the villages, tearing and ravening all they can find, so that the inhabitants are fain to fly for safeguard of their lives." Yet summer would bring a new face to the woods. Everything was "so fresh and so sweet, the pastures and meadows so green and well grown...such variety of flowers, such noise of birds...that a man shall not lightly travel in a more pleasant country."

The owls were uglier than in England, the soldiers did not march nearly so well, and the nation's religion was mired in superstition, although the concentration of political power in the hands of the tsar was a marvel to behold. Russia, Fletcher concluded, was, by turns, baffling, beautiful, and bizarre.[3]

Of course, ambassadors like Fletcher and Nepea rarely travelled out of sport or fascination (though a few, indubitably, did). Kings and queens hardly ever recruited them out of some benign commitment to enhancing the wealth of human knowledge. They were usually sent out of naked self-interest, to do their society's bidding. Often, they were greeted with fear, as the embodiment of an alien civilization. Their accounts could be flawed, sometimes mired in prejudice. Descriptions such as Giles Fletcher's portrait of Muscovy were always imperfect. Amid measured descriptions of flora and fauna, there would be diatribes against Russian drunkenness, cruelty, and poor hygiene.

Imperfect observations were better than no descriptions at all, however. Moreover, the forging of a crass, unfair stereotype was every bit as important to the interplay of cultures as a dispassionate survey of a nation's topography or diet. There would be moments of misunderstanding and embarrassment, but there would be just as many of clarity and insight. Through the efforts of ambassadors, civilizations would compare and contrast one another, prejudices and affinities would emerge, admiration or loathing would result. A staggering array of ideas and commodities, from coffee to perspective painting, from fashion trends to Galilean astronomy, from tulips to the theories of Ptolemy would be exchanged.

Isolated, exotic people that they often were, ambassadors rarely failed to make an impression on their hosts. Whether monks or noblemen, whether surgeons or Renaissance poets, such ambassadors carried the enormous burden of representing their entire culture. To Tudor England in 1557, Iosip Nepea *was* Russia. To Russia in 1588, Giles Fletcher *was* Tudor England. It was through their deeds and misdeeds that one society began to fashion an understanding of another.

In 1637, another unlikely ambassador journeyed to England. Jaurar Ben Abdella had been born in Portugal. Abducted as a child and sold into slavery, he had been taken to Morocco and, after "the manner of those nations," had been "distesticled, or eunuch'd." Happily, he had won favor with the emperor and become one of his most trusted counsellors. When he arrived in London as the Moroccan emperor's envoy, the writer George Glover took a moment to reflect on the benefits of such traffic between nations. It was good for trade, he quickly suggested, and it "conserves and makes peace, love and amity with princes and potentates, though they are far remote from each other." But it also "acquaints each nation with the language, manners, behaviour, customs and carriage of one another.... By these means, men are made capable of understanding and knowledge, and therefore prefer knowledge before wealth and riches, for the one soon fades, the other abides forever."[4]

Glover, hopelessly idealistic as he might sound, was entirely correct. By the time Iosip Nepea arrived in London in February 1557, there had been sixty centuries of ambassadorial endeavor. He was heir to the vibrant, neglected tradition which is the subject of this book.

———✦———

The book has a very simple purpose: to demonstrate just how influential ambassadors have been in the encounters, collisions, and rivalries among the world's disparate civilizations.

Negotiating a path through the history of the ambassadors is an awkward task and so it may prove helpful to briefly map out our itinerary. To help us find our bearings, we have quite deliberately begun close to the end of the story, in the relatively familiar world of Tudor England, with the journey of an ambassador who bears at least a passing resemblance to the diplomat of the modern world. As well as recounting the momentous cultural contributions of ambassadors, the book also examines how the business of embassy—the rituals and the protocols, the problems and the purposes—reached this point. How did issues such as diplomatic immunity, diplomatic precedence, or diplomatic gift-giving develop? How did societies decide what qualities an ideal ambassador ought to possess?

There are five sections to the book, progressing from ancient Greece to the European Enlightenment, each of which represents an extended historical moment to be explored. The first section, concerned with the ancient world, turns its gaze toward ambassadorial endeavor and its repercussions in classical Athens, Mauryan India, and Han Dynasty China—three of the storm centers of diplomacy from the fourth to the first century B.C. There are journeys that put Iosip Nepea's to shame and shifts in the political tectonics of the world, but there are also insights into the humdrum detail of the ancient ambassador's lot and the less-than-edifying spectacle of one such ambassador fighting for his professional life.

The next section moves the book forward to the ninth century A.D.—one of the high-water marks of diplomatic history—and takes the Byzantine Empire, the early Islamic caliphates, and the emperor Charlemagne as its points of departure. The places where diplomacy thrived, the crucibles of ambassadorial endeavor, had a habit of being the most important places in the world at any given time, and the history of the ambassadors maps out their rise, fall, and vicissitudes.

The next sections visit the Middle Ages—homing in on the ambassadorial adventures provoked by the Mongol invasions of the thirteenth century and the rise of the new diplomacy in fifteenth-century Italy—and the religious upheavals and worldwide explorations of the sixteenth century. A final section brings us to the dawn of the modern ambassadorial age in the period of the European Enlightenment.

What follows is a sketch of that vast history, and nothing more. It is a sketch that takes the European experience of diplomacy as its principal focus: a sketch that takes the very term ambassador in its broadest sense. Here, we aim for the marrow of the ambassadors' history, for the resonances and the fractures, for the things that remained the same and those that shifted: for the texture. That, and accounts of some of the most extraordinary episodes in human history.

If that is the structure, what is the purpose? To repeat, all that is really aimed at is a demonstration of the vital, very often surprising, role ambassadors have played in the encounters between civilizations. They offer a prism through which some of the grander themes of history—shifting worldviews, awakenings and reawakenings of cultural knowledge, the agonizing choices polities habitually face between isolation and engagement—can be explored.

The ambassadorial tradition is more ancient and various than is sometimes supposed. It is almost unfeasibly diverse. Embassy was about cultural encounter, and it would sometimes be wondrous. But it could just as easily be appalling, as when Hernando Cortez, posing as an ambassador, set about the destruction of Aztec civilization. Embassy brought peace, but it was often little more than the prelude to war or political takeover.

Those same Aztecs usually only sent out ambassadors to threaten their neighbors. First, they would demand the payment of tribute and the erection of a statue of one of their gods in the local temple. If their advances were still rebuffed after twenty days, more ambassadors would arrive, talking of the unhappy consequences of resistance and, to show how little they feared military engagement, providing their hosts with weapons. After another twenty days, a final party of ambassadors arrived, assuring their hosts that, very soon, their temple would be levelled and their entire population enslaved: a promise the Aztecs were especially good at keeping.

Embassy brought gifts, but then, even in the guise of gifts, it also brought threats and insults. When rumors spread that an Ottoman sultan lacked the wherewithal to complete the erection of a new mosque, the shah of Persia mischievously sent him chests of rubies and emeralds. This was not done out of generosity, but to sneer at the sultan's predicament. The sultan fully understood that an insult was intended, and he ordered the gems to be ground up and added to the mortar being used to build the mosque.

Embassy would forge marriages and alliances, but it sometimes left humiliated victims in its wake. In 1160 the Byzantine emperor

Manuel was looking for a new wife, and envoys were sent out to peruse the likely candidates. Melisend, the sister of Raymond III, count of Tripoli, had grown excited at the prospect of so prestigious a match. In truth, she had been kept in reserve in case a more suitable alliance with the ruler of Antioch failed to materialize. The ambassadors who had recently seen "the girl and admired her beauty" suddenly changed tack and abandoned negotiations when news arrived that the Antioch marriage had been confirmed.

The Byzantine chroniclers simply invented a story to conceal this rather disreputable episode of diplomatic matchmaking. "Severe illnesses beset the girl," the chronicles report, "and she was in serious danger…her body shuddered and shook extremely…The radiance of her appearance, which previously gleamed beautifully, was shortly altered and darkened. Seeing her, our eyes filled with tears at such a withered meadow." It was an utter fiction. Melisend had undergone no such transformations: She had simply, and suddenly, been supplanted in the emperor's affections.[5]

Sometimes embassy was spectacular. In 1162 that same Byzantine emperor received an ambassador in Constantinople "with magnificent banquets…charmed him with horse races, and according to custom set alight some boats and skiffs with liquid fire and absolutely gorged the man with spectacles in the hippodrome."[6] Sometimes it was dull, or even became a chore. The Venetian nobility were in the habit of retreating to their villas on the island of Murano whenever a new ambassador was about to be appointed.

The ritual was often splendid, but diplomatic dignity was just as often dispensed with. The Renaissance monarch Francis I was in the habit of accompanying visiting ambassadors on a horseback journey through the streets of Paris, where he set about pelting his subjects with eggs and rocks.[7] The history of the ambassadors was, ultimately, about this balance between the impressive and the mundane, the triumphs and the disasters.

It might also be assumed that the history of the ambassadors is one of ever-evolving sophistication and complexity, one that culminates in the clockwork diplomacy of the modern world. It would be an arrogant assumption to make. Almost every society that has opted to investigate rather than shun the rest of the world has mounted the same debates about what qualities a good ambassador ought to possess, about the elaborate rules and rituals of encounter. They have faced the same tensions between suspicion of the outside world and an urge to confront it; between behaving decorously toward other peoples and making sure to assert their cultural superiority.

Among the oldest surviving written records of diplomacy are the Amarna letters, several hundred clay tablets discovered at the end of the nineteenth century. Their faded cuneiform inscriptions record the relations between the rulers of Egypt and the greater and lesser kingdoms of the ancient Near East—Babylon, Assyria, and the rest—during the fourteenth century B.C.

The letters show kings dispatching ambassadors to complain about their fellow rulers' use of disrespectful language, about the failure to send envoys to inquire about their health. When the merchants of one king are robbed and killed by the subjects of another, swift justice is demanded: The culprits are to be bound and returned with the money they have robbed and the murderers are to be executed. If such measures are not taken, future travellers, ambassadors included, will be at risk, which threatens to bring diplomatic relations between the two kingdoms to an abrupt end. Nor are insults to the royal dignity any more likely to improve diplomatic relations. One ruler is utterly devastated when his brother's name is mentioned before his own on a tablet.

One monarch suggests to another that if he is going to take the trouble to send him gold, then it might as well be of a decent quality and in the same quantities as his father used to supply. A letter from the Cypriot kingdom of Alasiya warns the Egyptian king not to complain about receiving insufficient levies of copper. As a matter of fact, so prodigious an effort has been made that there is not a copper worker left alive on the entire island, and suitable gifts are expected in recompense—namely, silver, sweet oil, an ox, and a specialist in eagle omens.[8]

The Amarna letters reveal a consummate understanding of the value and vagaries of diplomacy. The motivations that would so often inspire ambassadors' missions—the fostering of trade, the payment of tribute, the search for alliances, the scolding of rivals—are all present, as are the pride, rivalry, and petulance, without which human diplomacy would be unrecognizable. Perhaps the story of the ambassadors provides an antidote to that thriving modern disease—the assumption that the past is either a quaint curiosity or an inevitable route-march to the present.

This, then, is a book of journeys, a book about the people who, far more tangibly than any impersonal force of history, wrote the human story: the men who did as much as any conqueror, merchant, scholar, or circumnavigating adventurer to help the world understand itself. Sometimes ambassadors would travel absurd distances, as did the thirteenth-century monks who trekked from Peking to Paris, and from Flanders to the Asian steppe. Sometimes they journeyed no farther than the nearest Greek city-state, or from one Renaissance court to another. They could be vile, snobbish, and stupid, or they could be astute, sympathetic, and wise, but throughout all their missions ambassadors were an inevitable facet of human history—offering an obvious way for squabbling rivals, potential allies and scattered civilizations to meet.

Ultimately, this book is a sampler of ambassadorial endeavor. A few decades after Iosip Nepea's mission to London, the otherwise unremarkable Francis Thynne pondered the meandering history of diplomacy. Perhaps weary of his culture's obsession with all things classical, he devoted a chapter of his book to proving that "other nations besides the Romans used ambassadors." Therein, he calculated that "the best kind of persuasion," the sort that allows us "to square our life, either in following virtue or avoiding vice…is to be drawn from the examples of others." Thynne's preachifying is best avoided, but his method was sound: "I will at this time set down the confirmation of the several matters belonging to ambassadors by examples, with short abridgement, drawn out of many histories."[9] As credos go, it serves.

THE AMBASSADORS

The Ancient World

I
"Glorious Hermes,
Herald of the Deathless Gods"

The World of Greek Diplomacy

I swear by Zeus, Gê, Helios, Poseidon, Athena, Ares and all the gods and goddesses. I shall abide in peace and I shall not infringe the treaty with Philip of Macedon. Neither by land nor by sea shall I bear arms with injurious intent against any party which abides by the oath, and I shall refrain from the capture by any device or stratagem of any city, fortification or harbour of the parties who abide by the Peace. I shall not subvert the monarchy of Philip and his successors... If anyone perpetrates any act in contravention of the terms of the agreement I shall render assistance accordingly as the wronged party may request and I shall make war upon him who contravenes the Common Peace... and I shall not fall short.

—The oath of the Greek city-states when joining the League of Corinth, 338 B.C.[10]

IN THE ELEVENTH CENTURY B.C., during the reign of Ramesses XI, an Egyptian envoy named Wen Amun travelled to Lebanon to buy timber for the sacred barque of the god Amun-re. Much like Iosip Nepea, his journey was plagued with bad fortune. At the port of Dor in the Nile delta he was robbed of all his money, although he quickly made good his loss by seizing an equivalent quantity of silver on board a ship bound for the Syrian port of Byblos.

The prince of Byblos was distinctly unimpressed by the arrival of an Egyptian envoy. He lacked written credentials, he had brought no gifts, so there was little incentive to provide him with precious timber. Wen Amun sent word to his superiors and they quickly dispatched four jars of gold, five jars of silver, five hundred ox hides, twenty sacks of lentils, and thirty baskets of fish. The gambit was successful, and Wen Amun purchased his timber from a suddenly much more amenable ruler.

Just before departing from Byblos, the men from whom Wen Amun had seized the silver arrived at court demanding justice. The prince took the night to mull over the envoy's fate, though he was sure to treat Wen Amun courteously during his temporary captivity—providing him with wine, food, and an Egyptian singer. The next morning the prince announced that since Wen Amun was an official envoy, he was immune from arrest.

Wen Amun embarked on his homeward journey only to encounter a storm that forced him to put ashore on Cyprus. The startled local people were intent on massacring the envoy and his crew, but Wen Amun begged for the right to plead for his life with the local princess, Hatiba. Mercifully, one of the locals could speak Egyptian, and he set about translating the envoy's threatening words. Wen Amun insisted on his ambassadorial immunity, and warned the princess that killing a Byblian crew would be a calamitous error of judgement. If she killed his crew, the ruler of Byblos would hunt down and kill ten of hers. Once again, Wen Amun skirted disaster and continued on his trek home.

His story is exceptional—a detailed ambassadorial adventure that just happened to survive on a roll of Egyptian papyrus. The sources are rarely so generous. In the centuries since the Amarna period, the work of envoys, messengers, and ambassadors continued, just as it always would. All of the civilizations of the ancient world—whether Vedic India, the Cretan Minoans and the Greek Mycenaeans of the Mediterranean, the Assyrians and Babylonians of the Near East, or the tribes of Bronze Age Europe—had need of envoys. They fostered trade, brokered alliances, carried tribute, and the rest. But almost without exception, they did so locally, with immediate or none-too-distant neighbors. The era of the continent-traversing ambassador had not yet dawned.

Across much of Eurasia, however, the second half of the first millennium B.C. can be understood as an era of consolidation. The first great, stable Chinese empires were emerging, coming to dominate the politics of East Asia, and in India, by the fourth century B.C., the first empire to genuinely hold sway across much of the subcontinent had appeared. In the Near East, the bridge between the two continents, the Assyrian Empire, had fallen by the end of the seventh century B.C., replaced by a series of redoubtable Persian empires—the Achaemenids, the Parthians, and finally, in the first centuries A.D., the Sassanids. The links between these civilizations were fragile, their knowledge of one another limited—but this was soon to change. As in much else, Greece led the way.

⊸⊷

Hermes, lover of Persephone and Aphrodite, protector of Perseus and Hercules, was the father of all ambassadors. God of gambling, trade, and profit, he traversed the earth like a breath of wind, carrying Zeus's messages, shepherding all travellers, escorting souls to the underworld. He would announce the weddings of the gods and execute their punishments, binding fire-thieving Prometheus to Mount Caucasus with iron spikes. He would visit all the communities of man to offer rewards for the return of Psyche, Aphrodite's errant handmaiden: "seven sweet kisses" from the goddess herself "and a particularly honeyed one imparted with the thrust of her caressing tongue." Ancient heralds, aspiring to his eloquence and cunning, would claim to be his offspring. They would carry his caduceus, his serpent-entwined staff, and it would grant them safe passage. Earnest and yet mischievous— stealing Apollo's cattle on the very day he was born—Hermes was to be the ambassadors' archetype and paragon.[II]

The caprices of diplomacy in classical Greece often demanded the talents of a Hermes. In southern Europe, Greece had enjoyed something of a resurgence from as early as the eighth century B.C. New cities had grown up, literacy and architecture had blossomed, and colonies had been established throughout the Mediterranean, and along the coasts of North Africa and the Black Sea. Political life was rooted in the polis, the proud, fiercely independent city-state. There was much that united the hundreds of communities across the Greek world, ties of religion, kinship, and, above all, of language, but just as much that divided them.

The mightiest states—Athens, Corinth, Thebes, and Sparta— were inevitable rivals, and while ancient Greece was not quite a theater of constant war (as is sometimes supposed), it was most certainly a place of shifting leagues, squabbles, and intrigue. The states were often willing to unite in the face of a common enemy— most often the Persian Empire—but diplomacy was just as likely to be concerned with territorial disputes, jurisdictional squabbles or cultural rivalry. It was fertile soil for the exploits of ambassadors. As so often, political rivalries and tensions provided the spark for diplomatic endeavor.

In the fifth century B.C. Athens led the resistance to the threat of Persian invasion and won famous victories at Marathon (490) and Salamis (480). She could now claim cultural superiority (it

was the age of Euripides and Sophocles) and ever-expanding dominion. Her leaders could be boastful. "Mighty indeed are the
marks and monuments of our empire which we have left," Pericles
(495–429 B.C.) declared. "Future ages will wonder at us, as the
present age wonders at us now. We do not need the praises of a
Homer…for our adventurous spirit has forced an entry into every
sea and into every land; and everywhere we have left behind us
everlasting memorials of good done to our friends, and of suffering inflicted on our enemies."[12] Here was a rare example of a
politician's swagger being both justified and prescient.

Athenian hegemony was offensive to her rivals. One of the sacred tasks of Greek diplomacy had always been to prevent any one
city from becoming unduly powerful. While the comparison may
be clumsy and anachronistic, the situation bore some resemblance
to that of seventeenth- and eighteenth-century Europe, when nations began to strive for a balance of power. Just as the great European states would frown at the pugnacity of Louis XIV's France,
so, centuries earlier, the Greeks had acted on their resentment of
Athens and, led by the Spartans, inaugurated the great Peloponnesian War (431–404 B.C.). By its end, Athens' dominance had
been shattered and her empire all but dismantled. The city-states
of Greece embarked on yet more decades of destructive feuding,
marked by periods of Spartan and then Theban dominance, but
most of all by political chaos.

To the north, in 359 B.C., Philip II ascended to the throne of
Macedon. With consummate timing (peppered with bribery and
assassination) he set about spreading Macedonian influence across
a confused, divided Greece, conquering lands and amassing tribu-
taries (many of them former Athenian allies). It was now the turn
of Athens to grumble at the rise of an overambitious rival, and it

fell to Demosthenes, the greatest orator of antiquity, to articulate his city's mounting trepidation.

In a speech before the Senate in 351 B.C., Demosthenes lambasted the arrogance of Philip II and the indolence of the Athenians who sat inactive as Philip was "casting his net around us." He was now "drunk with the magnitude of his achievements and dreams of further triumphs when, elated by his success, he sees that there is none to bar his way."

Demosthenes had a simple solution: Athens should recall its glorious past, cast off the marks of infamy and cowardice, and raise new and mightier armies to fend off the Macedonian assault.[13] Many of his fellow Athenians were less hawkish. They thought it wiser to negotiate with Philip, and so it was that Demosthenes found himself a reluctant member of an embassy to Macedonia in 346 B.C.

Athenian diplomacy was remarkably transparent. Tactics were debated in political assemblies before embassies set out, and negotiations (usually a series of set speeches and replies) were generally conducted in public meetings, although, as so often in the history of diplomacy, it was common for more private discussions between ambassadors and ministers to carry on behind the scenes. If agreement was reached there would be a formal exchange of oaths, and terms would be engraved on stone tablets. If the news was especially important, copies of such tablets would be displayed beyond the territories of the states most directly involved. After Athens and Sparta reached an accord in 421, copies of the treaty were set up at both Olympia and Delphi.

Given its importance, Greek diplomacy was astonishingly extemporaneous. There was no notion of a distinct arm of government dedicated to foreign affairs, nor of a permanent diplomatic establishment. Men were simply chosen for ambassadorial errands (usually bearing the title of *angelos* [messenger] or *presbeis* [envoy or elder]) as, and when, the need arose. There was scant financial reward, and envoys—typically drawn (as in many cultures) from the political classes—were obliged to bear all the expenses of their retinues, although service as an ambassador did tend to enhance a politician's reputation. There were few successful Athenian statesmen who had not, at one time or another, carried out diplomatic missions. Demosthenes, by the end of his career, would be a veteran of missions to Thebes and the Peloponnese as well as Macedon.

Greek diplomacy was also riddled with dissent. Unwilling to trust important errands to individuals or small groups, Athens generally favored the larger embassy, of three, five, or ten men. Although they were furnished with specific, detailed instructions, the potential for bickering among envoys was a perennial danger. Within the embassy of 346, Demosthenes was predictably hostile to Philip, insisting that any agreement with Macedon would have to be in the Athenians' best interests: Stringent conditions would have to be met before any treaty could be ratified. Some of his colleagues, notably the orator Aeschines, were more sympathetic to the Macedonian cause, and Demosthenes believed they were willing to give way on too many important points of negotiation. Some sources report that the rival factions even refused to sleep under the same roof during their journey. Upon returning to Athens, a furious Demosthenes charged some of his fellow ambassadors with receiving bribes from the Macedonian king.

One of the accused, Aeschines, sought to counter this threat by launching his own attack on the man expected to lead the prosecution—Timarchus. If he could damage Timarchus's reputation sufficiently, then Aeschines's own trial would, at the very least, be postponed. Aeschines opted for a spectacular strategy, accusing Timarchus of having been a gay prostitute. One of the most sensational jury trials in the ancient world would reveal, all at once, how seriously the Greeks took the business of embassy, and just how vulnerable their diplomacy was to the selfish machinations of individual ambassadors. Beyond all that, it furnished an extraordinarily intimate example of an ancient ambassador desperately struggling for political survival.

The Trial of Timarchus

The workings of Athenian justice, if we are to believe the comic playwright Aristophanes, were dangerously addictive. His scurrilous play *The Wasps* tells the story of Philocleon, who spends all his days serving on juries. He revels in the authority this bestows, enjoying the pathetic spectacle of defendants pleading for mercy: "Is there any creature on earth more blessed, more feared and petted from day to day, or that leads a happier, pleasanter life" than a juror, he asks? Some defendants "vow they are needy...and over their poverty wail and whine, some tell us a legend of days gone by, or a joke from Aesop...to make me laugh, that so I may doff my terrible rage." And when the "piteous bleating" is over, he can return home "with my fee in my wallet," to be greeted by his doting daughter and "my dear little wife [who] sets on the board nice manchets of bread in a tempting array."

His son, Bdelycleon, fears for Philocleon's sanity and locks him in the family home. His fellow jurors, dressed as a chorus of wasps, stage a rescue attempt and, although Bdelycleon manages to rout them in a debate, Philocleon's addiction is not so easily defeated. To ease his father's discomfort, Bdelycleon sets up a makeshift court and, for want of any human reprobates, the family dog is brought to trial for stealing a piece of Sicilian cheese. The creature is only saved by some trickery on Bdelycleon's part, whereby Philocleon unwittingly votes for acquittal. Devastated— he had never previously found a defendant not guilty—Philocleon ends the play by getting hopelessly drunk.[14]

The reality of Greek jurisprudence was more decorous, but Aristophanes had one thing exactly right: Athenian juries were gloriously powerful. In an attempt to check bribery, they were made up of hundreds, sometimes even thousands of members, drawn by lot. Even the wealthiest citizen, so it was supposed, lacked the resources to corrupt that many people. At trial, a water clock was set in motion, and both defendants and plaintiffs—who habitually represented themselves—would make lengthy speeches, cite the relevant laws, and call their witnesses. There was no judge (as we would understand the term) to coordinate proceedings, monitor objections, or offer summations. Success rested solely on whether a speaker had been persuasive: eloquence was everything.

A jury's verdict was final and there was no room for appeal. Jurors, who had to be over thirty years of age and free from any outstanding financial debt to the state, were chosen from a list of six thousand candidates, drawn up at the beginning of each year. They received a small daily stipend for their service and they knew, and revelled in, their own power. As the trial of Timarchus would demonstrate, to flatter a jury, to appeal to its patriotism, and to avoid the heckling in which jurors regularly indulged, were the lynchpins of any competent legal strategy.

"Fellow citizens," the embattled ambassador Aeschines began, "I have never brought indictment against any Athenian." However, "when I saw that the city was being seriously injured by the defendant, Timarchus, who, though disqualified by law, was speaking in your assemblies, and when I myself was made a victim of his blackmailing attack," he had been compelled to act. "I decided that it would be a most shameful thing if I failed to come to the defence of the whole city and its laws, and to your defence and my own." It was an irresistible opening salvo.

The city's lawgivers, Aeschines explained, had been unflinching when they established who might engage in public debate and hold civic office. There had been no attempts to "exclude from the platform the man whose ancestors have not held a general's office, nor even the man who earns his daily bread by working at a trade." Such citizens were welcome to participate. However, the same privilege did not extend to the man who "beats his father or mother, or fails to support them or to provide a home for them," or to the man who had failed to perform military service and had "thrown away his shield."

Nor did Athens tolerate the person who "because of his shameful private life the laws forbids from speaking before the people." The city's constitution was clear. "If any Athenian...shall have prostituted his person, he shall not be permitted to become one of the nine archons...nor to discharge the office of priest... nor shall he act as an advocate for the state...nor shall ever hold any office whatsoever...nor shall he be a herald or an ambassador." Aeschines intended to prove that Timarchus was just such a man, unworthy of holding office, and entirely disqualified from directing a legal proceeding.

Timarchus's profligacy had apparently begun early in life. "As soon as he was past boyhood he settled down in Piraeus [the port of Athens] at the establishment of Euthydicus the physician, pretending to be a student of medicine, but in fact deliberately offering himself for sale." Next came Misgolas, "a man otherwise honourable, and beyond reproach," aside for his penchant for male prostitutes. He had always been "accustomed to have about him singers or cithara-players" and, learning that Timarchus was "well-developed, young and lewd," he paid him a handsome sum of money to come and live with him. He was "just the person for the thing that Misgolas wanted to do, and Timarchus wanted to have done."

The most damning proof of Timarchus's guilt had been his unwavering ability to live far beyond his means. Certainly, he had once had wealth, but this had quickly vanished. He had sold his house, south of the Acropolis, to the comic poet Nausicrates, and disposed of his country estates and slaves. Yet he had still been able to enjoy "costly suppers" and maintain "the most expensive flute-girls and harlots....Does it take a wizard to explain all that?" Aeschines asked. Other men were obviously paying for Timarchus's excesses, and it was "perfectly plain that the man who makes such demands must himself be furnishing in return certain pleasures to the men who are spending their money on him."

Aeschines insisted that he was not launching an assault on the beauty of young men. All fathers hoped for sons who were "fair and beautiful in person, and worthy of the city." To be a pretty young boy was not the same thing as being a whore. Nor was Aeschines a stranger to love. As he warned the jury, his opposing counsel would doubtless remind them that Aeschines himself had sometimes "made a nuisance of myself in the gymnasia and... been many times a lover." He might even offer extracts from all "the erotic poems I have ever addressed to one person or another."

It was, Aeschines concluded, a foolish strategy: "As for me, I neither find fault with love that is honourable, nor do I say that those who surpass in beauty are prostitutes. I do not deny that I myself have been a lover and am a lover to this day." Love was one thing; love between men was one thing; but sex offered in return for monetary reward was quite another, and it did not befit the leaders of Athens.

Each juror placed his pebble in the appropriate urn (one to condemn, the other to acquit) and Timarchus was found guilty, his career now in tatters. The defense, mounted by Demosthenes, is lost to us. So, too, is any possibility of deciphering which of the charges levelled by Aeschines were justified. Nonetheless, the spectacle of an ambassador fighting for his political life still resonates down the ages. More poignantly, and not least by virtue of its grubbiness, the trial of Timarchus also seems to encapsulate the decline of Athenian grandeur and influence. A mighty power had entered its dotage.[15]

Three years later, in 343 B.C., Demosthenes would finally bring his original case against Aeschines, charging him with corruption during the embassy to Macedonia. Demosthenes realized just how sensational the trial had become. "I do not doubt," he told the jurors, "that you are all pretty well aware that this trial has been the center of keen partisanship and active canvassing, for you saw the people who were accosting and annoying you just now at the casting of lots."

They must not be swayed by such distractions, however. Aeschines was "trying to introduce into politics a most dangerous and deplorable practice." He had been criticized and so, three years earlier, he had turned his fire on Timarchus. This was a horrendous precedent, "for if a man who has undertaken and administered any public function can get rid of accusers not by his honesty but by the fear he inspires, the people will soon lose all control of public affairs."

There could be little doubt about Aeschines's guilt, Demosthenes suggested, and all the jurors had to do was call to mind the duties which any ambassador was expected to fulfil. "He is responsible, in the first place, for the reports he has made; secondly, for the advice he has offered; thirdly, for his observance of your instructions; and, to crown all, whether he has done his business corruptly or with integrity." Measured against this standard, Aeschines had been an abject failure.

There had been a time, Demosthenes reminded the jury, when Aeschines had been among Philip's harshest critics, making speeches against him and organizing conferences where the Greek states could formulate a united response to the Macedonian threat. But, in an instant, that had all changed. After an earlier mission to Philip's court, Aeschines had suddenly lent his support to a peace treaty with Macedon that was patently injurious to Athenian interests. After his earlier patriotism he began using language "for which, as heaven is my witness, he deserves to die many times over. He told you that you ought to forget the achievements of your forefathers; that you should not tolerate all that talk about old trophies and sea-fights." The only possible explanation for such a volte-face was that Aeschines had been bribed by the Macedonian regime, and as an Athenian jury was well aware, bribery was one of the heartbeats of Greek political life.

A second embassy had been dispatched to Philip with the aim of ratifying that peace treaty—the embassy which provoked the trial of Timarchus—but it failed to secure all of the conditions and provisos that the Athenian assembly had insisted on. A deeply unsatisfactory treaty had been reached. Aeschines was solely to blame, which is what Demosthenes had told the assembly upon his return to Athens, but it had been hoodwinked by Aeschines's eloquence. He offered no report, gave no reply to the charges levelled by Demosthenes, "but he made such a fine speech, so full of big promises, that he carried you all away with him." Through his efforts, Aeschines boasted, Philip had been entirely won over to the Athenian cause and would now be a valued ally.

This was hardly how Demosthenes remembered the embassy, so "I rose, and said that the whole story was news to me. I attempted to repeat the statement I had made to the council, but Aeschines and Philocrates posted themselves one on either side of me, shouting, interrupting, and finally jeering. You were all laughing; you would not listen to me, and you did not want to believe anything except what Aeschines had reported."

A dishonorable peace had been secured, and Philip of Macedon's ascendancy continued unchecked. "Men of Athens," Demosthenes suggested, "nothing more awful or more momentous has befallen Greece within living memory nor, as I believe, in all the history of the past." Athens had been duped by Philip of Macedon, a man who "has many claims to congratulation on his good fortune....Such achievements as the capture of great cities and the subjugation of a vast territory are, I suppose, enviable, as they are undoubtedly imposing; yet we could mention many other men who have done the like." But his "greatest stroke of good fortune...is that, when he needed scoundrels for his purposes, he found bigger scoundrels than he wanted." He had found Aeschines, who had not been cajoled into treachery but "had sold himself, and pocketed the money, before he made his speech and betrayed us to Philip. To Philip he has been a trusty and well-

beloved hireling; to you a treacherous ambassador and a treacherous citizen, worthy of threefold destruction."

It was not too late to make amends, however. "Today you are
not merely adjudging this case. You are legislating for all future
time, whether every ambassador is basely to serve your enemies for
hire, or without fee or bribe to give his best service to you." Philip
could be warned that "he will have to remodel his methods" when
dealing with Athens. "At present his chosen policy is to cheat the
many and court the few; but, when he learns that his favourites
have been brought to ruin, he will wish for the future to deal with
the many, who are the real masters of our state." "For the sake of
your honour, of your religion, of your security, of everything you
value," Demosthenes implored the jury, "you must not acquit this
man. Visit him with exemplary punishment, and let his fate be a
warning not to our own citizens alone but to every man who lives
in the Hellenic world."[16]

It was rousing stuff, but Aeschines had prepared a compelling
story of his own. From the outset he threw himself on the jury's
mercy. "I beg you, fellow citizens, to hear me with willing and
friendly mind, remembering how great is my peril, and how many
the charges against which I have to defend myself; remembering
also the arts and devices of my accuser." This Demosthenes was
hardly the most attractive of personalities, after all, Aeschines reminded the jury.

During the embassy to Philip he had been little more than a
nuisance. "All the way we were forced to put up with Demosthenes' odious and insufferable ways," and that was nothing compared to his boastfulness, "the over-weening self-confidence of
this fellow." When the ambassadors were discussing their tactics,
one of them had "remarked that he was afraid Philip would get the

better of us in arguing his claims." Demosthenes immediately "promised fountains of oratory, and said that he was going to make such a speech…that he would sew up Philip's mouth as with an un-soaked rush." Sadly, as Aeschines remembered it, events turned out differently.

When Demosthenes's turn came to address Philip,

> all were intent, expecting to hear a masterpiece of eloquence. For, as we learned afterwards, his extravagant boasting had been reported to Philip and his court. So when all were thus prepared to listen, this creature mouthed forth a proem—an obscure sort of thing and as dead as fright could make it—and getting on a little way into the subject he suddenly stopped speaking and stood helpless. Finally he collapsed completely.

Philip saw Demosthenes's plight and generously assured him that his faltering speech was not an "irreparable calamity." He was an ambassador, not an actor on the stage, and he should calm himself and "try gradually to recall his speech, and speak it off as he had prepared it." Unfortunately, "having been once upset, and having forgotten what he had written, he was unable to recover himself… and broke down again." Philip was deeply embarrassed and a herald ordered the ambassadors to withdraw. Demosthenes was mortified, at which point his sour feelings toward the entire embassy began to fester. To deflect attention away from his own risible performance, he suddenly began accusing the other ambassadors of negotiating against the best interests of Athens.

Throughout the rest of the ambassadors' stay in Macedon, Demosthenes oscillated between showering Philip in fawning speeches and behaving "with shameless rudeness" whenever he was invited to dinner. On the journey home his mood did seem to brighten. "Suddenly he began talking to each of us in a surpris-

ingly friendly manner," promising to lend his support to their political careers and even complimenting Aeschines on his oratorical
skills. One evening, "when we were all dining together at Larisa,
he made fun of himself and the embarrassment which had come
upon him in his speech, and he declared that Philip was the most
wonderful man under the sun." It was a ruse, however, an attempt
to make the other ambassadors say complimentary things about
Philip that he could later use as proof of their treachery.

Demosthenes had never been the warmest supporter of a
peace treaty with Philip, and his experiences in Macedonia had
only brought him humiliation. He was levelling charges of corruption, Aeschines suggested, as a political strategy, to rouse Athens
against Philip of Macedon and as a petulant gesture of revenge.
Aeschines allowed that "the peace failed to please some of our
public men," but "ought they not to have opposed it at the time,
instead of putting me on trial now?" "They say that Philip bought
the peace, that he overreached us at every point in the articles of
agreement, and that the peace which he contrived for his own interests, he himself has violated." Aeschines disputed the analysis
but, regardless, it seemed unfair that "although I was but one of
ten ambassadors, I alone am made to give account."

Finally, Aeschines invited the jurors to look around the court-
room. "Yonder is my father, Atrometus. There are few older men
among all the citizens, for he is now ninety-four years old. When
he was a young man, before the war destroyed his property, he was
so fortunate as to be an athlete. Banished by the Thirty [Athens'
oligarchic governing body after the Peloponnesian War], he served
as a soldier in Asia, and in danger he showed himself a man."
Then there was his mother, a woman of extraordinary courage,
who followed her husband into exile and shared in his disasters.

Aeschines was portraying himself as the child of proud Athenian parents, "and I myself, gentlemen, have three children, one daughter and two sons, by the daughter of Philodemus, the sister of Philon and Epicrates." He had brought them into court with the others "for the sake of asking one question and presenting one piece of evidence to the jury."

> For I ask, fellow citizens, whether you believe that I would have betrayed to Philip, not only my country, my personal friendships, and my rights in the shrines and tombs of my fathers, but also these children, the dearest of mankind to me. Do you believe that I would have held his friendship more precious than the safety of these children? By what lust have you seen me conquered? What unworthy act have I ever done for money? It is not Macedon that makes men good or bad, but their own inborn nature; and we have not come back from the embassy changed men, but the same men that you yourselves sent out.

"With all loyalty I have served the city as her ambassador," Aeschines declared. "My speech is finished. This, my body, I and the law now commit to your hands."[17]

Aeschines was acquitted, but only barely, and the damage done to his reputation would be catastrophic. He would always retain the whiff of scandal. He would end his career not as an elder statesman in Athens, but as a teacher of rhetoric on Rhodes. Demosthenes would even succeed in mobilizing public opinion against Philip of Macedon, but support came far too late (assuming it would ever have made any real difference). Just as Demosthenes had desired, Athens and Macedonia joined battle and, at Chaeronea in 338 B.C., Athens was crushed. In its aftermath, Philip established the League of Corinth, a pan-Hellenic league of mutual defense almost entirely dominated by Macedonian interests.

The trials of Timarchus and Aeschines were parochial affairs, but they intersected with momentous political events. Philip of Macedon, whose ascendancy was the catalyst for the whole affair, died two years after the battle of Chaeronea. His achievement was secure and Macedonia was now the greatest power in Greece. His son, Alexander, would extend that influence across much of the known world and, as skilled a warrior as he was, Alexander also knew the value of a diplomatic flourish. The insular relations of the Greek city-states were shortly to give way to ambassadorial encounters with the rest of the world that were as epochal as any that had yet been produced—epochal if, on occasion, boozy.

2
GREEKS AND *INDIKA*

Alexander

A PRODIGIOUS TOLERANCE FOR DRINK was always among the most useful of ambassadorial qualities. Writing in the middle of the eighteenth century, the Prussian monarch Frederick the Great offered unvarnished advice to anyone hoping to serve as an ambassador in London. He ought to be a "good debauchee who should preferably be able to drink wine better than the English and who, having drunk, would say nothing that should be kept quiet." Drinking wine better than the English was no easy feat. During a trip to Hanover in the winter of 1716, George I's secretary of state, James Stanhope, served no less than seventy bottles of wine to thirteen diplomatic dinner guests. At the end of the evening everyone but Stanhope—and he had certainly consumed his share—was hopelessly drunk. Stanhope left his guests to sleep off their excesses and went to compare notes with the representative of the French child-king Louis XV, Cardinal Dubois, who had been listening to the revelatory table talk from across the hall.[18]

Those with less robust livers risked moments of indiscretion and humiliation. In 1673, the French jeweller Jean Chardin attended a banquet at the Persian court in Isfahan. If he was impressed by the food—"a collation of fruits, both green and dried, and all sorts of sweet meats, wet and dry"—he was dazzled by the alcohol on display. Lavish flat-bottomed cups, each able to carry three litres of wine, were filled from fifty golden flagons, some enamelled, others encrusted with jewels and pearls. It all left Chardin with the feeling that "no other part of the world can afford anything more magnificent and rich or more splendid and bright." Impressed as he was, Chardin was also confused. None of the ambassadors present at the dinner seemed to be partaking of the wine, and while the Muscovite ambassador could be seen drinking, it was only from his private cache of Russian brandy. A nobleman at the dinner supplied Chardin with an explanation.

At a banquet ten years earlier, he revealed, two Russian ambassadors had "drank so excessively that they quite lost their senses." Unfortunately, the shah had then proposed a toast to the tsar, an honor that the ambassadors could hardly rebuff. The two men took long drafts from their massive cups but one of them, "not being able to digest so much wine, had a pressing inclination to vomit, and not knowing where to disembogue, he took his great sable cap, which he half filled."

His colleague was mortified by "so foul an action done in the presence of the king of Persia," and urged him to leave the banqueting hall at once. Instead, "not knowing either what was said to him nor what he himself did," he "clapped his cap upon his head, which presently covered him all over with nastiness." Mercifully, the shah and his retinue were not offended, but "broke into a loud laughter, which lasted about half an hour, during which time the companions of the filthy Muscovite were forcing him by dint of blows with their fists to rise and go out."[19]

Not that the debauched diplomatic banquet was an invention

of the modern era. In 327 B.C. Alexander the Great, heir to the man Demosthenes had so despised, crossed into India. There were those who cowered at his advance, those who resisted it, and still others who accepted it as inevitable. After suffering a humiliating defeat, two Indian kings decided to send a hundred envoys to offer their submission to the Greek invasion. "They all rode in chariots and were men of uncommon stature and of a very dignified bearing," the historian Curtius Rufus reports. In their gold and purple embroidered robes, they humbly offered Alexander "themselves, their cities, and their territories."

Alexander eagerly accepted and, in celebration, "gave orders for the preparation of a splendid banquet, to which he invited the ambassadors and the petty kings of the neighbouring tribes." Tapestry curtains, "which glittered with gold and purple," surrounded a hundred gilded couches. It was a majestic spectacle, one more demonstration of Macedonian paramountcy. Until, that is, alcohol intervened.

An Athenian boxer named Dioxippus was a guest at the festivities. Unfortunately, a Macedonian called Horratus was there, too. "Flown with wine," he began to taunt Dioxippus "and challenged him, if he were a man, to fight him next day with a sword." The challenge was gleefully accepted and Alexander, "finding next day that the two men were more than ever bent on fighting...allowed them do as they pleased."

Horratus arrived in full gladiatorial regalia, "carrying in his left hand a brazen shield...and in his right a javelin," with a sword by his side for good measure. Dioxippus carried nothing but a scarlet cloak and a "stout knotty club." To the large crowds that had gathered, "it seemed not temerity but downright madness for a naked man to engage with one armed to the teeth." They were mistaken.

Horratus launched his javelin, but Dioxippus evaded it "by a slight bending of his body" and proceeded to break Horratus's long pike with a single blow of his club. Next, he tripped Horratus, snatched his sword, and "planted his foot on his neck as he lay prostrate." Only Alexander's intervention prevented Dioxippus from smashing his challenger's skull. It was a huge disappointment for the assembled Macedonians, and they set about plotting their revenge. At another feast a few days later, they falsely accused Dioxippus of stealing a precious golden cup. He blushed at the suggestion, since "it often enough happens that one who blushes at a false insinuation has less control of his countenance than one who is really guilty." A proud man, Dioxippus "could not bear the glances which were turned upon him as if he were a thief," so he quit the banquet, wrote a letter of farewell to Alexander, and fell on his sword.[20]

Such unseemly events could hardly have impressed the envoys of the Indian kings, and Macedonian pride was doubtless bruised, but a brief moment of humiliation could not mar Alexander's spectacular achievements. He had quashed residual Greek resentment (even daring to raze the city of Thebes to the ground), conquered Persia, and by the time of his death at the age of thirty-two he had carved out an empire that stretched from the Danube, through Egypt, to the mouth of the Indus River. The pilgrimage he had reputedly made to Troy, to place wreaths on the tombs of the Homeric heroes Achilles and Patroclus, now seemed less like hubris and more like a fitting prelude to a glorious military career.

Redoubtable soldier that he was, Alexander had always honored diplomacy and had treated its officers with great respect. As a young man he had received a party of Persian ambassadors and had been so affable, and asked them such pertinent questions, that they thought the much-vaunted abilities of his father, Philip, were nothing in comparison with the precocious talents of his son. Years later, the envoys of some other defeated Indian towns visited Alexander to offer their submission. They were surprised to find him still in his armor and without anyone waiting in attendance upon him. At length, a cushion was brought in so that Alexander might rest his battle-wearied body. Instead, he made the eldest of the ambassadors take it and sit down upon it. Delighted by such courtesy, the envoys readily agreed to the terms of surrender that were proposed. Alexander could, as the occasion required, feast, charm, or flatter any and all ambassadors.

He had won his empire through a combination of military prowess and diplomatic politesse. The empire was as fragile as it was vast, however. When he died, Alexander's relatives, counsellors, and generals squabbled over his inheritance, and a series of smaller Macedonian states grew up. The easternmost of these was centered on Syria and Persia, where Seleucus Nicator, one of Alexander's most successful generals (358–281 B.C.), established a dynasty that would survive until the Roman invasion in 64 B.C. Seleucus dreamed of emulating Alexander's military forays into northern India. Unfortunately, in the period since Alexander's death, a formidable new power had arisen in that region.

Megasthenes

The Mauryan Empire does not enjoy the place it deserves in the popular historical imagination. Between 321 and 180 B.C., the Mauryans ruled over five hundred million people, easily matching the grandeur of either the Moghul Empire or the British Raj. By the fifth century B.C. the numerous tribal groups of India had been reduced to four dominant monarchies, or mahajanpadas, which set about battling for primacy. By the beginning of the fourth century, the kingdom of Magadha, with its capital at Pataliputra, had emerged victorious. In the wake of Alexander's military adventures in India, Chandragupta Maurya ascended to the Magadhan throne and, along with his successors, established the first genuine Indian empire, ranging from the borders of Persia to those of Afghanistan and Bengal.

Pataliputra (on the site of present-day Patna) was likely the largest city in the world at the time. Surrounded by 570 towers and a 900-foot moat, it boasted elegant houses, ponds, and orchards, plentiful food and hardly any crime. With an army of three thousand cavalry, nine thousand war elephants, and six hundred thousand foot soldiers, the Mauryans were fully equipped to repulse any Greek invasion. Seleucus realized that his plans to conquer India were stillborn. Instead, after suffering military defeat in 305 B.C., he made a treaty with the Mauryans, abandoning claims to the Punjab in exchange for several hundred war elephants. With the prospect of hostilities averted, diplomacy was able to flourish.

In 302 B.C. a Macedonian ambassador named Megasthenes travelled down the Kabul Valley, over the Kyber Pass, and headed across the Ganges Valley toward the Mauryan capital. He had been sent to formalize relations between two civilizations recently at war. He would stay for ten years, and while the workaday detail of his diplomatic encounters has vanished, the reports he brought home would define the West's understanding of India for centuries to come, endlessly cited, if not always uncritically, in the works of historians and scholars like Arrian and Pliny. India was suddenly more tangible: a land "of such vast extent, it seems well-nigh to embrace the whole of the northern tropic zone of the earth." It had "many huge mountains which abound in fruit trees of every kind, and vast plains of great fertility."

The Indian people were not hapless savages but, "distinguished by their proud bearing," were "well skilled in the arts, as might be expected of men who inhale a pure air and drink the very finest water." They were generally frugal, but entirely capable of appreciating finery, favoring robes "ornamented with precious stones" and "flowered garments made of the finest muslin." They had "a high regard for beauty, and avail themselves of every device to improve their looks."

There was much to admire in Mauryan culture. Even during military campaigns, those who worked the land were left unmolested, ensuring a steady supply of food. There were no slaves anywhere in the empire, and visitors like Megasthenes were guaranteed courteous treatment: "Officers are appointed even for foreigners whose duty is to see that no foreigner is wronged. Should any of them lose his health, they send physicians to attend him...and if he dies they bury him, and deliver over such property as he leaves to his relatives. The judges also decide cases in which foreigners are concerned, with the greatest care, and come down sharply on those who take unfair advantage of them."

The sophistication of Indian thought was perhaps the greatest revelation. "Truth and virtue they hold alike in esteem. Hence they accord no special privileges to the old unless they possess superior wisdom." Death was "a very frequent subject of discourse. They regard this life as, so to speak, the time when the child within the womb becomes mature, and death as a birth into a real and happy life for the votaries of philosophy." And when the old finally passed on, the Indians did not raise monuments in their honor but considered "the virtues which men have displayed in life, and the songs in which their praises are celebrated, sufficient to preserve their memory after death."

Like so many later visitors, Megasthenes was especially fascinated by Brahmin priests, men who "abstain from animal food and sexual pleasures, and spend their time in listening to serious discourse, and in imparting their knowledge to such as will listen to them." They were much revered, and any man who came to listen to their discussions was "not allowed to speak, or even to cough, and much less to spit, and if he offends in any of these ways he is cast out from their society that very day, as being a man who is wanting in self-restraint."[21]

Megasthenes's epic survey of Indian life, his *Indika*, did not survive antiquity intact. All that remain are fragments and the countless references to his work in later authors. His influence was profound, though not uncontroversial. Megasthenes would be criticized for his inaccuracies and wilder speculations. Unversed in Indian languages, he only ever heard stories and reports in, presumably, imperfect translation. He certainly made gross generalizations about a society made up of hundreds of millions of people and gave too much credence to the more fabulous stories he had heard. He told the Greek world about races of Indians who lacked noses, others who had backward feet, and still others who had heads like dogs and communicated by barking. He spoke of ants the size of foxes that dug for gold, and of bizarre flying serpents.

All such legends died hard. But Megasthenes also provided accurate accounts of Indian political and social life, Indian philosophy, the Indian judiciary, the Indian diet of rice and richly-spiced meat, and he depicted a mighty city about which almost nothing had previously been known. His description of the Indian caste system was flawed—he mistakenly divided society into seven rather than four groups—but the truly momentous thing was that he was introducing the West to that caste system for the very first time. Ultimately, it did not matter how good or bad his narrative was—although, on balance, it was remarkably good. It was, the justified carping of some critics aside, believed, and one civilization's understanding of another was forever transformed. India was suddenly far more than the mysterious place from which an occasional parrot arrived.

⟨⟩

Greek diplomacy was capable of outreach. Far more so, in fact, than its Roman equivalent. On the face of things, the ancient Roman worldview was unapologetically inclusive. Yes, Roman legions might tramp across most of the known world, but in due course conquered peoples would be exposed to the cultural and economic blessings of Roman civilization. The conquered, more often than not, could even aspire to Roman citizenship. Rome's lawyers had seemingly developed a code of international encounter that defined the procedures for waging war and making peace—the only good war was a just war.

All of this was true, but it hardly dampened Roman superiority and xenophobia. Diplomacy existed solely to expand the sphere of Roman influence. It did have much in common with its Greek counterpart. There was no specialized branch of government dedicated to foreign affairs, and ambassadors were chosen as the need arose, usually from the senatorial class. Like their Greek peers, they were given specific instructions, discouraged from showing undue initiative, and any agreements they reached had to be ratified by politicians back in Rome before coming into effect. Clearly, with such a vast empire, Rome was obliged to dispatch many ambassadors, whether to seek alliances, to mediate disputes or to deal with administrative problems. Sometimes, in the field, even an emperor such as Marcus Aurelius conducted his own negotiations.

Ultimately, though, Roman diplomacy was ruthlessly straight-forward. There were two preferred ways to deal with enemies and rivals. Ideally, they were to be terrified into submission, either through war or the threat of war. Alternatively, they could be bribed. The notion of cautious, respectful negotiation was often frowned on. Diplomacy, by many accounts, was the refuge of the weak emperor: the poor, even dishonorable relation to military conquest. In March 218, as one example among many, the senator Fabius Buteo and four other legates travelled to Carthage in North Africa. They announced that either Hannibal and his counsellors were to be handed over, or Rome and Carthage would be in a state of war. They avoided all discussion or negotiation and, when the Carthaginians refused to comply with the Roman demands, they blithely announced that the Second Punic War had now begun. Buteo "let war fall from his toga."[22]

And if there had to be diplomacy, if a foreign nation or tribe had something urgent to relate, the onus was on them to initiate proceedings. In the accounts of his military campaigns in Gaul, Julius Caesar makes few references to the dispatching of Roman ambassadors: Rather, we are told of foreign envoys, often weeping and prostrated, coming to the Roman camp. Foreign ambassadors, the bearers of congratulations, condolences, requests, or apologies, were expected to come to Rome, not vice versa. When the Senate was in session, there were regularly hundreds of envoys in the capital, the most illustrious among them being housed and fed, at the state's expense, in the Villa Publica.

Roman rulers took the number of envoys they received as an index of their prestige and power. Ambassadors from Germany, North Africa, and Greece were unexceptional. More noteworthy were the princes who acted as their own representatives—as when Tiridates of Armenia visited Nero to receive his crown from the emperor's own hands. The exotic ambassador was even more desirable. If envoys came from as far away as Ceylon, as happened in the reign of Claudius, this was a sure indication of an emperor's extraordinary fame.

The Roman view of the ambassador's role lacked nuance: It did not make for the inquisitive, scholarly ambassador. For the most part, while it was busy with the interstate rivalries of Athens, Thebes, and Sparta, neither did the Greek notion of diplomacy. But in Megasthenes, at least, a moment of genuine, lasting cultural dialogue had been achieved.

The Greeks were bemused by just how advanced and cultured Indian society seemed. Megasthenes was particularly impressed by its bureaucracy, by the number and quality of officials who oversaw a staggering range of domestic tasks. There was more to the Mauryan genius than this, however. Any fledgling empire, however exuberant, was obliged to look beyond its borders, to potential allies and likely adversaries. History in the West will always flatter classical Greece, but classical India had begun to hone its own ambassadorial skills and to meditate on the nature and ends of diplomacy. Mauryan civilization reached conclusions about its place in the world that were as startling as they were brilliant. Enter Kautilya.

3

A SANSKRIT MACHIAVELLI

Debating Diplomacy

Thus speaks the Beloved of the Gods: *Dhamma* is good. And
what is *Dhamma*? It is having few faults and many good deeds,
mercy, charity, truthfulness, and purity. I have given the gift of
insight in various forms. I have conferred many benefits on
man, animals, birds, and fish, even to saving their lives, and I
have done many other commendable deeds. I have had this inscription of *Dhamma* engraved that men may conform to it and
that it may endure. He who conforms will do well.
—2nd Pillar Edict of the Mauryan king Asoka[23]

ASOKA, BELOVED OF THE GODS, was the greatest of the Mauryan emperors. His reign (273–232 B.C.) began with a string
of bloody military campaigns, but tortured by pity for
the fallen and displaced he renounced martial glory and took to
the peaceful, reflective path of Buddhism. Legend tells of the Buddhist monk Nigrodha who went strolling in the gardens of the
royal palace one day and enchanted Asoka with his calm, almost
beatific demeanor. Everyone else struck Asoka as being confused
in mind, like perturbed deer, but the monk seemed utterly at ease,
perhaps possessed of some wondrous transcendent vision. The
emperor invited the monk into his palace and listened to his

account of a Buddhist faith that, after his conversion in c. 260 B.C., Asoka would help spread across the region.[24]

He decreed that a series of edicts should be promulgated across his dominions, as far as present-day Pakistan, Nepal, and Afghanistan. Sometimes etched on rock faces, sometimes on towering pillars, these inscriptions proclaimed Asoka's dedication to a life of virtue, his dream that he, "his sons, his grandsons and his great grandsons will advance the practice of *Dhamma* until the end of the world."

It was a benign vision. Charities, hospitals, and veterinary clinics were to be established, prisoners were to be treated more decently, and even the lot of animals was to be improved: "Formerly in the kitchens [of Asoka], many hundreds of thousands of living animals were killed daily for meat. But now, at the time of writing this inscription, only three animals are killed, two peacocks and a deer, and the deer not invariably. Even these animals will not be killed in the future." The edicts spoke of imperial officers who were to tour the countryside every five years to instruct people in the laws of piety, urging them to honor their parents and friends, to live frugally, and to maintain a bare minimum of personal property. Earlier kings might have indulged in endless "pleasure tours, consisting of hunts and similar amusements," but Asoka would only travel to meet with his people, to talk with the elderly, discourse with Brahmin priests, and distribute gifts.[25]

The rock and pillar edicts were tools of propaganda, and we might doubt that Asoka was quite as saintly as he wished history to believe. That he was enlightened and, by the standards of the time, compassionate cannot be doubted, however. He claimed that his task was to "promote the welfare of the whole world," and so he did. He abolished the death penalty, established a sprawling network of wells and rest houses for travellers, and planted shady trees along trade routes. As for ambassadors, they were to continue in their usual tasks—forging alliances and seeking tribute—but they were also to carry medicinal herbs to foreign lands.

The defining diplomatic policy of Asoka's reign had little to do with military aggrandizement or economic progress—it consisted of missionary-envoys being sent to Syria, Egypt, Macedonia, and Nepal to preach the tenets of Buddhism. And as we will see in the missions of men like John of Plano Carpini in the thirteenth century, the tradition of the monkish ambassador had a vibrant future ahead of it. When a new king, Tissa, came to the throne of Sri Lanka, he sent envoys to Asoka informing the emperor of his accession. Asoka responded by dispatching his son, Mahinda, as an "ambassador of righteousness," charged with winning the new king for the Buddhist faith. He succeeded, and King Tissa was soon erecting a Buddhist reliquary in one of the royal gardens.

Tissa's sister was an even more impassioned acolyte and announced that she desired to become a Buddhist nun. Lacking the authority to invest her in holy orders, Mahinda sent for his own sister, Sanghamitta, who was already a nun. She arrived in Sri Lanka with the requisite paraphernalia and a golden vase containing a branch of the Bodhi tree under which the Buddha had meditated for seven years before receiving enlightenment. The sapling was planted on a terrace in the royal gardens and to this day remains an object of veneration.

If this was one way to encounter the rest of the world, Asoka's grandfather had espoused quite another. Chandragupta (reigned 321–298 B.C.), the founder of the Mauryan dynasty, was a man of humble origins: by some accounts, the son of a peacock farmer.

One, presumably apocryphal, story perfectly encapsulates his fearful reputation. Ever wary of assassination attempts, Chandragupta was in the habit of taking a daily draft of poison with his meals, hoping to immunize himself against its effects. One day, when his pregnant wife accidentally imbibed some of the poison, the emperor immediately chopped off her head (hoping to stop the toxins progressing any further), ripped the unborn child from her belly, and placed the embryo in the womb of a goat.[26]

Such ruthless efficiency pervaded Chandragupta's entire political career. It was captured for posterity by one of his most trusted ministers, named Kautilya, who wrote an intricate treatise on how a wise king ought to govern. Kautilya's *Arthasastra* was not simply an abstract meditation on devious statecraft, but an account of actual political practice. It is one of the finest works of political philosophy ever written, though one that remains undervalued in the West. Its radical meditations on the nature and exercise of political power led the sociologist Max Weber to conclude that, by comparison, "Machiavelli's *The Prince* is harmless."[27] It made a refreshingly candid contribution to an enduring debate, and one that any history of the ambassadors is obliged to fathom. What was diplomacy for? By what rules should it be governed? Which is more important when conducting foreign affairs—moral rectitude or naked self-interest, courtesy or cunning, the urbanity of an envoy or the subtle skills of an assassin? Realism or idealism?

The great Roman orator Cicero (106–43 B.C.) offered one prescription:

> There will not be different laws at Rome and at Athens, or different laws now and in the future, but one eternal and unchangeable law will be valid for all nations and for all times, and there will be one master and one ruler, that is, God, over all, for He is the author of this law, its promulgator, and its enforcing judge.[28]

When expounding the rules and rubrics of diplomacy, the idealist insists, one must abide by the dictates of a universal moral order. This might be Cicero's God, Asoka's Dhamma, or even the modern notion of a binding Law of Nations, but in all cases ethical imperatives govern the parleys between societies. Of course, rulers invariably engage in diplomacy to further their own best interests, but there is still a right way and a wrong way to conduct foreign affairs. Justice and fair play are not only worth pursuing in and of themselves, they also foster dynamic, respectful relationships.

Realists regard this as naïve, and look instead to self-interest and contingency. Higher justice is a chimera, they suggest, and rather than genuflecting to a benign Law of *Nations*, political leaders ought to abide by the grittier realities of the Law of *Nature*. The strong will always dominate the weak, the pursuit of power and influence is both noble and necessary, and if you do not strive to rule over others then, in time, others will assuredly strive to rule over you.

Classical Athens, to look backward for a moment, is often credited with an uncompromisingly realistic outlook. In 416 B.C., during the Peloponnesian War, the city launched an expedition against the island of Melos, a Spartan colony that stubbornly refused to ally itself with the Athenian Empire. Envoys were sent to treat with the island's governors. "On our side," the Athenians began, "we will not use fine phrases" or claim that Athens deserves its empire because of past services to the Greek world. When reaching their decision, the Melians should eschew moralizing and "try to get what it is possible for you to get....When matters are discussed by practical people" the just outcome is always determined by the fact that "the strong do what they have the power to do and the weak accept what they have to accept."

In the present instance, "we rule the sea and you are islanders, and weaker islanders than the rest." Any appeal to "such a thing as fair play and just dealing" was given short shrift. The "path of justice and honour" led to danger, the path of self-interest to safety. "There is nothing disgraceful in giving way to the greatest city in Hellas when she is offering you such reasonable terms—alliance on a tribute-paying basis and liberty to enjoy your own property." Athens was simply behaving as a great power ought to: expanding its influence so that it might flourish.

The Melians were unconvinced. "Our decision, Athenians, is just the same as it was at first. We are not prepared to give up in a short moment the liberty which our city has enjoyed from its foundation for seven hundred years. We put our trust in the fortune that the gods will send…and in the help of men—that is, of the Spartans." The trust was misplaced and, after a period of siege, "the Melians surrendered unconditionally to the Athenians, who put to death all the men of military age, and sold the women and children as slaves."[29]

This account of the so-called Melian dialogue comes from the histories of Thucydides (460–400 B.C.), often claimed as a founding father of realist theorizing. Undoubtedly, he offers a skewed account of Greek statecraft. He had a particular view of the nature of Greek political life, a precise (and to some tastes compelling) theory about how the affairs of men were governed, and he shaped his history accordingly. But if he exaggerated, Thucydides, as great an historian as the world would know, was surely correct in diagnosing naked self-interest as one of the engines of Greek politics. However, the tradition he inaugurated (one that would be carried forward by philosophers such as Niccolo Machiavelli and Thomas Hobbes) had a less familiar, but no less vibrant, counterpart in the East, which brings us back to Kautilya's *Arthasastra*.

The Arthasastra

According to Kautilya's theory, in the Mauryan political world everything turned on the character of the king. If he "is energetic, his subjects will be equally energetic. If he is reckless, they will be reckless likewise." Kautilya advised any reputable monarch to divide his day into one-and-a-half-hour segments. His nighttime hours were to be every bit as regimented.

> During the first one-eighth part of the night, he shall receive secret emissaries; during the second, he shall attend to bathing and supper and study; during the third, he shall enter the bedchamber amid the sound of trumpets and enjoy sleep during the fourth and fifth parts. Having been awakened by the sound of trumpets during the sixth part, he shall recall to his mind the injunctions of sciences as well as the day's duties; during the seventh, he shall sit considering administrative measures and send out spies; and during the eighth division of the night, he shall receive benedictions from sacrificial priests, teachers, and the high priest, and having seen his physician, chief cook and astrologer, and having saluted both a cow with its calf and a bull by circumambulating around them, he shall get into his court.

An approachable king was likely to be a popular king. "When in the court, he shall never cause his petitioners to wait at the door, for when a king makes himself inaccessible to his people and entrusts work to his immediate officers, he may be sure to engender confusion in business, and to cause public disaffection." He should, therefore, "personally attend to the business of gods, of heretics, of Brahmans learned in the Vedas, of cattle, of sacred places, of minors, the aged, the afflicted, the helpless, and of women." Indeed, the *Arthasastra* is, in many ways, a primer in enlightened monarchy. Domestic affairs were to be conducted with justice and dispatch, measures were to be put in place to protect the population from natural disasters and to safeguard the rights and privileges of merchants.

Justice was never to be arbitrary, but it could sometimes be severe. Torture was a legitimate investigative technique, although it was not to be employed against certain classes of people: pregnant women, priests, "ignoramuses, youngsters, the aged, the afflicted, persons under intoxication, lunatics, persons suffering from hunger, thirst, or fatigue from journey, persons who have confessed of their own accord, and persons who are very weak—none of these shall be subjected to torture."

A terrifying variety of punishments awaited everyone else:

> blows with a cane: twelve beats on each of the thighs; twenty-eight beats with a stick of the tree; thirty-two beats on each palm of the hands and on each sole of the feet; two on the knuckles, the hands being joined so as to appear like a scorpion…burning one of the joints of a finger after the accused has been made to drink rice gruel; heating his body for a day after he has been made to drink oil; causing him to lie on coarse green grass for a night in winter.

Those adjudged guilty lost all hope of clemency. Anyone who stole a chicken, mongoose, dog, or pig could either pay a hefty fine or have the tip of his nose severed. "He who castrates a man shall have his generative organ cut off," while "any person who aims at the kingdom, who forces entrance into the king's harem, who instigates wild tribes or enemies against the king, or who creates disaffection in forts, country parts, or in the army, shall be burnt alive from head to foot."

The flinty character of domestic politics extended to the Mauryans' dealings with other kingdoms. The empire's fortunes were not determined by the randomness of fate, Kautilya insisted, but by the decisions rulers made. Kautilya offered a simple, but elegant analysis of Indian geopolitics. The king ought to regard his immediate neighbor as his enemy, and the neighbor beyond that as his ally, and so on, in a system of concentric circles. He should adjust his policy according to his potency and resources: When strong, he should strike, and when weak he should temporize.

At all times, however, he should do everything possible to gather reliable intelligence, both at home and abroad. A motley collection of spies were to be recruited to test the loyalty of his ministers and to infiltrate subversive factions within society. The state should

> employ spies disguised as persons endowed with supernatural power, persons engaged in penance, ascetics, bards, buffoons, mystics, astrologers, prophets foretelling the future...physicians, lunatics, the dumb, the deaf, idiots, the blind, traders, painters, carpenters, musicians, dancers, vintners, and manufacturers of cakes, flesh and cooked rice, and send them abroad into the country for espionage.

Agents should also be posted abroad to reconnoiter and sow discord. Astrologers might be dispatched to convince dissidents that it was an especially auspicious time to mount a coup. Prostitutes could be sent to seduce rival generals and foment animosity between them.

Ambassadors also had a vital role to play. An envoy's first duty was to "make friendship with the enemy's officers such as those in charge of wild tracts, of boundaries, of cities, and of country parts. He shall also contrast the military stations, sinews of war, and strongholds of the enemy with those of his own master. He shall ascertain the size and area of forts and of the state, as well as strongholds of precious things and assailable and unassailable

points." The ambassador's reception was an excellent way of gaug-
ing the intentions of a rival monarch. Promising signs included
respectful treatment, being given a seat close to the throne, and en-
quiries after the health of the emperor: "All these shall be noted
as indicating the good graces of the enemy and the reverse his
displeasure."

Whatever welcome the ambassador received, he was not to be
cowed by the "mightiness of the enemy" and he should "strictly
avoid women and liquor...for it is well-known that the intentions
of envoys are ascertained while they are asleep or under the influence of alcohol." During his mission he should establish his own
network of spies "to ascertain the nature of the intrigue prevalent
among parties favourably disposed to his own master, as well as the
conspiracy of hostile factions." If this proved impossible he could
"try to gather such information by observing the talk of beggars,
intoxicated and insane persons, or of persons babbling in sleep."
The precise objective of a mission would vary according to circumstances, but likely duties included "the maintenance of treaties, the
issue of ultimatums, gaining of friends, intrigue, sowing dissension
among friends, carrying away by stealth relatives and gems, [and]
gathering information about the movements of spies."

Of course, Kautilya realized that other potentates were always
likely to send their own devious ambassadors, so it was important
to remain vigilant. There were constant dangers associated with
being a Mauryan emperor, and the risk of assassination was taken
especially seriously, as Chandragupta's wife could attest, with poi-
soning being the regicide's preferred method. The alarm was to be
raised whenever

> the vapour arising from cooked rice possesses the colour of the
> neck of a peacock, and appears chill as if suddenly cooled;

when vegetables possess an unnatural colour, and are watery
and hardened, and appear to have suddenly turned dry…when
utensils reflect light either more or less than usual, and are covered with a layer of foam at their edges; when any liquid preparation possesses streaks on its surface; when milk bears a bluish
streak in the centre of its surface; when liquor and water possess reddish streaks; when curd is marked with black and dark
streaks, and honey with white streaks; when watery things appear parched as if overcooked and look blue and swollen; when
dry things have shrunk and changed in their colour; when hard
things appear soft, and soft things hard…when carpets and
curtains possess blackish circular spots, with their threads and
hair fallen off; when metallic vessels set with gems appear tarnished as though by roasting, and have lost their polish, colour,
shine, and softness of touch.

Poisoners were also apt to give themselves away, and the king's attendants should always be suspicious of "hesitation in speaking,
heavy perspiration, yawning, too much bodily tremor, frequent
tumbling, evasion of speech [and] carelessness in work." Whenever the king was presented with "water, scents, fragrant powders,
dress and garlands," servants "shall first touch these things by their
eyes, arms and breast."

It was a fitting response to a cynical political milieu. The Mauryans knew of every potential danger because of an unflinching
willingness to employ dubious strategies of their own. Just as ambassadors were expected to spy and agitate, so agents were sometimes sent to kill off offensive rivals. Pacts and pledges could be
negotiated, but it was also entirely legitimate to break them. A
trusted policy in the ancient world was for powers to exchange
hostages—often including a ruler's relatives—when they made
treaties: This provided some guarantee that the parties would abide
by the terms of an agreement. Kautilya recognized the usefulness

of such arrangements, but saw not the slightest reason to honor them. If a prince had been offered up as a hostage, that prince should do everything in his power to engineer his escape.

> Carpenters, artisans, and other spies, attending upon the prince (kept as a hostage) may take him away at night through an underground tunnel dug for the purpose. Dancers, actors, singers, players on musical instruments, buffoons, court-bards [and] swimmers previously set about the enemy [as spies], may continue under his service and may indirectly serve the prince. They should have the privilege of entering and going out of the palace at any time. The prince may therefore get out at night disguised as any one of the above spies... Or the prince may be removed concealed under clothes, commodities, vessels, beds, seats and other articles by cooks, confectioners, servants employed to serve the king while bathing, servants employed for carrying conveyances, for spreading the bed, toilet-making, dressing, and procuring water.

It might be necessary to serve sentinels with poisoned food, or to bribe them, or to create a diversion by setting "fire to a building filled with valuable articles." The strategies enumerated by Kautilya were seemingly endless. The prince could disguise himself as a shaven-headed ascetic, a diseased man, or even a corpse.[30]

Asoka and Chandragupta, grandson and grandfather, inhabited opposite ends of the same philosophical spectrum. Together, they offered a telling lesson in just how drastically, and rapidly, worldviews might change. Diplomacy was always the bellwether of a society's attitude toward the rest of humanity. The optimism and generosity of an Asoka, his policy of conquest through righteousness, were exceptional: In the phrase of H. G. Wells, among the monarchs that crowd the columns of history, Asoka shines almost alone. The encounters between cultures would more often be clouded by fear and suspicion.

Greeks were tolerated in the ancient city of Alexandria but, as Herodotus explained, "No Egyptian man or woman will kiss a Greek or use a Greek knife, spit or cauldron, or even eat the flesh of a bull known to be clean if it has been cut with a Greek knife."[31] Muscovite princes would accept the need for relationships with other nations but, well into the seventeenth century, they often refused to shake the hand of a foreigner for fear of infection. During the sixteenth century, Venetians would sell their wares in Ottoman Istanbul, and the Portuguese would trade in Macao, but both communities would be mistrusted and ghettoized.

Indeed, mention of the Portuguese in Macao brings us to China, the final destination in this survey of the ancient world, and a culture that has agonized more than any other over its dealings with the outside world. One of the duties of history is to puncture lazy orthodoxies, and the travels of one ancient ambassador do much to confound the notion of unwavering Chinese insularity and xenophobia. Before recounting his tale, however, it would be useful to ponder why that notion is so stubbornly embedded in the Western psyche. To that end, before visiting the Han dynasty of ancient China, a brief detour of twenty-one centuries is called for.

4
THE SON OF HEAVEN

The Boxers

> From now on, when barbarians come to the capital to present
> tribute, the military population and common people who dare
> to congregate in the streets to stare and make fun of them, or
> throw broken tiles and thus injure any of the barbarians, shall
> be punished with the cangue as a warning to the public.
> —Hui-t'ung-kuan Regulations, 1500[32]

FOR FIFTY-FIVE DAYS in the summer of 1900 the foreign
legations of Peking, crammed into the southern quarter of
the city, lay under siege. Resentment of the Western powers had been simmering in China for decades. They had brought
newfangled railways that tarnished the harmony of the natural
landscape, they had encouraged hordes of zealous Christian missionaries to chip away at the empire's ancient belief systems, and
they had demonstrated an unwavering ambition to dominate
China's political and economic life.

China had been slow to recognize the extraordinary technological advancements of eighteenth-century Europe. The Chinese
simply did not realize how mighty and wealthy the West had suddenly become until they tried to snuff out the illegal opium trade
in the late 1830s. China was crushed by British force of arms. In

the wake of the First Opium War (1839–1842), Britain opened seaports to foreign trade that were entirely removed from Chinese jurisdiction, and annexed Hong Kong. Further crises and humiliations followed. The Russians encroached on the empire's northern territories, internal rebellions scarred the middle years of the century, and in 1860 the French and British even temporarily occupied Peking. But despite all their successes, the Western powers were still impatient to carve out spheres of even greater influence and profit within the Celestial Empire.

In 1897 the murder of two Protestant missionaries gave Germany the ideal justification for seizing the bustling port of Jiaozhou. For several years, this same region had also seen a blossoming of enthusiasm for the so-called Boxer movement. Secretive, illegal martial-arts societies, the Boxers had abandoned their traditional antidynastic sentiment in favor of virulent anti-Western rhetoric. With their magical rituals and incantations, and their belief that they were immune from bullets, the Boxers offered an irresistible outlet for decades' worth of resentment. Their influence spread out across northern China during the late 1890s.

The population was in dire need of a rallying cry. A recent war with Japan had ended in humiliating defeat, the Yellow River had burst its banks in 1898, and two years later the northern reaches of the empire had been ravaged by drought. In Peking, power resided with a reactionary empress dowager, whose counsellors urged her to stop demonizing the Boxers as lawless bandits, and instead use them to reassert China's independence. Early in 1900 they were summoned to the capital.

The diplomatic community in Peking was understandably nervous. Ominous news began to rush in from all sides. The British summer legation outside the city was burned down, the Boxers severed the railway lines between Peking and the coast, and on the 11th of June the chancellor of the Japanese embassy was set on by an angry crowd. After being dragged from his coach he was hacked to pieces, his battered corpse thrown in the gutter and his heart presented to a popular general. By the thirteenth of the month, Boxers were flooding into the city, attacking churches and the homes of foreigners, digging up Christian graves. When the German ambassador, Clemens von Ketteler, set out for urgent talks with the government on June the 20th, he, too, was murdered in the street. An officially sanctioned siege of the legation quarter by imperial troops now seemed inevitable.

Outlying embassies were abandoned, and the 475 civilians, 450 guards, and 2,300 Chinese Christians, stranded in the diplomatic quarter, began their agonizing wait for the arrival of Western troops. Mercifully, they had a good supply of fresh water and rice, as well as ample stocks of pony meat and champagne. There was also a wealth of tobacco and, as one witness remembered it, "even some of the women, principally Italians and Russians, found relief in the constant smoking of cigarettes." Conditions were terribly crowded, however, and the Dutch minister was obliged to sleep in a cupboard belonging to the Russian ambassador. Morale was bruised when a Norwegian missionary went mad, and the French ambassador infuriated everyone by wandering around the compound, announcing that "we are all going to die tonight, we are all lost."[33]

The siege provided its edifying sights: Professors turning their hand to butchery, Catholic and Protestant missionaries filling defensive sandbags together. And for the most part, the imperial troops showed restraint, although during one day they did manage to discharge 200,000 rounds of ammunition in the direction of the legations. Finally, on August the 14th, relief came with the arrival of Western forces—8,000 Japanese, 4,800 Russian, 3,000 British, 2,100 American, 800 French, fifty-eight Austrian, and fifty-three Italian soldiers. "We heard the playing of machine guns on the outside of the city," someone recalled: "Never was music so sweet."[34]

It was an invincible force, and with the lifting of the siege, the Western powers set about exacting their revenge. By the terms of the Boxer Protocol of September 1901, China was to offer an abject apology, pay a huge indemnity for its outrageous behavior, and desist from importing arms for two years. It was a burden that the tottering Manchu dynasty could hardly withstand, and by 1911 imperial China had ceased to exist, a republic set up in its place. As for the Western powers, they seized every opportunity to expand their political and economic stranglehold on the country. Kaiser Wilhelm offered an especially bullish assessment of the changed situation: "Just as the Huns a thousand years ago, under the leadership of Attila, gained a reputation by virtue of which they still live in historical tradition, so may the name of Germany become known in such a manner in China that no Chinese will ever again even dare to look askance at a German."[35]

⸺⁓⸺

If the West still cherishes an image of Chinese insularity and xenophobia, one need look no further than the siege of the Peking embassies in 1900 for part of the explanation. The terror and privations suffered by ambassadors, their families, and retinues would not quickly be forgotten. In truth, the Boxer Rebellion was the culmination of decades of growing alienation. As early as the end of the eighteenth century, Europe had fallen out of love with China. Heady stories of the majestic Chinese court, revered during the sixteenth and seventeenth centuries as the most cultured and opulent place that might be imagined, were suddenly replaced by the niggardly accounts of ill-humored diplomats—as ever, the vessels for their cultures' prejudices.

When a Dutch ambassador travelled to Peking in 1796, there was precious little talk of silk, jade, or chinoiserie. Instead, he reported back on mandarins with "shrill voices" who rudely awakened visitors at three in the morning, and of "low and dirty" reception rooms stocked with "coarse rugs...a few common chairs [and] a piece of wood with an iron spike as a candlestick." The elaborate order and ritual of the court had apparently descended into chaos, and palaces were now "full of people, great and small, rich and poor intermingled, pressing and pushing without any distinction, so that we were struck by a scene of confusion."

The emperor's horses were "shaggy and rather dirty," and the food served at state banquets was an utter disgrace—pieces of game "looking as if they were remnants of gnawed off bones," that were unceremoniously "dumped on the table." Here, the ambassador suggested, was the "most conclusive proof of coarseness and lack of civilization."

> However incredible this may seem in Europe, it is too remarkable to pass over in silence. From the reports with which the missionaries have deluded the world for a number of years, I had imagined a very civilised and enlightened people. These ideas were deeply rooted and a kind of violence was necessary to eradicate them, but this reception, joined to all our previous experiences, was a radical cure.[36]

In fact, the Jesuits who had been tending the mission fields of China for the past two centuries had not been deluding anyone.

China was in a dozen sorts of decline, but it had not suddenly become an uncivilized backwater. Europe had simply experienced a shift in fashion, a cultural backlash. The Enlightenment adoration of Confucian philosophy, ceramics and the Chinese political genius had given way to talk of Chinese despotism, cruelty, and backwardness. The West had decided it was superior, the cradle and guardian of authentic civilization, and China was now a place to be feared, mocked, or exploited.

It was to prove a resilient perspective: one that still infects the European worldview, and one that a tragedy such as the Boxer Rebellion only served to reinforce. Millennia of Chinese history were reduced to a stereotype. China was—and always had been—odd, unwelcoming, and self-satisfied. But as other stories from the history of the ambassadors reveal, the image is at best a simplistic half-truth. The Boxer Rebellion does not epitomize the history of China.

Chang Ch'ien

Certain negative orthodoxies regarding China cannot be gainsaid. They persist because they are accurate. The Chinese emperor was always hailed as the Son of Heaven, the mediator between God and mankind, the overlord of all the earth's kings and princes, although this posture was hardly a Chinese preserve. The rulers of ancient Mesopotamia believed themselves to be gods, and Mongol khans would style themselves the lords of the universe. In 1525, when the Ottoman leader Suleiman the Magnificent sent a letter to Francis I of France, he referred to himself as, "by the sacred miracles of Muhammad...Sultan of Sultans, the sovereign of sovereigns, the dispenser of crowns to the monarchs of the face of the world, the shadow of God on earth...ruler of the White and the Black seas, of Rumelia and Anatolia, Kazakhstan,

Azerbaijan, Persia, Damascus, Aleppo, Cairo, Mecca, Medina, Arabia and Yemen."[37] When the client states of ancient Egypt sent their envoys to meet with the pharaoh, they were expected to prostrate themselves seven times on their bellies and seven times on their backs. Whenever letters were sent to the pharaoh, diplomatic convention required these same states to refer to themselves as the dust beneath his sandals.

It is also true that China would often be sublimely uninterested in affairs beyond Southeast Asia, and Chinese diplomacy would sometimes consist almost entirely of raking in tribute from Korea, Vietnam, and Japan. This proved to be a disastrous policy at the end of the eighteenth century, although in other periods one wonders why China *should* have been concerned with the intricacies of Western political life. Ancient Greece and Mauryan India were also preoccupied with their own regional politics, after all. Moreover, a sense of superiority did not always imply isolation. Throughout its twenty-five dynasties, China was usually delighted to welcome the envoys of distant nations.

As soon as two Persian ambassadors crossed the Chinese border in 1420, they were greeted by imperial officials. In "a delectable meadow" their hosts had set up a platform "with canvas awnings, over which were placed tables and chairs." A meal of "geese, fowls, roasted meat" and fruit was served and "after the repast various kinds of intoxicants were served up and all became tipsy." Drink and diplomacy once again.

A few days further into their journey, the ambassadors encountered a local viceroy, and he was just as determined to provide lavish hospitality. Once again, the ambassadors were ridiculously well fed. To the accompaniment of "organs, fiddles, Chinese fifes and two types of flute," they dined on muskmelons and watermelons, "walnuts, peeled chestnut, lemons, garlics, and onions pickled in vinegar." The feast was rounded off by an acrobatic display, with tricks being performed by "handsome boys, with their faces painted red and white in such a way that whoever happened to look at them took them for girls, with caps on their heads and pearls in their ears."

Festivities followed in every town through which the ambassadors passed until, in mid-December, they arrived in Peking. News reached the envoys that the emperor himself was planning a lunchtime banquet. They rode from their lodgings to the imperial palace and, having dismounted at the first gateway, they were "conducted to the foot of the throne" and "made prostration to the emperor five times." Led from his presence, the ambassadors were now advised to seek out a toilet, "lest they should unexpectedly feel the necessity to rise in the middle of the banquet for some need when it would not be possible to go out."

With such matters attended to, the ambassadors returned to the scene of the banquet, "a very extensive courtyard paved most beautifully and exquisitely with cut stones." Inside a canopy they discovered a "magnificent throne, higher than the height of man with silver staircases on its three sides." Incense burners and eunuchs were posted on either side, and next to them "stood stalwart Chinese officers armed with quivers." Farther back came "soldiers with long halberds in their hands and behind them yet another body of men with drawn swords."

The Yongle emperor made his entrance and took his seat beneath a canopy of yellow satin decorated with images of fighting dragons. All was silence as the ambassadors, "on the tiptoe of expectation," approached the throne. Having prostrated themselves five more times, the meal got underway. There were yet more acrobats—a troupe of dancers, made up of boys "as beautiful as the moon"—and with the arrival of each new course an orchestra struck up and an ocean of colored umbrellas were spun around. With the meal of lamb, goose, and rice wine complete, the emperor doled out rewards to the performers and retired to his harem.[38]

The Persian ambassadors had been treated with the greatest courtesy, but the Chinese did not perceive them as representatives of a political equal. From the earliest days of imperial China in the second millennium B.C., whenever envoys came to China, whether from Persia, Rome, or the courts of Europe, they were seen as the bearers of tribute and homage to the greatest ruler in the world. Such visits flattered the emperor, they were a fitting sign of respect and submission, and it behooved the Chinese court to respond with grace and generosity.

But the world over, and certainly not only in China, diplomacy has always been a game of power and one-upmanship. When an insult was called for, rulers would turn to less than impressive men to serve as their envoys. Louis XI of France once sent a barber on a diplomatic errand to Margaret of Burgundy; another French king disparaged Edward III of England by conveying a message of defiance via a kitchen hand; the citizens of ancient Rhodes were furious when Rome supplied an ambassador who not only lacked the customary rank of senator but was also a lowly gymnastics instructor.

Conversely, when one ruler wished to show respect to another he would select skilled, very often noble ambassadors, and kings and princes have usually interpreted the arrival of such men as a reflection of their own grandeur. The Roman emperor Augustus would boast of how "embassies were sent to me from the kings of India who had never been seen before in the camp of any Roman general."[39] One of Elizabeth I's more devoted subjects reported how English sailors refused to transport Moroccan ambassadors in

1600, "because they think it is a matter odious and scandalous to the world to be too friendly or familiar with infidels." Nevertheless, it remained "no small honour to us that nations so far remote and every way different should meet here to admire the glory and magnificence of our Queen of Sheba."[40]

China was no different, and was always pleased to receive envoys. Dispatching ambassadors of its own was an infinitely more troubling proposition, however. Would it not be a sign of weakness or of parity with the barbarian hordes beyond its borders? Often, China decided that it would—but, to return to the ancient world, sometimes it did not.

There have been many epic diplomatic journeys. The distances travelled and the time such journeys took are likely to bewilder the modern reader. Envoys sent from ancient Babylon to Egypt traversed thousands of miles of caravan routes, usually only covering forty or fifty miles a day. When the ambassadors of an Indian king sought out the Roman emperor Augustus in 20 B.C., their outward journey lasted more than four years—a respectable achievement given the curious cargo with which they were burdened: a serpent ten cubits long, a partridge larger than a vulture, and an armless youth who could play the trumpet with his feet.[41] The journey of the Han ambassador Chang Ch'ien was every bit as impressive.

The Han dynasty ruled China, a seventeen-year hiatus excepted, from 206 B.C. to 220 A.D. It was a civilization that easily bears comparison with either fourth-century Athens or Mauryan India. Paper was invented, ideologies were forged, and a fiercely efficient bureaucracy developed. Specialized, well-trained ministers oversaw everything from tax collection, to religious ceremony, to the observation of the stars. The marketplaces of the Han capital, Ch'ang-an, bustled with merchants from across Asia; Buddhist missionaries travelled throughout the empire; and the Han embraced a policy of expansion and discovery. Their armies ploughed south of the Yangtze River, eastward to Korea, and even into the mysterious western regions of Central Asia. China was no less assured of its plenitude, but it was open to the world.

The Han emperor had many enemies, notably the aggressive Hsiung-nu tribe on China's northern frontier. Traditionally, it had seemed more sensible to contain the Hsiung-nu threat than to engage them in battle. Supplying them with luxurious goods—offering them bribes, in effect—also served to blunt their hawkish tendencies. One Han courtier talked of the various "baits" with which the Hsiung-nu could be seduced: "To give them elaborate clothes and carriages in order to corrupt their eyes; to give them fine food in order to corrupt their mouth; to give them music and women in order to corrupt their ears; to provide them with lofty buildings, granaries and slaves in order to corrupt their desires."[42]

The Han emperor Wu-ti grew weary of this passive, and to his mind ignoble, variety of diplomacy. He decided it was time to join battle against the Hsiung-nu. He would require allies, and who better than a people known as the Yueh-shih? They had been defeated by the Hsiung-nu and forced into exile, though not before the skull of their king had been fashioned into a drinking cup. They would surely crave revenge. Unfortunately, no one knew where they had fled. And so, in c.140 B.C., the courtier Chang Ch'ien was dispatched as an ambassador to locate their whereabouts.

A man of strong physique and of considerable generosity, Chang was accompanied by a hundred attendants as he set out on his embassy, but he was almost immediately captured by the Hsiung-nu. He spent the next ten years in captivity, although he seems to have been treated decently, and even acquired a Hsiung-nu wife and son. Finally, he managed to escape and embarked on a journey that would take him farther west than any previous Chinese ambassador. He even located the Yueh-shih in present-day Kazakhstan, only to find they had no interest in forging an alliance with the Han. Chang spent the next year travelling around the region. On his homeward journey he was again captured by the Hsiung-nu but quickly escaped and reached the Chinese court in 126 B.C. Only two of the hundred servants who had originally set out with him returned alive.

Chang was elevated to the office of grand counsellor of the palace, but not before providing the emperor with a report of the western regions that shattered the Chinese worldview. He had visited lands that no earlier Chinese ambassador had reached. His verbal report was enshrined in the imperial histories and provoked decades of further exploration beyond the traditional sphere of Chinese diplomatic interest, usually limited to Japan, Korea, Vietnam, and the various tribes on the empire's frontier. The assumption had always been that the farther one travelled from China, the more barbaric the people became, until one came to the edge of the world and a limitless ocean was reached. But Chang talked of people in the West, in the central Asian regions of Ferghana and Bactria, who actually lived "in houses, in fortified cities," who were "settled on the land, ploughing the fields and growing wheat and rice," who made wine from grapes and tended the finest horses Chang had ever seen. Even more astonishingly, he had heard of empires, most likely Persia, even farther to the west, that had developed the art of writing and traded with metal coins.[43]

As a direct result of Chang's mission, more ambassadors would be sent out in search of allies in the coming years—to northern India, to Samarkand, as far as the Persian Gulf. Each journey brought more revelations, and the trade routes into central Asia—the fabled silk roads—were refined and extended. As a direct result of such missions, China would be flooded with new imports, whether grapes or pomegranates, sesame seeds or broad beans.

By 92 B.C. a Chinese ambassador was laying silks at the feet of the Parthian monarch Mithridates II, who returned the compliment, dispatching ambassadors to China with an ostrich egg and a troupe of conjurers. Two hundred years after that, the envoys of a Roman emperor brought elephant tusks, rhinoceros horns, and tortoise shells to the Chinese court. The links that had been forged in the wake of the Han ambassadors would be sustained. The enduring relationship between diplomacy and gift-giving was already thriving—in 638 A.D. the Persians were sending the Chinese a ferret that was an expert mouse-catcher; a century later, they sent the Chinese four leopards. In the next phase of the ambassadors' story, this aspect of diplomacy would soar.

The Middle Centuries

5
CHARLEMAGNE'S ELEPHANT

Gift-Giving

> *Enter the French Ambassadors*

KING HARRY
> Now are we well prepared to know the pleasure
> Of our fair cousin Dauphin, for we hear
> Your greeting is from him, not from the King.

AMBASSADOR
> May't please your majesty to give us leave
> Freely to render what we have in charge.
> Or shall we sparingly show you far off
> The Dauphin's meaning and our embassy?
> [...] Your highness lately sending into France
> Did claim some certain dukedoms, in the right
> Of your great predecessor, King Edward the Third.
> In answer of which claim, the Prince our master
> Says that you savour too much of your youth,
> And bids you be advised, there's naught in France
> That can be with a nimble galliard won:
> You cannot revel into dukedoms there.
> He therefore sends you, meeter for your spirit,
> This tun of treasure, and in lieu of this
> Desires you let the dukedoms that you claim
> Hear no more of you. This the Dauphin speaks.

KING HARRY
> What treasure, uncle?

EXETER (*opening the tun*)
    Tennis balls, my liege.
KING HARRY
    We are glad the Dauphin is so pleasant with us.
    His present and your pains we thank you for.
    When we have matched our rackets to these balls,
    We will in France, by God's grace, play a set
    Shall strike his father's crown into the hazard...
    ...I will rise there with so full a glory
    That I will dazzle all the eyes of France,
    Yea strike the Dauphin blind to look on us.
    And tell the pleasant Prince this mock of his
    Hath turned his balls to gunstones, and his soul
    Shall stand sore chargèd for the wasteful vengeance
    That shall fly from them—for many a thousand widows
    Shall this, his mock, mock out of their dear husbands,
    Mock mothers from their sons, mock castles down...
    —*Henry V,* I.ii

BEFORE THE DRAFTING of the United States Constitution, potentates were free to lavish tokens of esteem on American worthies whenever they chose. In 1785, the king of Spain sent two especially handsome donkeys to General George Washington in recognition of his military exploits, and they were graciously received. Article I, section 9 of the Constitution immediately made such gestures suspicious, even illicit. Henceforth, no American public servant was to "accept of any present, emolument, office or title of any kind whatever, from any king, prince or foreign state."

So when, in 1839, the emperor of Morocco decided to present the United States with a lion and lioness (a prodigious gift by any standard), the local consul Thomas Carr faced an awkward decision. He could either offend an influential monarch or transgress the new rules of American diplomatic conduct. Carr valiantly tried to reject the gifts, but was forced to relent when the emperor's messenger threatened to release the animals into the street. After a few months' sojourn in the consulate buildings, the lions were shipped to Philadelphia and quietly sold off at auction.[44] Intended as a necessary check on bribery and corruption, the constitutional prohibition had managed, at a stroke, to jeopardize one of the most venerable of diplomatic rituals—the exchanging of meaningful, preferably spectacular, gifts.

For millennia, such exchanges had succeeded in capturing the tensions inherent in any ambassadorial encounter. Those giving the gifts often sought to demonstrate their affection or admiration for the recipient—see what we are *willing* to give—but they also hoped to hint, rather loudly, at their superiority, at their own wealth, ingenuity, and influence—see what we are *able* to give. To dispatch too meagre a gift was a snub, to send too exotic a gift was a boast. Polities were always much more likely to err on the side of boastfulness. Upon receiving presents from the Byzantine emperor in Constantinople, one tenth-century Muslim ruler immediately declared: "Send him a gift one hundred times greater than his so that he may recognize the glory of Islam and the grace that Allah has bestowed upon us."[45]

The Romans won favor by presenting gold necklaces to British tribal leaders, while the courts of Enlightenment Europe fastened on the idea of trading elegant Sèvres and Meissen porcelain. Fidel Castro would even limit the distribution of certain brands of luxury cigar to enhance their cachet as diplomatic gifts. In the eighteenth century, Frederick William I of Prussia went so far as sending an entire room, a candlelit Baroque confection of amber panels, mirrors, and mosaics, to Peter the Great of Russia. Peter had admired what became known as the Amber Room during a visit to Berlin in 1712. The Prussian king, eager to cement an alliance against Sweden, ordered the room's dismantlement. In 1717 it was packed into eighteen boxes and made the precarious journey between the Charlottenburg Palace and St. Petersburg. Until Hitler's invading troops tore it down during the Second World War, it came to symbolize the amity between two great nations.

Presenting something that was particularly evocative of one's own culture was another shrewd strategy. The Ottoman rulers of Turkey looked to fragrant soaps and carpets, the Chinese to precious silks. In the seventeenth century, the Polish city of Gdansk routinely selected the engraved amber for which it was so renowned, just as the burghers of Nuremburg favored their city's humble but much-coveted Lebkuchen cakes. Japanese emperors sent a full suit of Shogun armor to James I of England in 1613, and an elaborate Samurai sword to Queen Victoria two-and-a-half centuries later.

Comparison was everything in the world of diplomatic gift-giving. Monarchs endlessly contrasted themselves with their peers and predecessors. When a Russian ambassador presented James I of England with a "rich Persian dagger and knife" in 1617, "the king was very much pleased, and the more so when he understood Queen Elizabeth never had such a present thence."[46] They also compared the different gifts offered up by rival ambassadors. In 1614, when the East India Company looked to recruit an ambassador to send to the north Indian court of the Moghul emperor Jahangir, its gaze settled on Sir Thomas Roe—"a gentleman of pregnant understanding, well-spoken, learned, industrious, of a comely personage."[47] He left for India in February 1615 with a suitably impressive retinue—a chaplain, physician, apothecary, secretary, and cook.

Unfortunately, his diplomatic gifts were decidedly uninspiring. Upon receiving a scarf, swords, and some leather goods, Jahangir turned to a visiting Jesuit priest to ask whether James I was really the great monarch he purported to be. "Presents of so small a value" did little to bolster the English king's reputation. Jahangir had hoped, at the very least, for a cache of precious jewels. As for the coach that Roe also presented to the emperor, it simply did not measure up to the exacting Moghul standard of opulence. Jahangir had his servants dismantle it, replacing lackluster velvet fittings with silk, and "instead of the brass nails that were first in it, there were nails of silver put in their place."

Roe's embarrassment turned to utter humiliation with the arrival of a Persian ambassador. Here was a diplomat who truly knew how to impress a Moghul emperor. As well as twenty-seven Arabian horses, nine mules, and two chests of "Persian hangings," he offered Jahangir "forty muskets, five clocks, one camel laden with Persian cloth of gold…twenty-one camels of wine of the grape, fourteen camels of distilled sweet water, seven of rose water, seven daggers set with stones…[and] seven Venetian looking glasses." Roe contrasted the two assortments of gifts and confessed to being "ashamed of the relation."[48]

In this delicate game of cultural dialogue and rivalry, nothing was ever quite as impressive as the animals—whether the camels, bears, and monkeys dispatched to Frederick II of Sicily by the sultan of Cairo in 1228, the ten greyhounds taught to sit on horses' backs that ambassadors from India brought to the Mongol court a few years later, or even the pandas Ching-Ching and Chia-Chia that Peking gave to Britain in 1974. Animals, especially when transported over long distances or into strange climates, did have a tendency to perish en route. In 1514, when the king of Portugal sent a rhinoceros to Pope Leo X, the creature drowned on its way to Rome. Even when they arrived in perfect condition, the animals were not always wonderfully well behaved. In the tenth century, dogs sent as gifts from the Hungarian king almost bit the Byzantine emperor's hand and an unfortunate diplomatic incident was only narrowly avoided.

Such risks were well worth taking, however. Animals flattered even the greatest monarch. Very rarely was the gift of a curious animal rejected. In 693 A.D., Arab rulers suggested sending a lion to the Chinese empress. Unfortunately, it was a time of scarcity and famine in the East, and one of the empress's advisors suggested that an animal that ate such a prodigious amount of fresh meat every day would be an unwelcome strain on the court's limited resources.[49] This was an aberration. Throughout the world's history, possessing exotic creatures was a hallmark of power and influence. The pharaohs of Ancient Egypt sent out hunting parties as far as Somalia to capture monkeys and leopards, and rulers—whether Solomon or Kublai Khan, the Bourbons or the Medici—lavished untold wealth on their menageries.

Giraffes always made for unusually extravagant gifts. The Chinese emperor was delighted with the creature sent as tribute, via Bengal, from East Africa in 1414, and four centuries later, in 1827, the pasha of Egypt scored a notable diplomatic triumph by dispatching giraffes to the rulers of England, France, and Austria. Two of the animals soon perished, but the giraffe that had been shipped to Marseilles and then marched through the French countryside would continue to delight crowds of Parisians at the Jardin des Plantes for the next sixteen years.

Most prized of all, however, was the elephant—a creature that had charmed and fascinated Europe for centuries. To the ancient world, elephants were "of all the brutes the most intelligent," known to "have taken up their riders when slain in battle and carried them away for burial." They were invested with the full gamut of human faculties and emotions. "It understands the language of its country," the Roman naturalist Pliny explained. "It obeys commands, and it remembers all the duties which it has been taught. It is sensible alike of the pleasures of love and glory, and, to a degree that is rare even among men, possesses notions of honesty, prudence, and equity." It had "a religious respect for the stars, and a veneration for the sun and the moon," and, according to the Greek historian Arrian, "there was even one that died of remorse and despair because it had killed its rider in a fit of rage."[50]

The typical elephant enjoyed "his bath with all the zest of a consummate voluptuary" and was endearingly temperamental. If his keepers did not fill his manger with just the right kinds of flowers, he would begin roaring in protest. Even when the requisite flowers had been located, he would refuse to eat if they were not properly arranged, "for he loves to have his sleep made sweet and pleasant." A suitor's promise of an elephant, Arrian revealed, had even been known to seduce chaste Indian women away from the path of virtue. To present an elephant to a coy mistress served as an irresistible flirtatious gambit.

Elephants carried an air of menace, of course. They were formidable engines of war, able to turn the tide of any battle and to terrify the hardiest soldier. They would always be associated in the Western imagination with Hannibal's crossing of the Alps in 218 B.C., but their fabled military prowess only added to their mystique. As a result, there was obvious capital to be made from exhibiting mastery over such fearsome creatures.

In 55 B.C., the Roman general Pompey treated crowds at the Circus Maximus to a banquet of cruelty and bloodshed, overseeing the slaughter of five hundred lions and four hundred leopards. Roman audiences were hardly squeamish, but the culling of seventeen elephants that came next was too brutal even for them. Realizing that their lives were in the gravest danger, the elephants sought to gain the compassion of the crowd by letting out desperate cries and wails. Suddenly, the formerly bloodthirsty crowds turned against Pompey and showered him in curses and abuse. It was perhaps wiser to treat elephants with greater respect: making use of them, for instance, as the very finest of diplomatic gifts.

In 1552, Suleyman the elephant trekked across central Europe from Genoa to Vienna. A present from the Portuguese king to the Holy Roman Emperor, it attracted huge crowds in all the towns and villages through which it passed and inspired dozens of adoring songs and poems. Three centuries earlier, Louis IX of France had presented Henry III of England with an elephant, the first such creature to be seen on British soil since the Roman invasions of the first century A.D. It took up residence in the menagerie at the Tower of London, already home to leopards sent by the German emperor, and from the Norwegian king, a polar bear that fished for its supper in the Thames each evening. Sadly, the elephant died within two years, most likely from overindulgence in the red wine prescribed to warm its blood. Not the worst of deaths, perhaps, but the English king was heartbroken and is said to have nursed his outrageously unusual pet through its final death agonies.

Some elephants travelled even farther.

Greece, India, and China were the triple pillars of our survey of the ancient world. Turning to the early medieval centuries, Charlemagne's Europe, the Abbasid caliphate of Baghdad, and the Byzantine Empire take center stage. All three mistrusted one another, and such mistrust sometimes engendered hatred. But, as three of the greatest powers in the world, they all realized that they were obliged to maintain diplomatic relations. Their encounters forced a collision between Islam and Christianity, between the two squabbling halves of the Christian commonwealth—and, in the year 801, the dispatching of yet another diplomatic elephant.

⬸⫙⫙⫙⫙⬳

The death of Muhammad in 632 ushered in the era of the Rashidun, the first four Islamic caliphs, all of them trusted companions of the prophet. From their Arabian stronghold in Medina, in present-day Saudi Arabia, they oversaw decades of staggering territorial expansion. Jerusalem was taken in 638, and by 641 the Muslim conquest of Syria, Palestine, and Egypt was all but complete. Persia's armies were crushed at the battle of Qadisiyyah in 637 and its capital, Ctesiphon, seized: the prelude to the wholesale takeover of the entire Sassanid Persian Empire. Within a few more years, Cyprus would be snatched from Byzantium, and Muslim armies would march as far as Tripoli in the west and Afghanistan and the Indus River in the east.

Military adventures abroad could not disguise factionalism and theological bickering at home, however. Towards the end of the Rashidun, rebellion brought Muhammad's son-in-law Ali to power in 656. His authority was not universally recognized across the Muslim world, and a period of civil war was only ended by the arrival of the Umayyads, the first great Islamic dynasty descended from one of Muhammad's closest companions. A new period of expansion began. By 750, Sicily and Crete had been welcomed into the Islamic fold, and a Muslim kingdom had been established in Spain. It was in the year 750 that a new dynasty wrested control of the empire from the Umayyads. The Abbasid caliphate, descended from an uncle of the prophet, transferred the capital from Damascus to Baghdad and ushered in one of the golden ages of Islamic history.

Under Abbasid rule, Baghdad was to become a wonder of the early medieval world, a circular city of science and poetry, famous for its bookshops and bathhouses, its chess games and secret cabarets. One observer calculated that it had "no equal on earth either in the Orient or the Occident, it is the most extensive city in area, in importance, in prosperity, in abundance of water, and in healthful climate." Merchandise flooded in from as far away as India, China, and Tibet, and one might imagine that "all the goods of the earth are sent there, all the treasures of the world gathered there, and all the blessings of the universe concentrated there." The water was sweet, the trees flourished, the fruit was of perfect quality, and the people were all blessed with bright countenances and open intelligences. No one was "better educated than their scholars…more solid in their syntax than their grammarians, more supple than their singers…more eloquent than their preachers, more artistic than their poets." The only possible conclusion was that "Iraq is indeed the centre of the world."[51]

Harun al-Rashid (reign 786–809), was the most famous of the Abbasid caliphs, his opulent court familiar to history through the pages of *The Thousand and One Arabian Nights*. A ruthless politician, patron of the arts, builder of magnificent palaces, Harun was an expert diplomatist.

During the reign of the Byzantine empress Irene, he had marched his troops to within sight of Constantinople and demanded the payment of a handsome yearly tribute in exchange for not attacking the city. Irene had acquiesced, but her successor,

Nicephorus I, thought it far below Byzantium's dignity to humble itself before a Muslim ruler. In 802 he dispatched an envoy to Iraq with a strongly worded letter, replete with an analogy to the game of chess that any Abbasid caliph was certain to appreciate:

> The queen who reigned before me gave you the position of the tower and placed herself in the position of a simple pawn. She paid the tribute that was once imposed upon you…This was the result of the frailty and foolishness of women. When you receive my letter, send back the money that you have received from her, and ransom yourself by paying the sums that are incumbent on you. Otherwise, the sword will decide between us.

For added emphasis, the Byzantine envoys then threw swords at the caliph's feet. A furious Harun took up his saber, smashed the swords to pieces and then penned the tersest of replies. "From Harun, commander of the faithful, to Nicephorus, the Roman dog: I have read your letter, son of an infidel woman. You will not hear my reply but will see it with your own eyes." Sure enough, Harun marched his army northward, and the emperor, distracted by other affairs, agreed to recommence tribute payments. But even before Harun had returned to Raqqa (his new capital), he learned that Nicephorus had reneged on his promise. Having lost all patience, Harun led his troops toward the Black Sea coast where he besieged and conquered the Byzantine city of Heraclea.[52]

Happily, some of Harun's other dealings with Christianity were more polite. In 801, Charlemagne's representative Isaac the Jew returned from a diplomatic mission to Iraq with an elephant named Abu'l Abbas—named for the founder of the Abbasid dynasty. It was a present from Harun to Charlemagne, king of the Franks.

The caliph was eager to recruit allies against rival Muslim rulers in Spain, Charlemagne hoped to make travel safer for Christian pilgrims in the Holy Land, and both rulers shared a mighty rival in the Byzantine Empire. Crossing the Alps so late in the year was impractical, but after wintering at Pisa, Isaac escorted the elephant to Charlemagne's capital at Aachen. The emperor would dote on Abu'l Abbas for years to come, regularly bringing him along on military expeditions. The creature would die in 810 while crossing into Saxony, although his bones would be preserved at Lippenheim until the eighteenth century.

At other times Harun would send Charlemagne ivory chessmen, water clocks, and perfumes, but Abu'l Abbas was his most precious diplomatic gift, exchanged between two of the greatest powers in the ninth-century world. Harun referred to himself as the shadow of God on earth, but he did not underestimate the talents of his compeer in the West.

Aachen

> He was broad and strong in the form of his body and exceptionally tall without, however, exceeding an appropriate measure. As is well known, his height was equal to seven of his feet. The top of his head was round, his eyes were large and lively. His nose was somewhat larger than usual. He had attractive grey hair, and a friendly, cheerful face. His appearance was impressive whether he was sitting or standing, despite having a neck that was fat and too short, and a large belly. The symmetry of his other limbs obscured these points. He had a firm gait, a thoroughly manly manner of holding himself, and a high voice which did not really correspond to the rest of his body.
> —Einhard's description of Charlemagne[53]

In April 799, Pope Leo III approached the Flaminian Gate in Rome. An armed band descended on him, threw him to the ground, and after trying to pluck out his tongue and eyes, left him bleeding in the street. His assailants, supporters of the previous pope, had hoped to disfigure Leo so severely that he would be unable to continue in his papal duties. They failed, and after recuperating at a nearby monastery Leo travelled north, to Paderborn, to recruit the help of Charles the Great, king of the Franks. A few months later the pope returned to Rome in the company of an armed escort. It was not the first time that Charlemagne had served as guardian and protector of a vulnerable papacy.

The Franks, however temporarily and belatedly, had filled the political vacuum left by the demise of the Western Roman Empire. Between 370 and 470, Asiatic Huns, perhaps the descendants of the Hsiung-nu that had so troubled Han China, pushed westward, forcing Germanic tribes into Roman territory. Over the following decades these tribes spread across Europe—the Visigoths into Spain, the Ostrogoths into Italy, the Vandals as far as North Africa.

Rome sought to establish workable relations with these newcomers, even allowing them to settle on lands within the empire. Diplomacy and accommodation had their limits, however, and by 410 the German chieftain Alaric was sacking Rome. The empire, now based in Ravenna, tottered on, but by 476 the last Roman emperor in the West, the sixteen-year-old Romulus Augustulus, had been forced to abdicate and begin his premature retirement in the Bay of Naples. The barbarian Odoacer was now the king of Italy, and the future of Roman civilization lay in the East, in the city founded on the Bosporus by the emperor Constantine—the capital of the new Byzantine Empire.

There were many beneficiaries of this dramatic shift in Western politics, among them the Franks who, under Clovis, moved into the territories of Gaul. In the eighth century the Merovingian dynasty established by Clovis was displaced by the Frankish aristocrat-turned-usurper Pippin the Short (Pippin III), and the center of Frankish power moved three hundred miles to the east, from Paris to the Carolingian capital of Aachen, in present-day Germany. Pippin's son, Charlemagne, proved to be the greatest of all Frankish rulers. Through a combination of military might and subtle diplomacy, he outflanked his immediate neighbors—the Bavarian, Breton, and Aquitanian tribes of northern Germany—and waged successful campaigns against more distant opponents, among them the Saxons of Germany and the Avars of Hungary. At its height, Charlemagne's empire stretched from the Spanish border and central Italy in the south, to Saxony in the north, to Bavaria in the east.

He also rescued the papacy from the intrusions of the Lombard kings of northern Italy, conquering Lombard possessions from the German border to the lands south of Rome. The Holy See had a new champion, and Charlemagne was the mightiest king in western Europe. On Christmas Day, 800, in the church of St. Peter in Rome, Leo III crowned Charlemagne Holy Roman Emperor. The pope, in keeping with tradition, prostrated before the new emperor's feet and the crowds let up a shout: "Life and victory to Charles the most pious Augustus," they chanted three times, "crowned by God, the great and pacific emperor."[54]

The future kings and emperors of western Europe would always dream of emulating Charlemagne's achievement. Napoleon Bonaparte was no exception. Napoleon, much like Charlemagne, was always well supplied with detractors. One of them wrote a scurrilous, rather far-fetched account of Napoleon's trip to Aachen, Charlemagne's ancient capital. Napoleon summoned the entire French diplomatic corps to bear witness to this act of imperial pilgrimage. He apparently visited all the places where Charlemagne had walked, slept, eaten or prayed, dragging the foreign ministers behind him.

Napoleon was apparently so intoxicated by the place that he allowed himself to be duped by local entrepreneurs who, in return for handsome rewards, offered up supposed relics of the great Frankish king—a stone on which Charlemagne had once knelt, a document bearing his signature, a contemporary portrait, a ring he had worn, a crucifix he had used in his devotions.

One German professor wrote to Napoleon, urging him to be less credulous and suggesting that all the items were latter-day forgeries. Napoleon was not amused and, upon reading the professor's note, dispatched officers to his rooms. They woke the professor, forced him to dress, and then bundled him into a covered cart which carried him to the left bank of the Rhine where he was ordered never to return to France, on pain of death.[55]

If the story was a fabrication or, at best, an exaggeration, it was one that hinted at just how long a shadow Charles the Great cast over European history. Perhaps only an Arthur or an Alexander bequeathed a more intoxicating legend.

Charlemagne's diplomatic acumen was certainly part of that legend, but the one thing that medieval Europe enjoyed even more than celebrating its heroes was denouncing Islam. The *Song of Roland* was the most famous of the medieval *chansons de gestes* (songs of deeds) that flourished from the twelfth century, and which made such efficient work of denouncing Muslims as duplicitous, avaricious scoundrels. The *Song of Roland* would principally be remembered for its fanciful account of the murder of a heroic Frankish knight at the pass of Roncesvalles. It also offered a typically unflattering portrayal of Muslim statecraft, and depicted an Islamic penchant for subverting the protocols of diplomatic encounter. This would prove to be a staple of medieval European discourse. The elephant, sent from Islam to Christianity, was dismissed as an aberration. Muslim ambassadors managing to deceive as mighty an emperor as Charlemagne were surely more representative of Islamic "treachery."

At the beginning of the poem, Charlemagne and his armies have been ensconced in Spain for seven years. They have won endless victories, but the town of Saragossa still remains under Muslim control. On his blue marble throne, King Marsile calls forth his counsellors and asks if there is any way to avert military defeat by Charlemagne's armies. One of his counsellors proposes a devious plan. The king should pretend to submit to Charlemagne. He should reveal that he is willing to be baptized as a Christian in the emperor's own kingdom, and promise to pay tribute, only to renege once his troops have departed.

Charlemagne will doubtless require hostages as guarantee of payment, and he will likely execute them when he realizes that he has been deceived, but surely this is a price worth paying. Better that the hostages' heads be shorn away than the Muslims lose the whole of Spain. Marsile chooses ambassadors from among his most cunning followers, and sends them off to Charlemagne on ten snow white mules, bridled with gold and saddled in silver.

Charlemagne is in high spirits when the Muslim ambassadors arrive. His catapults have recently battered down the walls of Cordoba, and a mighty haul of plundered treasure has been secured. All pagans have been slain or made to convert to Christianity. He is relaxing in an orchard, surrounded by his fifteen thousand followers. The older knights are lying on white carpets playing checkers, while the younger squires fence beneath an eglantine-embowered pine tree.

The ambassadors approach Charlemagne on foot and launch into a fawning address. Marsile will send him lavish gifts—lions, bears, greyhounds, and seven hundred camels—provided Charlemagne returns to France.

It is approaching sunset, so Charlemagne tells the ambassadors to tie up their mules and retire to the tents he has provided for them. The next morning, after hearing mass, Charlemagne summons his counsellors to a spot beneath a pine tree to discuss the events of the previous day. Opinion is divided. The knight Roland reminds Charlemagne of a worryingly similar situation seven years earlier, when Marsile had also sent ambassadors bearing olive branches. In reply, two imperial envoys were sent to the king, only to have their heads severed from their bodies. The Christians have been fighting for seven years, Roland insists, and they should complete their campaign by besieging Saragossa. As Charlemagne clasps his chin and tugs at his beard, another of his advisers suggests that such counsel of pride is wrong. Receiving Marsile's homage would be victory enough.

Charlemagne is convinced, and all that remains is the selection of the ambassador to be sent to Marsile. Some are rejected because they would be too dearly missed; Roland is regarded as far too hotheaded for such delicate negotiations. He does succeed in nominating his stepfather, Ganelon, one of his worst critics, however. Ganelon is far from happy with being chosen for such a treacherous mission. He asks Roland why he would be so wrathful as to nominate his own stepfather. Roland offers to go in his stead, fully aware that Ganelon would never accept so insulting a proposal.

Charlemagne calls Ganelon before him and presents his staff and glove, symbols of his authority, but Ganelon drops the glove—an unhappy omen. And so the ambassador sets out for Saragossa.[56]

The Muslim ambassadors have succeeded in hatching their plan: Charlemagne has been utterly deceived. They have also managed to sow dissent within the Frankish camp, and Ganelon will not forget the treachery of his stepson. He will turn to plotting with the Moorish king and help to bring about Roland's death.

—————

The historical Charlemagne was less gullible, and he developed an efficient, wide-ranging diplomatic apparatus. The Carolingian ambassador—usually referred to as *missus* or *legatus*—was a familiar figure throughout the courts of Europe and beyond. Under Charlemagne, and during the reigns of his predecessor and successor (Pippin III and Louis the Pious), there was a steady stream of envoys to Rome, Constantinople, Bulgaria, and Scandinavia, to the kings of Northumbria, the emir of Cordoba, and the patriarch of Jerusalem. There was no professional diplomatic class, and men—whether clerics, palace officials, or nobles—were chosen as the need arose. However, there was a tendency, and a very sensible one, to return envoys to places they had previously visited and learned something about: Gervold, the abbot of St. Wandrille on the Seine, for instance, would make a series of embassies to the English kings of Mercia.[57]

There was more to diplomacy than industry, of course. It also demanded glamour. The wonderfully named Notker the Stammerer most likely spent his entire adult life sequestered in a Benedictine monastery. In his biography of Charlemagne, the emperor is portrayed as a master of diplomatic ritual. When a party of

Greek ambassadors arrived in Aachen in 812, the palace's courtiers decided to have a little sport at their expense. They took turns dressing as the emperor, allowing the envoys to think they were speaking with the mighty Charlemagne. The exhausted Greeks doubtless grew impatient but suddenly, with the appearance of the true emperor, all weariness and irritation evaporated. "Charlemagne, of all kings the most glorious was standing by a window through which the sun shone with dazzling brightness. He was clad in gold and precious stones and he glittered himself like the sun at its first rising." His sons stood around him "like the host of heaven," next to them his wife and daughters, adorned alike with wisdom and pearls. "Had David been in their midst," Notker suggested, "he would have had every reason to sing out: 'kings of the earth and all people, princes and judges; both young men and maidens, old men and children; let them praise the name of the lord.'" The Greek envoys, overcome by such a majestic sight, "fell speechless and senseless to the ground."

Charlemagne realized that the art of diplomacy was the art of spectacle. Envoys had to be convinced of a ruler's power and charisma. When Persian envoys arrived at Aachen in 803 with gifts of monkeys, balsam, and spices, the glamour of the court won them over at once: "Until now", they said, "we have seen only men of clay: now we see golden men." They were less certain of the extent of Charlemagne's political influence, however. After all, they had arrived in Tuscany, in lands supposedly under Charlemagne's jurisdiction, and had asked dozens of locals the way to Aachen. Instead, they had repeatedly been given false directions, delaying their arrival at court for several weeks.[58]

Having had too much to drink one evening, the ambassadors suggested to Charlemagne that if he really was such a feared and respected monarch, his subjects would not have dared to behave so mischievously. Charlemagne realized that his dignity had been undermined and immediately ordered the seizure of any lands belonging to the Tuscans who had deceived the ambassadors. The envoys, sent home with gifts of Spanish horses and hunting dogs, were now fully assured of Charlemagne's plenitude within his domains.

What Charlemagne did well, his great rival, Byzantium, did better, exhibiting diplomatic panache the like of which the world had never seen and, in all likelihood, will never see again.

6
BYZANTIUM

Attila

Indeed, ambassadors were continually arriving from all nations,
bringing for his acceptance their most precious gifts. I myself
have sometimes stood near the entrance of the imperial palace
and observed a noticeable array of barbarians in attendance,
differing from each other in costume and decorations, and
equally unlike in the fashion of their hair and beard. Their aspect truculent and terrible, their bodily stature prodigious:
some of a red complexion, others white as snow, others again
of an intermediate colour. For in the number of those I have
referred to might be seen specimens of the Blemmyan tribes, of
the Indians, and the Ethiopians...All these in due succession,
like some painted pageant, presented to the emperor those gifts
which their own nation held in most esteem: some offering
crowns of gold, others diadems set with precious stones, some
bringing fair-haired boys, others barbaric vestments embroidered with gold and flowers...These presents he separately received and carefully laid aside, acknowledging them in so
munificent a manner as to enrich those who bore them. He also
honoured the noblest among them with Roman offices of dignity; so that many of them thenceforward preferred to continue
their residence among us, and felt no desire to revisit their native land.
      —Eusebius Pamphilius, "Life of Constantine"[59]

THE ROMAN EMPIRE survived the loss of Rome. Ultimately, its loss—an event that also paved the way for the
rise of Charlemagne—*saved* the Roman Empire, an institution that had grown factious and weary. A city on the Bosporus,
founded by the emperor Constantine in the fourth century A.D.,
emerged as the hub of a new, Greek-speaking, Christian civilization. From the outset, Constantinople was both a rival and an ally
of Rome. The two cities served as the twin capitals (each with its
own ruler for long spells) of the eastern and western halves of the
empire of the Caesars. With the abdication of the last western
emperor in 476, Constantinople became the sole inheritor of a
centuries-old imperial tradition, God's own city, the new Rome,
and perhaps the most glamorous, talked-about metropolis in the
world—the center of an empire, rooted in Anatolia and Greece,
whose influence was felt as far away as Venice, Carthage, and
Memphis.

There were efforts to regain the western patrimony. In the sixth
century, the emperor Justinian wrested control of Italy and North
Africa away from the Ostrogoths and the Vandals, but his victories
were fleeting. Justinian only really succeeded in emptying Constantinople's coffers, and within a few years of his death Italy had fallen
to the Lombards. The future, resoundingly, lay in the East.

The Byzantine Empire flourished for a more than a thousand
years, if flourished is the word. It is hard to think of another civilization that has endured such muddled fortunes. Byzantium
would bequeath a legacy of astonishing cultural, artistic, and intellectual achievements, as well as a history littered with imperial
usurpers, plotters, and pretenders. But the scheming and treachery
of dynastic politics were nothing compared to the external threats
and pressures to which Byzantium was endlessly subjected. There

has perhaps never been a polity with quite so many enemies and rivals—Persia and the Islamic powers to the east; the Avars, the Slavs and, later, the Bulgarians in the Balkans; then the Normans in Sicily and the Turkish invaders of Anatolia. In such a jumbled, hostile political world the ministrations of ambassadors were of supreme importance.

Byzantine diplomacy did not enjoy the most illustrious of beginnings, however. Throughout his reign, the emperor Theodosius II (408–450) was obliged to confront the Huns, the Asiatic intruders whose arrival had forced the disruptive barbarian tribes into western Europe. He was unlucky enough to be a contemporary of the most famous Hun of all: Attila, "a man born to shake the races of the world, a terror to all lands," and master of an empire that ranged from the Danube to the Baltic to the Black Sea. The Huns would eventually overreach themselves, and their campaigns in France would lead to demoralizing defeat by an army made up of Romans and Germanic tribesmen, at the battle of the Catalaunian Plains, near Champagne, in 451. But in the middle decades of the fifth century the Huns were utterly dominant in central Europe, in the plains that comprise much of modern-day Austria and Hungary. They were the worst imaginable neighbors for the Byzantine Empire.

By one account, Attila did not die well:

He took in marriage a very beautiful girl, Ildico by name—after numerous other wives according to the custom of his race. Worn out by excessive merriment at his wedding and sodden with sleep and wine he lay on his back. In this position a haemorrhage which ordinarily would have flowed from his nose, since it was hindered from its accustomed channels, poured down his throat in deadly passage and killed him. So drunkenness put a shameful end to a king famed in war.

He was discovered by his young bride, who let out a scream and fell to weeping. Servants rushed in and, "as is the custom of that race, they cut off part of their hair and disfigured their faces horribly with deep wounds so that the distinguished warrior might be bewailed, not with feminine lamentations and tears, but with manly blood."

A sordid death could not blot out a magnificent life, however. The Huns honored Attila with the most dignified of funerals. In the middle of a plain, his body was laid out in a silk tent and "solemnly displayed to inspire awe."

> The most select horsemen of the whole Hunnish race rode around him where he had been placed, in the fashion of the circus races, uttering his funeral song as follows: "Chief of the Huns, King Attila, born of Mundiuch his father, lord of the mightiest races, who alone, with power unknown before his time, held the Scythian and German realms and even terrified both empires of the Roman world, captured their cities, and, placated by their prayers, took yearly tribute from them to save the rest from being plundered. When he had done all these things through the kindness of fortune, neither by an enemy's wound nor a friend's treachery but with his nation secure, amid his pleasures, and in happiness and without sense of pain he fell.

His body was placed in the ground, surrounded by the weapons he had seized in battle, precious stones and "ornaments of every kind and sort whereby royal state is upheld." The place of burial was to be kept a secret, so the men who had dug Attila's grave were executed—"a grim payment for their work. And so sudden death covered the buriers and the buried."[60]

On the day Attila died, the Byzantine emperor was visited in his dreams. A divinity stood before him holding Attila's now-broken bow, a fitting signal for the demise of as mighty and infuriating an enemy as Constantinople had ever faced. Just as the mourners had boasted, he had "terrified both empires of the Roman world."

⟨ornament⟩

In 434 Attila, with Greek translators in tow, met with Byzantine ambassadors at Pozarevac, a town in modern-day Serbia. Byzantium was hopelessly vulnerable in these early years and had little choice but to trade tribute (an annual payment of three hundred pounds of gold) for guarantees that the Huns would not ransack the empire's borderlands south of the Danube. Constantinople also agreed to return any Europeans who sought sanctuary from the Huns in Byzantine territory. Attila was well satisfied with the terms of the treaty and spent much of the next five years campaigning (with an untypical lack of success) in Persia, but when he returned to Europe in 440 he promptly, and with some justification, announced that the Byzantines had breached the agreement. In retaliation, he led a force across the Balkans in 443 and laid siege to Constantinople. The city's walls withstood the assault, but only barely, and the emperor was compelled to ratify a new, even more oppressive treaty: The annual tribute levy was tripled, and a one-off punitive payment of almost four thousand pounds of gold was demanded.

Throughout history, the securing and delivery of tribute has been one of the key tasks of diplomacy. The demands of ascendant rulers could sometimes be curious, as when the Chinese Mongol ruler Kublai Khan demanded Confucian scholars, doctors, and astrologers from the ruler of Vietnam in 1260.[61] They could sometimes be refreshingly sensible, as when, in 556, the

Frankish king Clotaire I imposed an annual tribute of five hundred cows on the Saxon tribes he had recently defeated.[62] And they could sometimes be exorbitant. In 857 B.C. the Assyrian king Shalmaneser III collected thousands of kilograms of silver, bronze, and iron from his subjects and clients, along with plentiful supplies of sheep, cattle, cedar, and "one hundred noble girls."[63]

Against this backdrop, Attila's terms were not unreasonable, but they were terms that Constantinople, already ravaged during these years by plague and famine, could barely sustain. Attila was always one to press his advantage, however, and he believed that still more concessions might be wrung from the embattled Byzantine emperor. In 447 he once more crossed into Byzantium and, with formidable armies at his back, suggested that a swathe of land to the south of the Danube, three hundred miles long and a hundred miles deep, be depopulated and handed over to the Huns.

It was an audacious request and one that called for the exchange of a succession of embassies between the two rulers. One of these, from the year 448, was recorded in unusually rich detail by of one of its participants, the historian Priscus of Panium. It proved to be a troubled diplomatic encounter, not least because of a clumsy assassination attempt dreamed up by desperate Byzantine officials. But the significance of an ambassadorial mission did not reside solely in its political success or failure. The embassy of 448 also provided one of those pregnant moments when cherished assumptions about an alien people were utterly confounded.

"The people called Huns," one Byzantine historian reported, "lived beyond the Sea of Azov, on the border of the frozen ocean, and are a race savage beyond all parallel." He went on to summarize his culture's prejudices. "They are certainly in the shape of men, however uncouth, but are so hardy that they neither require fire nor well-flavoured food, but live on the roots of such herbs as they get in the fields, or on the half-raw flesh of any animal." They did not live in roofed houses, or even thatched cottages. Rather, they avoided such dwellings, "as people ordinarily avoid sepulchres as things not fitted for common use." Totally bereft of the civilizing potential of settled towns and cities, "they wander about, roaming over the mountains and the woods, and accustom themselves to bear frost and hunger and thirst from their very cradles."

Nor was their moral code any more reputable. "Like brute beasts, they are utterly ignorant of the distinction between right and wrong," lacking any religious sensibilities and "immoderately covetous of gold." As diplomatic partners they were famously untrustworthy. "In truces they are treacherous and inconstant, being liable to change their minds at every breeze of every fresh hope which presents itself, giving themselves up wholly to the impulse and inclination of the moment."[64]

Priscus of Panium subscribed to many of these prejudices but, unlike almost all of his contemporaries, he saw some things in the Huns that were worthy of praise, especially in the character of Attila, who emerges from his narrative as something more than the cruel, unthinking monster of legend.

As Priscus recalled, in 448 an ambassador named Edeco, a native of the East European lands overrun by the Huns, arrived at the Byzantine capital. He was there to relay Attila's demand "that envoys should come to him to discuss controversial points—not just ordinary individuals but the most outstanding of those with consular rank." Like so many other visitors, Edeco was overwhelmed by Constantinople's architectural beauty. One day he paid a visit to Chrysaphius, the emperor's chamberlain, and "marvelled at the

splendour" of the royal palaces. The chamberlain was quick to notice Edeco's rapture and wondered whether the wealth and luxury
of Constantinople might not be capable of seducing the ambassador away from loyalty to Attila.

Through the ambassador's interpreter, Bigilas, he announced
that "Edeco might also be the lord of a golden-roofed house and
of such wealth" if he pledged allegiance to Byzantium. When
asked whether "admission to Attila's presence was easy for him,"
Edeco revealed that he was an intimate friend of the king of the
Huns, and "that he was entrusted with his bodyguard along with
men chosen for this duty.... On specified days," he boasted, "each
of them in turn guarded Attila with arms." The chancellor was in-
trigued and invited Edeco to a private meal ("without his other fellow envoys"), where he promised to "make him very important
and advantageous proposals."

When the two men met for dinner they "gave their right hands
and oaths to each other" and Edeco promised not to reveal anything that was discussed. It was a vital precaution since the chancellor proceeded to tell Edeco that if "he should slay Attila and
come back to the Romans, he would have a happy life and great
wealth." With astonishingly little hesitation, Edeco agreed to the
proposal. His price was fifty pounds of gold. After consultation
with the emperor, it was agreed that this attempt at regicide should
be concealed under cover of the embassy that Attila had requested.
Edeco, accompanied by the interpreter Bigilas, would join the retinue of the ambassador Maximinus, who was to know "nothing of
the things planned by them." It was at Maximinus's bidding that
his friend Priscus also joined the embassy and kept his precious
record of what transpired.

The embassy reached Attila some eight miles west of the
Danube. A group of the king's advisors "came and asked us what

we were seeking to gain by making an embassy." The ambassador and his party were baffled by such a question. After all, they had only travelled five hundred miles because Attila had demanded their presence. The Huns went to consult with their leader and returned with the most unexpected of ultimatums: "They ordered us to depart as quickly as possible unless we had anything else to say."

Fortunately, it was close to nightfall and travel was plainly too dangerous. Although the Byzantines' baggage was already packed up and loaded onto their horses, Attila sent word that they should postpone their departure until tomorrow. The ambassador and his retinue dined on ox meat and fish and took to their tents. The next morning they tried to fathom some way of gaining access to Attila. A conversation with a Hun named Scottas provided a solution. In return for gifts and the promise of an ambassadorial posting for his brother, he managed to secure the Byzantines an audience.

"When we made our entrance we found Attila sitting on a wooden seat. As we stood a little apart from the throne Maximinus went forward, greeted the barbarian, and gave him the letters from the emperor, saying that the emperor prayed that he and his followers were safe and sound." Attila responded in kind but then started berating the interpreter Bigilas, "calling him a shameless beast": Had he not been told that no ambassadors were to come before him until all the refugees who had fled to Byzantium were turned over? "Bigilas said that there was not a single refugee... among the Romans, for all of them had been surrendered."

It was an unfortunate comment. "Attila became even angrier and, railing at him violently, said with a shout that he would have impaled him and given him to the birds for food if he had not thought it an outrage to the law of embassies to exact this punishment from him for his effrontery and recklessness of speech."

There were still dozens of refugees in Byzantium, he bellowed, and to prove his point he ordered his secretary to recite their names from a list. Bigilas was ordered to return to Constantinople and demand their immediate return.

Bigilas was petrified. What if Attila's outrage was a signal that he had discovered the plot against his life? It is likely that this is precisely what had happened, that the ambassador Edeco had turned informant. Bigilas was probably being sent back to Byzantium because Attila knew he would collect the gold that had been promised to Edeco, the would-be assassin. As Priscus recalled, shortly after the meeting in the tents "some of Attila's retinue came and told both Bigilas and ourselves not to buy any Roman prisoner or barbarian slave or horses or anything else except things necessary for food until the disputes between the Romans and Huns had been resolved." It was a cunning maneuver. From now on the Byzantine party would only have need of very modest amounts of money and yet, if things fell out as was expected, Bigilas would soon be returning to the Hun's territories with fifty pounds of gold. This would be enormously difficult to explain.

The truly remarkable thing, however, was that Attila restricted his invective to Bigilas. He continued to treat the rest of the ambassadorial party with courtesy. It was not the last surprise that Priscus and his travelling companions would enjoy.

After several weeks at the Huns' camp, word came to Priscus and Maximinus that "Attila invites you both to a banquet and this will start about the ninth hour of the day." The whole affair was infinitely more regimented, stratified, and decorous than Priscus could have expected. It was decidedly unbarbaric:

> All the chairs were ranged along the walls of the house on either side. In the middle sat Attila on a couch, another couch being set behind him, and [behind that] steps that led up to his

bed, which was covered with white linens and coloured embroi-
deries for ornament, just as the Greeks and Romans prepare for
those who marry. The position of those dining on the right of
Attila is considered most honourable, and second the position
on the left, where we happened to be…When all were arranged
in order a cupbearer approached and offered Attila an ivy-wood
cup of wine. He took it and saluted the first in rank, and the
one honoured by the greeting stood up. It was not right for him
to sit down until the king had either tasted the wine or drunk
it up and had given the cup back to the cupbearer.

Servants came in with platters of food, and while Priscus and his
fellow guests ate from silver plates, "for Attila there was nothing
but meat on a wooden trencher." But this did not strike Priscus as
a mark of Attila's barbarity. Rather, it signalled his humility and
temperance. All the guests drank from gold and silver goblets, but
Attila used a wooden mug. The guests sat in their finery, but Attila wore the plainest of clothes, "having care for nothing other
than to be clean," with a simple sword by his side and humble
boots on his feet, all bereft of the gold and gems so favored by his
peers.

"As evening came on, pine torches were lit up, and two barbarians, advancing in front of Attila, sang songs which they had composed, chanting his victories and his virtues in battle….Some took
delight in the verses, some, reminded of wars, were excited in their
souls, and others, whose bodies were weakened by time and whose
spirits were compelled to rest, gave way to tears."

The next round of entertainment was markedly less dignified.
"After the songs, a certain crazed Scythian came forward, who
forced everyone to burst out laughing by uttering monstrous and
unintelligible words." After him, Zercon the Moor entered the
fray. "On account of the deformity of his body, the lisp of his
voice, and his appearance, he was an object of laughter. He was

somewhat short, hump-shouldered, with distorted feet, and a nose indicated only by the nostrils, because of its exceeding flatness."

Priscus looked over to Attila, who "remained unmoved and his expression unaltered, nor in speech nor action did he reveal that he had any laughter in him." Or so it seemed until his youngest son, Ernach, came in and stood before him. "He pinched the lad's cheeks and looked on him with serene eyes." Attila, "short of stature, with a broad chest and a large head, small eyes and a thin beard sprinkled with grey" had proved to be a more complicated man than any Byzantine ambassador could have imagined.

It was time for the embassy to return home. After being dismissed by Attila and "honoured with suitable gifts," the party set off for Constantinople. What had Priscus learned? Throughout the mission he had done everything in his power to promote the dignity of Byzantium and to protect it from calumny. One day, as he was strolling through Attila's camp, someone had said hello to him—in *Greek*. Priscus was startled to hear his native tongue so far from home, and it turned out that the man was a Greek by birth who had worked as a merchant in Moesia, a town on the Danube. With the arrival of the Huns, "he had been stripped of his prosperity and enslaved," but through years of hard work had managed to win his freedom.

Priscus was astonished, and appalled, to learn that the man adored his adopted country and claimed to lead "a better life at present than he had formerly." The Byzantine Empire, he explained, was riddled with inequality. In wartime only the generals had the privilege of bearing decent weapons, while the ordinary foot soldier entered the battlefield in a hopelessly vulnerable condition. In peacetime, ordinary people were crippled by heavy taxes and all but ignored by a corrupt legal system: "No-one will even grant a court to a wronged man unless he lays aside some money for the judge and his attendants." By contrast, in his new home, "men are accustomed to live at ease…each enjoying what he has, causing no trouble and not being troubled."

Priscus rushed to the defense of Byzantium. A perennial duty of the ambassadors would be to uphold their culture's reputation and to defend it from calumny.

> I said that the founders of the Roman constitution were wise and noble men, with the result that affairs are not carried on haphazardly. They appointed some to be guardians of the laws and others to pay attention to arms and to practice military exercises…The laws are imposed on everyone—even the emperor obeys them—and it is not true (as was part of his charge) that the well-to-do assault the poor with impunity.

He was half right, the man admitted. The constitution of the empire was indeed exemplary, "but the rulers were ruining it by not caring for it like their predecessors."

Priscus never doubted Byzantine superiority, and a single journey to the Huns could not dispel a hundred prejudices. He was left in no doubt that Huns and their allies could be petulant. On the homeward journey the Byzantines had been joined by Attila's ambassador Berichus who, at least at first, proved an affable travelling companion. "He seemed mild and friendly, but as soon as we crossed the Danube he adopted the attitude of an enemy toward us." He took back the horse that had been presented to Maximinus and refused to eat with the Byzantines.

Nor was the Huns' reputation for cruelty entirely unjustified.

> As we were on our journey and encamped at a certain village, a Scythian was caught who had crossed from Roman territory into the land of the barbarians in order to spy. Attila ordered

him to be impaled…On the next day, as we were proceeding through other villages, two men who were slaves of the Scythians were brought in, their hands bound behind them, because they had destroyed their masters during the war. They crucified them, putting the heads of both on two beams with horns.

But for all that, his attitudes had undoubtedly shifted, and his assumptions challenged. When he had dined with one of Attila's wives, he had been greeted not with barbarian vulgarity but "with gracious words and food." When he and his party had lost their way during a storm, the central European villagers they encountered did not rob, mock, or slaughter them. Rather, they "sprang out of their tents and lit fires and fed them," and sent "good-looking girls to console us." The next day, when their rain-soaked clothes had dried and it was time to set out, the Byzantines gave their gracious hosts presents of palm fruit and Indian pepper.

And then there was the enigma of Attila. A barbarian still, by Priscus's reckoning, but also the man who had hosted that elegant banquet, humbling himself before his people and playfully pinching his son's cheeks. A man of cruelty but also, against all expectation, a man with the bearing of majesty, and the pride of a father.

But what of the traitors who had conspired to kill Attila? When Bigilas returned from his mission to Constantinople, carrying Edeco's fifty pounds of gold, Attila's men "surrounded and held him, having been prepared for this, and took the money." He was dragged before the king and asked why he had returned with such a prodigious quantity of gold. "He answered that it was for provisioning himself and those accompanying him…It was also supplied to purchase fugitives, for many in Roman territory had begged him to liberate their kinsmen."

Attila was having none of it: "No longer, you worthless beast, will you escape justice by deception. Nor will there be any excuse sufficient for you to avoid punishment. Your supply of ready money is greater than necessary for your provisioning, or for the horses and baggage animals to be bought by you, or for the freeing of prisoners."

Priscus reports that Attila next informed Bigilas that his son would be killed unless he revealed the truth. "When he beheld his son under threat of death he took to tears and lamentations and called aloud on justice to turn the sword against himself and not against a youth who had done no wrong." He told of the plans he had concocted with Edeco, the chamberlain, and the emperor, "and begged unceasingly to be put to death and his son set free." Bigilas was placed in chains, only to be freed if his son could raise a ransom of, fittingly enough, fifty pounds of gold.

Attila next sent two of his own ambassadors, Orestes and Eslas, to Constantinople. Orestes was ordered to hang a bag, containing Bigilas's gold, around his neck. He was to come before the emperor and the chancellor wearing this bag and ask them if they recognized it. This done, the second ambassador, Eslas, was to recite a chilling speech:

> Theodosius is the son of a nobly born father. Attila also is of noble birth, having succeeded his father Mundiuch, and he has preserved his high descent. Theodosius, since he has undertaken the payment of tribute to him, has cast out his own nobility and is his slave. Therefore, he does not act with justice

toward his superior—one whom fortune has shown to be his master—because he has secretly made an attack like a miserable house slave. And Attila will not free of blame those who have sinned against him unless Theodosius should hand over the [chamberlain] for punishment.

It was a humiliating moment in the history of Byzantine diplomacy. The emperor had been outmaneuvered and the empire brought into disrepute. Barbarian ambassadors had come to Constantinople with mocking, menacing tidings. The future would bring much more illustrious moments.[65]

Liudprand

Debates about the attributes of the ideal ambassador are almost as old as human civilization. The bards of ancient Mesopotamia, in the cities that sprang up between the Euphrates and Tigris Rivers in the fourth millennium B.C., praised those envoys who could run like the wild ram and fly like the falcon: "Like a wild donkey…he runs over the mountains, like a large powerful donkey he races…like a lion in the field at dawn…he goes, like a wolf seizing a lamb he runs quickly."[66] For the ancient Greeks, eloquence was paramount, and the oratory of Odysseus, whose words "fell fast, like snow in winter," would always be a paradigm to be emulated. One of the earliest recorded European diplomatic encounters comes from the mid-sixth century A.D., when Aethelbert, the future king of Kent, was pursuing a marriage with Bertha, the daughter of King Charibert of Paris. None of the parties could read or write and the negotiations were entirely oral. In such a world, the diplomatist who lacked an excellent memory would have been at a huge disadvantage.[67]

Some commentators took a more mundane approach. It was best, so one Renaissance authority explained, if an ambassador was not deaf, blind, a ravisher of sacred virgins, or a despoiler of churches.[68] Nor, Philippe de Béthune added, should he have any conspicuous imperfection "as to have one eye, to be purblind, squint-eyed, lame, crook-backed, or extremely foul or deformed." "He must not likewise be sickly or dainty, lest the discommodity of the ways, or the change of air make him unprofitable for his masters' affairs." Physical beauty was always to be admired, Béthune concluded, and an ambassador's countenance "must be grave and serious, yet mingled with a pleasing aspect."[69] Sometimes, of course, the need for experience outweighed the value of good looks. In 1539 the Venetian Senate chose the eighty-five-year-old Pietro Zen for delicate negotiations with the Turks. When he died en route to the Levant he was replaced by Tommaso Contarini, only one year his junior.[70]

A talent for languages, a solid knowledge of current affairs, a calm head, and a good stomach—these were among the most commonly cited qualities expected of a successful ambassador. As were discretion, affability, and charm—and in such a context it might seem bizarre that a crotchety, badly behaved envoy was sometimes called for. But in Byzantium, in the middle of the ninth century, that was precisely what circumstances demanded.

Liudprand had been raised at the court of King Hugh of Italy. After service as a deacon in Pavia, he rose to the ecclesiastical dignity of bishop of Cremona. He had been on a diplomatic mission to Constantinople before, back in 949, and had rather enjoyed himself, watching horseraces in the Hippodrome and the rest. Twenty years later, his experiences were to be somewhat less agreeable. He was sent by Otto I of Saxony to try to convince Emperor

Nicephorus Phocas to countenance a marriage between Otto and the daughter of the emperor's predecessor.

On June 4, he arrived at the gates of the city in a pouring rain but despite such inclement conditions was made to dismount and make the rest of his way on foot. "It was a miserable reception," he reported to Otto and his court, "meant as an insult to yourselves." By the time he reached his lodgings he was soaked through, and the sight that awaited him did little to brighten his mood. He had been allotted "the most miserable and disgusting quarters" in the city, replete with brackish water and a bed as hard as marble. His rooms were so far from the imperial palace that whenever he walked there he arrived completely out of breath.

Not that visiting the imperial palace was a task the ambassador relished. On the 6th of June he had a meeting with the emperor's brother that descended into absurd bickering over which monarchs were entitled to use which royal titles. The next day Liudprand was granted an audience with the emperor himself, but he was dumbfounded by the individual who confronted him. Nicephorus, so Liudprand informed Otto, was "a monstrosity of a man, a dwarf, fat-headed and with tiny mole's eyes, disfigured by a short, broad thick beard half going to grey." He had tiny legs, a ludicrously small neck, and piglike bristles all over his head. As Nicephorus stood there in his ancient, stinking linen robe, Liudprand could not help but compare the emperor to his own master. "You always seemed comely to me," the ambassador declared, "but how much more comely now!"

And that, in essence, was the whole point of Liudprand's scornful remarks, perhaps even an ulterior motivation for his entire embassy. To insult the emperor was a way of praising Otto. To criticize Constantinople was, by inference, to eulogize Otto's own lands and cities. A curmudgeonly ambassador was the ideal candidate for such work.

As for the much-vaunted ceremony and ritual of the Byzantine capital, Liudprand was similarly unimpressed. When the emperor made a progress through the city, the ambassador saw none of the richly dressed soldiers and courtiers he had been led to expect. "A numerous company of tradesmen and low born persons lined the sides of the roads with thin little shields and cheap spears." There was a contingent of noblemen, but they marched in bare feet wearing tatty robes that must surely have been owned by their grandfathers.

At length, the emperor made his appearance, walking along "like some crawling monster." The crowds were obviously delusional, Liudprand suggested, since they launched into paeans of adulation: "Behold the morning star approaches," they chanted, "the day star rises. In his eyes the sun's rays are reflected...adore him you nations, worship him, bow the neck to his greatness." Liudprand wondered whether it might not have been more appropriate for them to shout out, "Come you miserable burnt out coal; old woman in your walk, wood-devil in your look; clodhopper, haunter of byres, goat footed, horned, and double limbed."

There was hardly anything that Liudprand failed to criticize during his four months in Constantinople. The food was "foul and disgusting, washed down with oil after the fashion of drunkards and moistened also with an exceedingly bad fish liquor." The wine "we found undrinkable because of the mixture in it of pitch, resin and plaster." When the imperial guards were not following Liudprand wherever he went (a sure sign that the ambassador was not trusted), they were insulting Otto's armies and navies.

The emperor apparently treated him with similar effrontery. Admittedly, Nicephorus had invited Liudprand to visit the imperial zoo and to accompany him on hunting trips. On one occasion he had even sent over fish from his own table for the ambassador's delectation. But, for the most part, he had been appallingly ungracious. The crowning insult came one night at dinner, when a Bulgarian ambassador was seated much closer to the emperor than Liudprand—showing total disregard for his diplomatic precedence. Liudprand simply walked out of the banquet and was unlikely to have been appeased by the goat stuffed with garlic and onions that the emperor had sent by way of an apology.

Otto's ambassador had seen enough and, certain that the proposed marriage was a lost cause, he sought permission from the emperor, as all envoys were required, to leave Constantinople on July 22nd. As one last humiliation, he was only allowed to leave two and a half months later. Before he did, he vandalized his rooms, scrawling verses on the walls and tables that warned future visitors "not to trust the Greeks."

How tragic, Liudprand mused, when a city "that was once so rich and prosperous" becomes "such a starveling, a city full of lies, tricks, perjury and greed, rapacious, avaricious, and vainglorious." Having announced that he looked forward to meeting various Byzantine officials in hell, he set off for home, finally reaching his destination, Otranto, in the heel of Italy, after forty nine days of "ass riding, walking, horse riding, fasting, weeping and groaning."

Liudprand's report to Otto was a masterpiece of propaganda: less an accurate piece of reportage and more a way of undermining Byzantine claims of cultural superiority. One of the reasons ambassadors existed was that they allowed civilizations to contrast themselves—favorably, for the most part—with their rivals. It was simply that Liudprand was infinitely, and gloriously, less subtle than many of his confreres.[71]

But in truth, Constantinople was more accustomed to astounding visiting envoys than offending them. By the ninth and tenth centuries, its intricate mechanisms of diplomacy had moved a long way on since the clumsy encounters with Attila the Hun.

<hr />

From its earliest days, Constantinople had set out to impress. Official visitors would enter to the west of the city, through the ceremonial Golden Gate, nestled in the fourteen miles of Theodosian walls that stretched uninterrupted from the channel of the Golden Horn to the Sea of Marmora. They would be escorted down the city's grand central avenue, passing arcades and arches, imposing squares and buildings—the Church of the Holy Apostles, the Aqueduct of Valens, the forums of Theodosius and Constantine. After a trek of three miles, they would finally reach the Augustaion square, the hub of the Byzantine world, surrounded by the great cathedral of St. Sophia, the Senate, and the Imperial Palace: a vast complex of galleries, courtyards, meadows, prisons, and churches.[72]

The outward grandeur of the city was matched by the nimble inner workings of its bureaucracy. Unlike the Greeks, the Romans, or Charlemagne, the Byzantine Empire established permanent diplomatic institutions. From as early as the fifth century, the Scrinium barbarorum, or "Barbarian Bureau," coordinated Byzantium's dealings with the tribes on its borders. Its officials coped with everything from the housing, feeding and surveillance of envoys, to the ceaseless gathering of vital information across the Byzantine world and beyond. They quizzed all returning merchants, immigrants and pilgrims about the places they had visited. And at the head of this bureaucracy stood the logothete of the drome, an official whose duties had expanded from supervising the empire's postal routes to supervising its entire diplomatic apparatus. Ambassadors, much as in ancient Greece, would usually be selected ad hoc— the modern-day career diplomatist was still far into the future— although the scope of their missions, ranging from the rival Muslim caliphates of Persia, Egypt, and Spain, to the Balkan tribes, to the princes of western Europe, was nonetheless impressive.

Diplomacy in Byzantium was about more than efficiency, however. Its heartbeat was ritual. The empire had inherited its love of ceremony from the Western Roman Empire. When Rome was poised to go to war, it did not simply announce the fact. It sent out diplomatic representatives, priests known as *fetiales*, to air its grievances and provide its enemies with an opportunity to repent. They would explain Rome's reasons for war three times: once at the border, then to the first person they met in enemy territory, and finally, in the nation's forum. The potential enemy would be given thirty-three days to apologize for whatever crime or misdemeanor it had committed and to promise that Rome's rights would now be respected. If this opportunity was not seized, the fetiales would return to Rome, a formal declaration of war would be made, and the envoys would go back to the border. The declaration would be loudly pronounced and a fire-hardened blood-colored spear launched into enemy territory.[73]

The Eastern empire prized and augmented this ritualistic tradition. The tenth-century emperor Constantine Porphyrogenitus went so far as to compose his own *Book of Ceremonies*, which outlined the specific rites and protocols that were to accompany every aspect of Byzantine court culture. "Many things are apt to disappear in the process of time," he explained, "among them a great and precious thing, the exposition and description of imperial ceremony." This would represent a catastrophic loss to any ruler. "To neglect this ceremony, and to sentence it as it were to death, is to be left with a view of the empire devoid of ornament and deprived of beauty."

Power was not just about wealth or force of arms. A great civilization had to be able to fill its rivals, and their ambassadors, with awe. "Through the praiseworthy system of ceremonial," Constantine continued, echoing the sentiments of Charlemagne, "the imperial power is displayed in greater beauty and magnificence, thus filling with admiration both foreign nations and our own citizens."[74] And if it was to function properly it had to be organized and codified with forensic precision. The state was like the human body: Without order it perished.

And so Byzantium set about ranking and regimenting the rest of humanity. Every nation was evaluated according to its might, its degree of independence, its cultural achievements, and, tellingly, its usefulness to the empire. According to these calculations, whenever the ambassadors of these nations visited Constantinople, they would enjoy differing levels of access, more or less freedom of movement, and a specific position in the hierarchy of precedence, even down to the details of where they sat during an imperial banquet or how many invitations to dinner or the Hippodrome they might expect to receive. The rulers of different nations would be addressed in diplomatic correspondence according to their prestige: Some would be hailed as the emperor's brothers, others as his sons, or simply as his friends. Even the amount and quality of gold to be used in the seals on letters was determined according to the recipient's status. The Persian emperor and the

Egyptian sultan were held in highest esteem, with the pope and the rulers of western Europe coming further down the diplomatic pecking order.

What the ambassadors of all such nations shared, however, was exposure to Byzantine theatricality. When they were led into the emperor's presence at the beginning of their missions, they would be greeted in a chamber decked with tapestries and intricate metalwork, filled with automata powered by air and water. Golden lions roared and birds sat on golden trees, fluttering their wings. The ambassadors would be expected to throw themselves to the floor three times—a floor most likely strewn with laurel and ivy, myrtle and rosemary—and while their gaze was averted, the throne of Solomon would rise up, transporting the emperor still further above the realm of ordinary humans.

To transgress the rules of imperial ceremony or disrupt the hierarchy of the imperial court was a cardinal mistake, but part of the Byzantine code (sometimes adhered to, sometimes not) was to respond to such blunders with quiet dignity. In the twelfth century, during the crusades, Anna Comnena (the sister of an emperor) recalled that so many soldiers rushed into Constantinople that "one might have likened them to the stars of heaven or the sand poured out along the edge of the sea." For the most part, they exhibited due deference, but one day "a certain venturesome noble sat down on the emperor's seat." The emperor did not respond, but the knight's companions quickly berated him for committing such an outrage.

The knight ignored them, "darted a fierce glance at the emperor and muttered some words to himself in his own language, saying 'look at this rustic that keeps his seat while such valiant captains are standing round him.'" By chance, the emperor's interpreter—

an accomplished lip reader—had been able to make out what the knight had said and informed the emperor. But there were to be no accusations or punishments, merely regal stiffness tempered with gentle mockery. When the "haughty-minded, audacious Latin" was about to leave, the emperor called him over. He politely asked who he was and where he was from. The knight proved as boastful as he was ill-mannered. "I am a Frank of the purest nobility," he declared. As for his homeland, "all that I know is that at the crossroads in the country whence I come there stands an old sanctuary, to which everyone who desires to fight in single combat goes ready accoutred…and there prays to God for help while he waits in expectation of the man who will dare to fight him." An ominous place for some, perhaps, but not for him: "At those crossroads I too have often tarried, waiting and longing for an antagonist, but never has one appeared who dared to fight me."

With an eye to the horrors the knight was likely to encounter in the Holy Land, the emperor suggested that "if you did not find a fight when you sought for it then, now the time has come which will give you your fill of fighting." Perhaps the knight would do well not to stand at the front or the back of his regiment, where he would be most exposed to the enemy's attack, but seek refuge in the middle ranks. It was the perfect blend of generous advice and condescension: a supremely kingly, imperious moment that encapsulated Byzantine statecraft.[75]

Of course, there was always a difference between imperial pretensions and political realities. At the level of theory and propaganda the emperor was God's vicar on earth, the descendant of the Caesars who boasted imperium over the entire world. His crown and ceremonial robes were not of human origin but had been donated by an angel. He was a man who never even stood on the ground in public, but was always lifted that inch or two above humanity by a footstool or podium. He was Christ's imitator, who dined each Christmas with twelve guests, posing as latter-day apostles.[76]

Very often, however, the emperor was also an embattled politician, short of money or harried by enemies. At such times diplomacy was less about gorgeous ceremony and more about dispatching envoys to tribes on the borders with tribute dressed up in the guise of freely given gifts. The remarkable thing is that even during the empire's darkest days, the myth of invincible, almost divine superiority was still given lip service. Rulers would continue to address the emperor as their revered father, they would continue to seek prestigious Byzantine wives for their sons and honorific Byzantine titles for themselves.

The Byzantine diplomatic machine was wonderfully efficient. Visiting envoys would bask in ceremony, and Byzantine envoys would spread their civilization's art, religion, and culture across eastern Europe and the Caucasus. In the tenth century, Vladimir, the ruler of Russia, willing to abandon paganism, dispatched ambassadors to find out more about the world's great religions. Much of the news they brought back was bitterly disappointing. Converting to Islam was out of the question because one would have to give up alcohol. Judaism could hardly be considered a reputable faith because its adherents lacked even so much as their own independent homeland. Christianity, by contrast, had much to offer.

Vladimir's ambassadors, like so many others, had been overwhelmed by the magnificence of Constantinople, especially the glories of St. Sophia. "They led us to where they worship their god and we knew not whether we were in heaven or on earth: for on earth there is no such beauty or splendour...we know only that in that place God dwells among men, and their service is more beautiful than that of other nations: for we cannot forget that beauty." Vladimir, eager to adopt a religion that might unify his people, and keen to recruit a powerful ally, converted to the Christian faith. In 988 he smashed every pagan idol in Kiev and had the city's entire population forcibly baptized in the River Dnieper.[77]

As diplomatic coups go, this was an extraordinary moment. What diplomacy could not hide, however, were the resentments that Byzantium's influence provoked and the cultural chasms that separated Byzantium from the rest of the Christian commonwealth.

Medieval

7
THE CROWN OF THORNS

But isn't this relic matter a little overdone? We find a piece of the true cross in every old church we go into, and some of the nails that held it together. I would not like to be positive, but I think we have seen as much as a keg of these nails. Then there is the crown of thorns; they have part of one in Sainte Chapelle, in Paris, and part of one also in Notre Dame. And as for bones of St. Denis, I feel certain we have seen enough of them to duplicate him if necessary.

—Mark Twain, *The Innocents Abroad*[78]

As any diplomat will tell you, diplomacy, for the most part, is dull: vital, but dull. It involves the same endless round of chores and protocols. Perhaps even the spectacular ritual of the Byzantine court—dazzling to ambassadorial eyes that had never seen it before—eventually began to fatigue those charged with dusting down the automata month in and month out. Of course, diplomacy had its quirks. Some ambassadors were blessed with the most curious of missions and errands: being sent by Antiochus I of Syria to ask the pharaoh for sweet wine, dried figs, and a sophist philosopher; or by a fourteenth-century king of Moldovia to beg the Venetian Senate for a doctor specializing in leg ulcers.[79] In the middle of the thirteenth century, ambassadors even had the opportunity to rescue one of Christendom's most precious talismans.

The Crown of Thorns, fashioned from rushes of the jujube tree, was the most potent of relics. Mockingly placed on the head of Jesus at his crucifixion, it was the choicest, most poignant icon of the Passion. An item purporting to be the crown was transferred from Jerusalem to Constantinople in 1063, along with the nails which had pinned Christ's hands to the cross and the lance which had pierced his naked side. Prior to this, individual thorns had regularly been conveyed across Europe, often as diplomatic gifts. Charlemagne, an avid collector of relics, had received a thorn from the Byzantine empress Irene, and one of his successors duly passed it on to the English king Athelstan I in 927 during important marriage negotiations. Medieval Europe laid claim to some seven hundred authentic thorns—a mathematical absurdity that Protestant reformers of the sixteenth century were eager to exploit—and entire churches, including Pisa's ornate Capella della Spina (on the wrong side of the Arno for most tourists to visit), were sometimes built around them.

Constantinople was fiercely proud of the crown and yet, in 1238, it surrendered the relic. Desperately short of funds, the city had offered the crown as security against a loan from Genoese and Venetian merchants. The money was quickly spent, so another deal was struck with the Venetian banker Niccolò Quirino. The terms of this second arrangement were much more stringent than the first. If the Byzantines did not repay their debt within a month, Quirino would be permitted to take the crown to Venice and parade it before the doge and Senate. If another four months went by, Quirino would gain outright possession and be free to dispose of the crown as he saw fit.[80]

Meanwhile, the heir to the Byzantine throne, the future Baldwin II, was visiting Louis IX in France. Baldwin was, in effect, a princely ambassador hoping to recruit allies against the empire's enemies. The undignified treatment of holy relics was hardly unheard of during the Middle Ages. The body of St. Agatha had been stolen at night from a church in Constantinople, and the two thieves, to make their booty easier to carry, had chopped the body up and divided it into smaller parcels.[81] Nonetheless, Baldwin was especially scandalized (or more likely embarrassed) to hear that so holy an object as the Crown of Thorns was facing the most uncertain of futures. Aware of Louis's pious reputation, he suggested to the king that the crown might make an excellent addition to his already impressive collection of relics. Predictably, Louis agreed, and he sent two Dominican monks as his ambassadors to Constantinople. When they arrived, the crown was just about to be shipped to Venice. They secured permission to accompany it, leaving Constantinople on Christmas Day, 1238. Upon reaching Venice one of them sped to Paris to inform Louis of the crown's whereabouts. The king immediately sent yet more ambassadors to Venice with sufficient money to redeem the loan and take possession of the crown.

A few weeks later the ambassadors brought the precious item back to Paris. Louis and his entire court went out to meet them and the barefoot king carried the relic into the city. He would erect the most beautiful church in Paris, the Sainte-Chapelle, to house the crown, and the relic would remain a focus of adoration and a source of miraculous intervention for the next five centuries, even curing Blaise Pascal's niece of an ulcer in 1656. During the Revolution, an unhappy time for Christian relics, it would be moved to the Bibliothèque Nationale, later finding a home in the cathedral of Notre Dame, where it still resides, with not a single thorn remaining intact.

It was a respectful end to a sordid affair, but how had the Byzantine Empire come to such a pitch that it was willing to part with one of its most treasured possessions? Forty years earlier, in 1200, a Russian named Dobrinia Iadreikovich, the future archbishop of Novgorod, visited the "city guarded by God." He scoured Constantinople's endless shrines and churches and carefully noted down everything he saw. As well as the Crown of Thorns, he came across Christ's sandals, his swaddling clothes, the basin he had used to wash his disciples' feet, the sponge from which he had drunk during the crucifixion, and even a chart that had been used to keep a record of his height while growing up. He saw the gold brought by the Magi, the right hand of John the Baptist, the trumpet Joshua had blown at Jericho, the rod of Moses, and a cross made from the wood of Noah's ark. There were any number of saintly arms and legs and entire bodies of, among so many others, Saint Andrew, Saint Luke, Saint Timothy, and the prophet Daniel.[82]

Only four years later, much of this ravishing collection would be dispersed, and Byzantium would fall into the very decline that provoked the unseemly business dealings of 1238. Ambassadors would help set in motion the bungled events of 1204, known to history as the Fourth Crusade.

—————

The crusades had begun through the efforts of ambassadors. In 1095, the Byzantine emperor had sent an embassy to Pope Urban II asking for help against the Seljuk Turks, who were making steady incursions into Asia Minor. European armies succeeded in capturing Antioch and Jerusalem in 1098 and 1099 and set about establishing crusader states in the region. A second crusade (1147–1149) was raised after the Turks captured Edessa in 1144, and a third

(1189–1192) in the wake of the capture of Jerusalem and many of the Levantine crusader states by Saladin, the ruler of Egypt and Syria. Many of the crusader states and ports were recaptured, but Jerusalem remained in the hands of the infidel. In 1201, Innocent III preached that "all who should take the cross and serve in the host for one year, would be delivered from all the sins they had committed, and acknowledged in confession." As one contemporary, Geoffrey of Villehardouin, reported, "Because this indulgence was so great, the hearts of men were much moved, and many took the cross for the greatness of the pardon."

The nobility of France had been especially receptive to the pope's call to arms. A meeting was held at Soissons "to settle when they should start, and whither they should wend. But they could come to no agreement, because it did not seem to them that enough people had taken the cross." The plan was to sail to Egypt—an ideal base for an incursion into Saladin's territory and also a rich source of supplies and booty. All that was lacking was the wherewithal to mount such an ambitious expedition. After more discussions, it was decided to dispatch ambassadors to seek out ships that could be used to ferry the Christian forces to Egypt.

"It was agreed that envoys should be sent, the best that could be found, with full powers, as if they were the lords in person, to settle such matters as needed settlement." Thibaut, the Count of Champagne, chose the knights Miles of Brabant and Geoffrey of Villehardouin (the author of a detailed narrative of the crusade) to serve on the embassy. Baldwin, the count of Flanders, supplied Conon of Bethune and Alard Maquereau, and they were joined by John of Friaise and Walter of Gaudonville, the two representatives of the count of Blois and Chartres.

Each of the men was supplied with "charters, with seals attached, to the effect that they would undertake to maintain and carry out whatever conventions and agreements the envoys might enter into, in all sea ports, and wherever else the envoys might fare." These documents granted the ambassadors full power to negotiate on behalf of their masters, and bound the nobles to abide by any agreements that were reached. After some discussion, the ambassadors agreed that the most promising destination was Venice, where they "might expect to find a greater number of vessels than in any other port."

They arrived in Venice in the first week of Lent 1201, and they seem to have been impressed by the doge, Enrico Dandolo. He "was very wise and very valiant," and "did them great honour, both he and the other folk, and entertained them right willingly." "Sirs," Dandolo, speaking in Latin, explained to the ambassadors, "I have seen your letters. Well do we know that of men uncrowned your lords are the greatest, and they advise us to put faith in what you tell us, and that they will maintain whatsoever you undertake. Now, therefore, speak, and let us know what is your pleasure." They asked the doge if he would assemble his council so that they might consider the crusaders' request. They wondered if a meeting might be arranged for as soon as the next day. The doge asked for a little longer to prepare, and four days later the ambassadors entered the doge's palace, "which was passing rich and beautiful, and found the Doge and his council in a chamber." Here they made their plea:

> Sire, we come to thee on the part of the high barons of France, who have taken the sign of the cross to avenge the shame done to Jesus Christ, and to reconquer Jerusalem, if so be that God will suffer it. And because they know that no people have such great power to help them as you and your people, therefore we pray you by God that you take pity on the land overseas and the shame of Christ, and use diligence that our lords have ships for transport and battle.

The doge seemed sceptical. "It is a great thing that your lords require of us," he suggested, "and well it seems that they have in view a high enterprise. We will give you our answer eight days from today. And marvel not if the term be long, for it is meet that so great a matter be fully pondered." After this delay, another meeting was arranged at the palace and the doge proposed his terms.

> We will build transports to carry four thousand five hundred horses, and nine thousand squires, and ships for four thousand five hundred knights, and twenty thousand sergeants of foot...
> And the covenants we are now explaining to you, we undertake to keep, wherever we may be, for a year, reckoning from the day on which we sail from the port of Venice in the service of God and of Christendom. Now the sum total of the expenses above named amounts to 85,000 marks...For the love of God, we will add to the fleet fifty armed galleys on condition that, so long as we act in company, of all conquests in land or money, whether at sea or on dry ground, we shall have the half, and you the other half. Now consult together to see if you, on your parts, can accept and fulfil these covenants.

They could, and three days later the doge assembled his forty-strong Great Council. "By his wisdom and wit, that were very clear and very good, [he] brought them to agreement and approval." Next, the general population had to be convinced. Ten thousand Venetians were gathered together in St. Mark's, "the most beautiful church there is," and a mass was celebrated. At its conclusion "the doge desired the envoys to humbly ask the people to assent to the proposed covenant."

> The envoys came into the church. Curiously were they looked upon by many who had not before had sight of them. Geoffrey of Villehardouin...acted as spokesman and said unto them: "Lords, the barons of France, most high and puissant, have sent us to you; and they cry to you for mercy, that you take pity on

Jerusalem, which is in bondage to the Turks, and that, for God's sake, you help to avenge the shame of Christ Jesus. And for this end they have elected to come to you, because they know full well that there is no other people having so great power on the seas, as you and your people. And they commanded us to fall at your feet, and not to rise till you consent to take pity on the Holy Land which is beyond the seas."

The envoys kneeled before the people, "weeping many tears," and "the doge and all the others burst into tears of pity and compassion, and cried with one voice, and lifted up their hands, saying: 'We consent, we consent.'" The noise was so great, Ville-hardouin remembered, that "it seemed as if the earth itself were falling to pieces." A proud doge strode to the lectern and addressed his people with "good and beautiful words:...Behold the honour that God has done you; for the best people in the world have set aside all other people, and chosen you to join them in so high an enterprise as the deliverance of our Lord!"

When the treaties had been prepared, the ambassadors visited the doge's palace one final time: "When the doge delivered the treaties to the envoys, he knelt greatly weeping, and swore on holy relics faithfully to observe the conditions thereof, and so did all his council, which numbered fifty-six persons." Messengers were sent to Rome to secure the pope's approval of the covenant, "which he did right-willingly," and the ambassadors borrowed five thousand marks "and gave them to the doge so that the building of the ships might be begun."[83]

⟶⟶⟫∫⟪⟵⟵

Here was a diplomatic triumph that very quickly descended into political farce. It became increasingly clear to the crusaders that they would be unable to pay Venice all that she was owed. The doge and Senate, rather than bemoaning the situation, saw an opportunity to turn it to their advantage and arranged for the indebted crusaders to help them recapture the city of Zara, recently conquered by Hungary. Zara fell in November 1202, and the crusaders settled down in the city for the winter.

The new year did not bring any upturn in their fortunes. They still lacked the wherewithal to pay off their debts to Venice, and the crusade was in real danger of petering out before it had even gotten underway. At this juncture, the complexities of Byzantine court politics intervened.

In 1195 the emperor Isaac II had been deposed by Alexius III. Isaac's son, another Alexius, had managed to escape Constantinople and had found an influential ally in the German ruler Philip of Swabia. The two men approached the desperate crusaders with an outlandish idea. Alexius would provide them with generous donations of both men and money if they agreed, before undertaking their tasks in the Near East, to remove the impostor on the Byzantine throne. Many crusaders were appalled at the prospect of a Christian crusading army descending on a Christian (albeit Orthodox) city, but others saw the proposal as the only likely way out of their impasse.

The crusading fleet, made up of almost five hundred ships, arrived in the Bosporus in June 1203. Ambassadors were dispatched to meet them and were informed of the Westerners' intention to depose the sitting emperor, Alexius III. An inconclusive assault was launched on the city in July and then, quite unexpectedly, the emperor fled the city. The crusaders immediately installed Isaac II but were sure to remind him of the troops and money that had been promised them. Fearing for the safety of his son, who was now a virtual hostage, Isaac pledged to honor the agreement, and his son was crowned as co-emperor with the title of Alexius IV.

The crusaders were wildly unpopular. They behaved haughtily, looted the countryside outside Constantinople, and continued to demand payment of what they were owed. Desperate measures were taken, with many churches and imperial buildings being stripped of whatever precious fittings could be melted down. Such indignities only served to further alienate the Byzantine population. By January 1204 it seemed increasingly likely that open war between the Byzantines and the crusading fleet would break out. A courtier named Alexius Ducas seized his moment, declared himself emperor and had Alexius IV strangled. With little to lose, and all prospect of payments now vanished, the crusaders launched a series of attacks. By the middle of April they had breached the Byzantine defenses and begun their sack of the city. Thousands were killed, altars were smashed, ancient statues reduced to rubble. It was an event that appalled the whole of Europe. This was not what crusading armies were for.

We will never really know whether the attack on Constantinople had been part of an elaborate Venetian plan all along. It seems a far-fetched notion. There had certainly always been tensions between Byzantium and Venice. The two powers coexisted. Venetian doges sent their sons to Constantinople for an education. Byzantine princesses married into Venetian families. Byzantium increasingly relied on Venetian military intelligence and assistance. Venice was dependent on Byzantine trade. Coexistence and interdependency were not the progenitors of affection, however.

To many Byzantines, the West was a dissolute, uncultured wasteland. According to the contemporary historian John Kinnamos, Venice was utterly "corrupt in character," the rudest nation in

Christendom.[84] To many in the West, Byzantium was self-satisfied and decadent, summed up by the story told by St. Peter Damian in the eleventh century, about a Byzantine princess who had come to Venice and refused to drink the local water, eat with her hands, or tolerate the smells of the city. Instead, she had rain water collected in barrels, only ate with a golden fork, and doused her apartments in perfume. This was self-indulgent to the point of absurdity, and so typically Byzantine. God, despairing of such behavior, had decided to intervene, inflicting a disease on the princess that left her with a putrified body and withered limbs.[85]

Byzantium struck Venice as pompous. To Byzantine eyes, Venice had transformed itself from a feeble imperial colony to the richest, most influential power in the Mediterranean. Defusing such tensions was precisely what diplomacy was for. When diplomacy stalled, however, the consequences could be devastating. In 1182, decades of growing antipathy between Byzantium and the Italian city-states had culminated in a massacre of the westerners living in Constantinople. When they sought refuge in the city's Catholic churches, the churches were burned. A papal legate was decapitated, his head tied to the tail of a dog. Those who survived, perhaps as many as four thousand souls, were sold as slaves to the Turks.[86]

And then came the terrible events of 1204. "How shall I begin to tell of the deeds wrought by these nefarious men?" one outraged contemporary asked.

> Alas, the images, which ought to have been adored, were trodden under foot! Alas, the relics of the holy martyrs were thrown into unclean places! Then was seen what one shudders to hear, namely, the divine body and blood of Christ was spilled upon the ground or thrown about. They snatched the

precious reliquaries, thrust into their bosoms the ornaments
which these contained, and used the broken remnants for pans
and drinking cups

The great church of St. Sophia also suffered terribly. Horses and
mules were "led to the very sanctuary of the temple" and loaded
with vases and ornaments. A common prostitute sat in the patriarch's seat, "singing an obscene song and dancing frequently."

> No one was without a share in the grief. In the alleys, in the
> streets, in the temples, complaints, weeping, lamentations, grief,
> the groaning of men, the shrieks of women, wounds, rape, cap-
> tivity, the separation of those most closely united. Nobles wan-
> dered about ignominiously, those of venerable age in tears, the
> rich in poverty. Thus it was in the streets, on the corners, in the
> temple, in the dens, for no place remained unassailed.[87]

In the wake of the sack of Constantinople, the Latin conquerors
set up their own emperor and began parcelling out Byzantine territory among themselves. The regime would not survive, and by
1261 Western control came to an end. The Fourth Crusade marked
the beginning of dark decades for Byzantium, perhaps best summed
up by the loss of the Crown of Thorns. Ambassadors had set the
events leading up to the sack of Constantinople in motion. But, as
unhappy as their mission turned out to be, it had a significance beyond the world of thirteenth-century dynastic politics.

To return to those weeks of negotiations in Venice, the doge
and his counsel had been surprised by the letters the ambassadors
carried. It was typical for envoys to take along very detailed instructions, itemizing their employers' demands, expectations, and

suggestions. In this way, the parameters of any negotiation were immediately apparent, and it was virtually impossible for ambassadors to stray far beyond the intentions of those who had sent them. In this instance, however, "the letters were letters of credence only, and declared no more than that the bearers were to be accredited as if they were the counts in person, and that the said counts would make good whatever the six envoys should undertake."

At the moment when an agreement had almost been reached, the asymmetry of the situation was striking. The doge had needed to secure the consent of the great council and the commons before making any definitive commitment. As for the crusaders, the decision as to whether to undertake one of the most significant business transactions of the Middle Ages—whether to launch a crusade—was left to six men who lacked any opportunity to consult with their leaders back in France. They thanked the doge for granting an audience and "said that they would consult together and give their answer on the morrow." They consulted, "and talked together that night, and agreed to accept the terms offered. So the next day they appeared before the Doge, and said: 'Sire, we are ready to ratify this covenant.' The Doge thereon said he would speak of the matter to his people, and, as he found them affected, so would he let the envoys know the issue."

The burden of responsibility that had been placed on the shoulders of the six ambassadors was colossal. That single phrase—"with full powers, as if they were the lords in person"—marked a paradigm shift in the history of European diplomacy. The role of ambassadors was in a process of transformation. Before the later medieval period, they had almost always been thought of as representatives of their rulers, lacking autonomy. They might double for their monarchs on important occasions, as when Peter della

Vigna stood in for the emperor Frederick II when he was unable to attend his marriage to Isabella of England in 1235. In the fifteenth century, Galleazzo Maria Sforza was also unable to attend his own wedding; he dispatched his cousin Tristan as his ambassadorial proxy—a duty that Tristan carried out with exemplary thoroughness, even entering the wedding bed and touching the bride's thigh. In the more sober world of negotiation, ambassadors simply carried the wishes, demands, and instructions of their superiors. They were, as a common phrase had it, "living letters," and little more. But now, suddenly, there was talk of initiative, of plenipotentiary powers.[88] This model of the autonomous ambassador would remain the norm in Europe into the Modern Era.

Over the coming years, with the arrival of the Mongol threat on Europe's borders, ambassadorial initiative would prove vital.

8
A Rooftop in Naples:
Europe and the Mongols

The Road to Karakorum

> To the most excellent lord and most Christian Louis, by the grace of God illustrious king of the French, from Friar William of Rubruck, the meanest in the order of minor friars, greetings, and may he always triumph in Christ. It is written in *Ecclesiastes* of the wise man: "He shall go through the land of foreign peoples, and shall try the good and evil in all things." This, my lord king, have I done, and may it have been as a wise man and not as a fool; for many do what the wise man doth, though not wisely, but most foolishly; of this number I fear I may be. Nevertheless in whatever way I may have done, since you commanded me when I took my leave of you that I should write you whatever I should see among the Tartars, and you did also admonish me not to fear writing a long letter, so I do what you enjoined on me, with fear, however, and diffidence, for the proper words that I should write to so great a monarch do not suggest themselves to me.
>
> —William of Rubruck to Louis IX of France[89]

THE MONGOL HOMELANDS, deep in the Asian steppe, made for an austere existence. Aside from a handful of oases in the river valleys of central Mongolia, there was scarcely a tree to be found, barely a crop that had the slightest hope of flourishing. Grass, however, grew in abundance. It was a paradise for livestock. From wool and sheepskin, the Mongols fashioned their clothes and their famously portable felt tents, or yurts. Sheep provided mutton and cheese, and their dung could be burned for fuel. Horses allowed the Mongols to hunt, to trade, and to fight, and, for better or worse, their fermented milk gave the Mongols *qumis*, as potent an alcoholic drink as might be imagined.

The Mongols were nomads, moving between pastures as the seasons turned. They had always maintained links with other cultures. One could not hunt without weapons, and the manufacture of weapons demanded metal. One could hardly subsist on animal flesh alone, so one required grain. Trade with northern China had always provided such staples. For all that, the Mongols were inward-looking. What was more, they were divided, fragmented into hundreds of proud, independent tribes, until the advent of Genghis Khan, that is: the founder of a Mongol Empire that would eventually stretch from Hungary to Korea. The rise of the Mongols would turn the thirteenth-century world upside down. At that century's outset many of the ancient empires—the Abbasids in Persia, the Sung dynasty in China, the Byzantines in Constantinople—were faded but still influential. They would all either be bruised or overturned by the Mongol advance. The emerging civilization of Kievan Russia and the older kingdoms of eastern Europe would all suffer.

In 1206, at a meeting of the Mongol nobility, or *khuriltai*, the title of Genghis Khan was first bestowed: It was an illustrious title meaning "ruler of everything between the oceans." This was only the culmination of years of brilliant statecraft. Since his emergence at the end of the previous century, Genghis had succeeded in bringing vast swathes of the Mongol population under his control, winning admirers through martial prowess and the booty that military victory brought with it. Tribal allegiances had been displaced by personal loyalty to a single ruler: For the first time, tribalism had been superseded by a transcendent Mongol identity.

Genghis had an irrepressible sense of Mongol superiority and a vision of a vast Mongol empire. In the decades after 1206, the Mongols' horseback armies streamed out of Mongolia in all directions. Many reasons are proffered for this sudden flowering of Mongol expansionism. Perhaps climate change had curtailed the grass-growing season, making it harder to sustain the nomadic lifestyle. Perhaps trade with northern China had declined to such a degree that new economic ventures—a euphemism for sack and pillage—had to be explored.

Genghis himself led expeditions into northern China and central Asia. His son Ogedei took victorious Mongol armies as far east as Korea, and as far west as Georgia, Armenia, and Persia. One of his grandsons, Kublai Khan, would conquer the whole of China and establish an imperial dynasty that would flourish for a hundred years. Farther west, Baghdad would fall in 1258, and the Abbasid caliphate would perish. At its height, the Mongol Empire, home to one hundred million people, stretched over fourteen million square miles.

The lands farther to the west would not be spared such intrusions. Europe simply did not know what to make of the Mongols when they first began to encroach on its territory. Were they potential allies? Were they the lost ten tribes of Israel or the demonic residents of hell? The years between 1237 and 1242, when Mongol troops under the great general Batu swept through Russia, Poland, and Hungary, had provided unwelcome answers.

An English cleric who had witnessed the ruthless Mongol advance into eastern Europe wrote of "a barbarous and inhuman people, whose law is lawless, whose wrath is furious." The Lord, he decided, was punishing Christendom for its moral shortcomings. In fact, Europe knew almost nothing about the Mongol Empire. As a Russian chronicler explained, "For our sins, unknown tribes came...no-one exactly knows who they are, nor whence they came, nor what their language is, nor of what race they are, nor what their faith is." Nonetheless, a grotesque stereotype was beginning to fester in the Western imagination. Mongols (often referred to as Tartars by contemporaries) were cannibals, the Englishman announced, "glutting themselves and leaving nothing for vultures but the bare bones." And they were discriminating cannibals at that: "The beautiful devoured they not, but smothered them with forced and unnatural ravishments. Like barbarous miscreants they quelled virgins, and cutting off their tender paps to present for dainties unto their magistrates, they engorged themselves with their bodies."[90]

In 1241 Ogedei Khan died, and all Mongol leaders were obliged to return to Asia to elect his successor. The Mongol armies left Europe in 1242, withdrawing into Russia (whose princes would recognize Mongol overlordship for the next two centuries), but Europe's relief was tinged with the fear that they might one day return. At the Council of Lyons in 1245, Pope Innocent IV decreed that envoys should be dispatched to the Mongol homeland to dissuade the new khan from launching fresh attacks on Europe, and to try and win him over to the Christian faith.

So it was that John of Plano Carpini, a Franciscan friar, departed Lyon in April 1245 as the pope's ambassador. He travelled through Bohemia, Poland, and the Ukraine, only to fall so ill that he had to be carried by cart to Kiev. Having encountered an army of 60,000 Mongol troops at the River Dnieper, he moved farther into Asia, destined for the khan's camp, close to the Mongol capital at Karakorum. Eight years later, at the behest of the French king Louis IX, another envoy would approach the khan: The Flemish Franciscan William of Rubruck would leave Constantinople armed with little more than "fruits, muscadel wine and dainty biscuits" with which to bribe local officials. In the company of a translator, and a slave boy purchased in the Byzantine capital, he would travel through the Crimea and the steppes of Kazakhstan, sometimes through cold that was so harsh "it split stones and trees." So far from home, it seemed to Rubruck "that I had been transported into another century."[91]

Both missions were diplomatic fiascos. Rubruck was informed that, the world over, those who resisted Mongol supremacy were likely to lose their eyes, hands and feet. To the pope's suggestion that the Mongols convert to Christianity, a reply came back: "You in person, at the head of the monarchs, all of you without exception, must come to render us service and pay us homage." The leaders of Western Europe should realize that "thanks to the everlasting heaven, all lands have been given to us from sunrise to sunset." Mongol pride did not countenance the feeble overtures of feeble Western rulers.[92]

But the journeys of these monkish ambassadors also provided accounts of Mongol life and manners that were endlessly more reliable, nuanced, and incisive than the more famous observations of the Venetian Marco Polo two decades later. In an echo of Priscus's embassy to Attila the Hun back in the fifth century, they revealed that the Mongols were far more than bloodthirsty barbarians.

Rubruck caused something of a sensation in his friar's garb, especially when he began walking through the Mongol emperor's camp without any shoes—a mark of gross disrespect: "They surrounded us and gazed at us as if we were monsters, especially because we were barefooted, and they asked us if we had no use for our feet, because they supposed that we would at once lose them." Rubruck was always more concerned with evangelism than with diplomacy. His narrative comes most vividly to life when recounting his awkward attempts to explain the tenets of his faith. Early in his journey he seemed close to winning a Mongol over to Christianity: "When he heard of the blessings of God to man in the incarnation, the resurrection of the dead and the last judgment, the washing away of sins in baptism, he said he wished to be baptized." Unfortunately, "while we were making ready to baptize him he suddenly jumped on his horse saying he had to go home to consult with his wife." Returning the next day he regretfully announced that conversion was out of the question because "the Christians of these parts say that no true Christian should drink alcohol."

The defining image of Rubruck's mission was surely the moment when he mounted a remarkable display of Christian worship for another potential convert. Having secured an audience by sending him a hamper of biscuits and a bottle of "muscadel wine which had kept perfectly well during the whole long journey," Rubruck eagerly donned his costliest vestments. He entered the Mongol's tent "with a most beautiful cushion against my breast, and took the Bible, and the beautiful Psalter which my lady the Queen had presented me with, and in which were right beautiful pictures." Surrounded by missals, crosses, and censers, Rubruck must have cut an impossibly incongruous, irredeemably optimistic figure.

He was a monk first and an ambassador second, and he said as much. In fact, on at least three separate occasions he said he was not an ambassador at all. This was disingenuous. His mission, however religiously motivated, was indubitably part of the European campaign to prevent future Mongol invasions, and he was carrying letters from Europe's mightiest king. It was impossible for his mission to lack a diplomatic aspect, a fact that Rubruck's own behavior sometimes betrayed.

During one audience with the khan, Rubruck grew extremely angry when, however jokingly, the prospect of the Mongol's revisiting Europe was mooted. Rubruck was offered a drink—a choice between rice wine or fermented milk. He opted for the "rice drink, which was clear and flavoured like white wine, and of which I tasted a little out of respect for [the khan]." Unfortunately, Rubruck's interpreter showed less restraint. He was "standing by the butlers, who gave him so much that he was drunk in a very short time."

In fact even the khan "appeared to be tipsy." In their cups, the Mongols "began to question us greatly about the kingdom of France, whether there were many sheep and cattle and horses there, and whether they had not better go there at once and take it all." Rubruck "had to use all my strength to conceal my indignation and anger; but I answered: 'There are many good things there, which you would see if it befell you to go there.'" However well he had risen above the Mongols' taunts, Rubruck, in that moment, encapsulated the mingled fear and frustration of an entire continent. He was, undoubtedly, that continent's representative.[93] That said, it is the worldlier John of Plano Carpini, an unapologetic ambassador, who warrants most of our attention.

———

After departing from Lyon on April 16, 1245, Carpini and his travelling companion, a fellow Franciscan named Benedict, headed for southern Germany and the court of the king of Bohemia. They sought advice about what route they ought to follow on their long, perilous journey to the East. The king suggested travelling via Poland. He had relatives there who could help facilitate their entry into Russia. Medieval diplomacy was reliant on the largesse of influential kings, princes, and nobles. John and Benedict were not salaried bureaucrats, but poor monks, chosen not only as diplomatists but as men who might carry the Christian message to the pagan Mongol hordes. The Bohemian king was well aware of his duties and provided the two monks with letters of safe conduct, an armed guard, and some funds to help defray their travelling expenses.

When they reached the king's nephew in Poland, the duke of Silesia, he, too, offered the ambassadors provisions and a fresh escort, and sent them on to the court of the Duke of Lenczy. Here, John and Benedict were fortunate enough to meet a Russian nobleman who had recently sent his own ambassadors into Mongol territories. He was full of useful information—perhaps most gratifying of all was the news that his ambassadors had returned home safely—and was delighted to dispense advice. It was absolutely imperative, he explained, that the two monks should carry a good stock of gifts for any Mongol dignitaries they might encounter. "He told us that if we wanted to go to them we must have rich presents to give them, for they were in the habit of asking for them most importunately, and if they were not given them...an ambassador could not conduct his business satisfactorily, and that furthermore he was looked upon as a mere nothing."[94]

Carpini set about buying up beaver pelts and others assorted animal skins. Word spread of Carpini's impending mission, and additional gifts were supplied by the duchess and bishop of Cracow. Just as importantly, the Russian duke offered to personally escort the two monks into his territories.

They rested at his court for several days, taking the opportunity to deliver papal letters to Russian Orthodox bishops, in which the Holy Father urged them to return to the fold of the Roman Catholic Church. They then set off for Kiev, "the metropolis of Russia," with some of the duke's servants, although their journey was plagued by the unwelcome attentions of Lithuanian bandits and spells of bad health. Carpini remembered being ill "to the point of death," but he bravely had himself "carried along in a cart in the intense cold through the deep snow, so as not to interfere with the affairs of Christendom."[95]

Upon their arrival, they were advised by the merchants of Kiev to rethink their means of transport. "They told us that if we took into Tartary the horses which we had, they would all die, for the snows were deep, and they did not know how to dig out the grass from under the snow like Tartar horses, nor could anything else be found for them to eat, for the Tartars had neither straw, nor hay, nor fodder." More robust packhorses were acquired, and the ambassadors set off on the three-thousand-mile journey to the Mongol heartlands.[96]

Their itinerary led them through a series of modest Mongol settlements, at each of which they were obliged to secure permission to continue their journey. Not all of them were particularly welcoming. One Mongol governor named Micheas had sent servants to Kiev, specifically inviting the ambassadors to travel via his camp. An act of apparent generosity had actually been a ruse. He was "a man full of all malice and iniquity," who had only lured John and Benedict to his lands to relieve them of some of their possessions.

When we reached him, he made himself most disagreeable, and unless we promised him presents, would in no wise agree to help us. Seeing that we would not otherwise be able to go further, we promised to give him some presents, but when we gave him what appeared to us suitable, he refused to receive them unless we gave more; and so we had to add to them according to his will.[97]

Finally, late in February 1246, the monks encountered their first sizeable Mongol encampment. Things did not begin well. "While we were stopping for the night, as the sun went down, the Tartars broke in on us in arms in horrible fashion, asking us who we were." John explained that he was an envoy of the pope and, after helping themselves to some of the monks' evening meal, the Mongol soldiers returned to their camp. The next morning it was the turn of more senior Mongol officials to interrogate the strange visitors about their intentions. John, with no little courage, offered a blunt and bullish reply:

We answered them that we were the envoys of the lord pope, who was the lord and father of Christians; that he had sent us…because he desired that all Christians should be friends of the Tartars and at peace with them…The lord pope also advised them, by his letters, that they should become Christians and receive the faith of Our Lord Jesus Christ, for otherwise they could not be saved. He told them, furthermore, that he was astonished at the slaying of human beings done by the Tartars, and especially of Christians and above all of Hungarians, Moravians and Poles, who were his subjects, when they had injured them in nothing nor attempted to injure them. And as the Lord God was gravely offended at this, he cautioned them to abstain henceforth from such acts, and to repent of those they had done.

Mercifully, John's provocative statement caused no offense, and, after receiving a sufficient supply of gifts, the Mongols provided him with new packhorses and a guide to an even mightier encampment on the banks of the frozen Dnieper River.[98]

The governor of this next settlement was reputed to be in charge of some sixty thousand troops. He reacted cautiously to the ambassadors' arrival, insisting that they set up their tents at a secure distance from his own. He demanded presents and finally granted the envoys an audience, during which they would enjoy their first encounter with the complicated ritual of Mongol diplomacy.

After being made to kneel down three times outside the governor's tents, they were told "to be very careful not to put our feet on the threshold of the door; and this we were attentive to observe, for sentence of death is on those who knowingly tread upon the threshold of a chief's dwelling." Safely inside, they once more fell to their knees before the governor and his assembled counsellors. A letter from the pope was proffered, but sadly no one had the first idea how to translate it. The fraught issue of linguistic incompetence was a recurrent theme in the history of the ambassadors. Within the confines of western Europe, envoys benefited from a common diplomatic language—Latin and, later, French. In Turkey, a unique professional class of interpreters, the dragomans, grew up. Farther east, everything depended on whether, as a matter of pure chance, a local could be found who knew something of European languages. On this occasion, no such person was forthcoming. Nonetheless, the governor was at least able to explain that the ambassadors would be allowed to continue their journey farther east. Their next destination was the camp of the illustrious general Batu, the very man who had led the military campaigns in Europe a decade earlier.[99]

The pace of the ambassadors' journey suddenly quickened. From February 26 to April 4 they traversed three of Russia's great rivers, the Dnieper, the Don, and the Volga, riding "as fast as horses could go trotting" from dawn until dusk. Each set of animals was quickly exhausted by this regimen, and horses were changed as many as three or four times a day.

Upon reaching Batu's encampment the ambassadors experienced another curious Mongol ceremony.

> Before we were taken to his court we were told we would have to pass between two fires, which we refused to do under any consideration. But they told us: "Fear not, we only make you pass between these two fires lest perchance you think something injurious to our lord, or if you carry some poison, for the fire will remove all harm." We answered them: "Since it is thus we will pass through, so that we may not be suspected of such things."

John and Benedict were interrogated by Batu's officials and, predictably, made to offer up yet more gifts. On Good Friday, after their letters of introduction had been translated, they finally met with the general. There was much for the ambassadors to resent. They were offered nothing to eat during their stay apart from endless bowls of millet. But they were clearly surprised by Batu's bearing and dignity and by the orderliness of his court. Perhaps he was not some vulgar savage, after all.

> This Batu holds his court right magnificently, for he has doorkeepers and all the other officials like unto their emperor. He sits also in a raised place, as on a throne, with one of his wives, but every one else, his brothers and his sons as well as others of lesser degree, sit lower down on a bench in the middle of the tent. All the other people sit behind them on the ground, the men to the right, the women to the left.

As befitted any powerful ruler, Batu inspired respect and trepidation. No one dared enter his presence uninvited, "no matter how great and mighty he may be." On occasion he struck the visitors as almost civilized. He would not dream of drinking alcohol without the accompaniment of singing or guitar playing, and "when he rides out, there is always carried over his head on a pole an umbrella or little awning." Added to that, as Europe well knew, "he is very shrewd and extremely crafty in warfare, for he has been waging war for a long time." William of Rubruck would later admire Batu's diplomatic sophistication. "At Batu's court there is an [official] on the west side who receives all those who come from the west, and it is arranged in like fashion for the other quarters of the world...At the court of Batu [the various ambassadors] do not know each other, and one knows not whether another is an envoy, for they know not each other's lodgings, and only see each other at court."[100]

Impressive as he was, Batu was not the ultimate objective of the ambassadors' journey. They were intent on meeting with the emperor. On April 8th, with Batu's permission, they recommenced their journey, heading out of Russia into the lands of present-day Kazakhstan, their final destination still more than two thousand miles to the east. They were anything but optimistic about their prospects. "We started out most tearfully," John remembered, "not knowing whether we were going to life or death." For the whole of Lent they had eaten little more than millet cooked with salt and water, "nor had we anything else to drink but snow melted in the kettle....We were so feeble that we could hardly ride."

But ride they did, and at a breakneck speed, changing horses five, six, or even seven times a day. With their Mongol escorts at their sides, they rose at dawn and "travelled until night without stop....Often we arrived so late that we did not eat at night, but that which we should have eaten was given us in the morning."

The landscape through which they travelled was eerie and desolate. They "found many human skulls and bones scattered about on the ground like cattle-dung" and a grim procession of ruined cities and villages—ominous reminders of the Mongols' devastating military progress through the region. Finally, after their surroundings began turning "exceptionally mountainous and cold," they reached the vast plains of Mongolia, and on July 22, the feast of Mary Magdalene, they approached the khan's camp.[101]

They were given a tent and provisions, but were forbidden from meeting with Guyuk (son of Ogedei Khan) before his election and coronation. Prior to that, the Mongol establishment had spent many hours deep in discussion and negotiation. They assembled in "a great tent...ornamented with diverse designs... which in our opinion was large enough to hold more than two thousand persons." Electoral proceedings would usually take up the whole morning, after which the delegates "began drinking mare's milk, and they drank until evening so plentifully that it was a rare sight." Only the great and the good of the Mongol political establishment were allowed inside the tent, and if anyone else came too close "he was beaten if caught, or shot at with headless arrows if he ran away."

It was, therefore, something of a privilege for Benedict and John to be invited inside, though they were not the only outsiders present for the election. Two sons of the kings of Georgia, an envoy from the caliph of Baghdad, and a dozen other Indian and central Asian ambassadors were all in attendance, along with "those bringing tribute" and "sultans and other chiefs who had come to present themselves in person."[102]

After four weeks of deliberation, Guyuk was elected khan. His coronation was scheduled for August 15 but had to be postponed until the 24th, "on account of the hail which fell." After several days of feasting, a meeting with the new emperor was finally arranged. Before entering Guyuk's tent, a scribe recorded John and Benedict's names and had them searched for knives. Upon entering the tent, the ambassadors were once more bewildered by the opulent surroundings. Silks, golden girdles, and splendid furs were strewn around the emperor. "It was a marvel to see," John recalled.

Little was achieved. Guyuk was accustomed to ambassadors offering him sumptuous gifts, and officials asked the monks "if we wished to make any presents; but we had already used up nearly everything we had, so we had nothing at all to give him." This was not the best way to endear themselves to a Mongol emperor. But at least John would finally be able to tell Europe exactly what a Mongol emperor looked like: "He may be forty or forty-five years or more old; he is of medium stature, very prudent and extremely shrewd, and serious and sedate in his manners; and he has never been seen to laugh lightly or show any levity." There was even a rumor that he had considered abandoning his pagan ways: "We were also assured by Christians who were of his household that they firmly believed that he was about to become a Christian. As signal evidence of this he keeps Christian clerks and gives them allowances."

Life could be perilous at the Mongol court. John heard of a Russian duke who had recently met with a very suspicious end. The emperor's mother had invited him to her tent and fed him "with her own hand, as if to honour him." "He went back to his lodgings straightway and fell ill, and after seven days he was dead, and all his body became livid in strange fashion; so that everyone believed that he had been poisoned, that they might get free and full possession of his lands."

John and Benedict were spared such intrigues, but their time at Guyuk's camp was still something of a trial. After the bountiful days of the election and coronation, the monks were reduced to the most meagre of diets: food that would have fed one man having to be shared among four. They were "in such hunger and thirst that we were barely able to keep alive...and we could find nothing to buy, the market being too far away. Had not the Lord sent us a certain Ruthenian called Cosmas, a goldsmith, and a great favourite of the emperor, who helped us a little, I verily believe we should have died."[103]

The pope's letters had been delivered, Guyuk's irascible reply had been secured, and there was little reason for the monks to prolong their stay. Before they departed, however, Guyuk raised the possibility of sending his own ambassadors back with John and Benedict. It was the most unwelcome of proposals:

> There were various reasons for which it seemed to us inexpedient that they should come. The first was that we feared they would see the dissensions and wars among us, and that it would encourage them to march against us. The second reason was that we feared they were intended to be spies. The third reason was that we feared lest they be put to death, as our people for the most part are arrogant and hasty...and it is the custom of the Tartars never to make peace with those who have killed their envoys till they have wreaked vengeance upon them. The fourth reason was that we feared they would carry us off. The fifth reason was that there was no need for their coming, for they had no other order or authority than to bring the letters of the emperor to the lord pope and the other princes of Christendom, which we already had.

The monks succeeded in dissuading Guyuk from dispatching ambassadors (a notable diplomatic triumph in itself) and started on their homeward journey. "We reached Kiev fifteen days before the feast of Saint John the Baptist [June 9, 1247]. The people who had heard of our arrival all came out to meet us rejoicing, and congratulated us as if we had risen from the dead."[104]

John of Plano Carpini had enjoyed endless conversations in the East. He had met French and Latin-speaking soldiers and merchants who had lived among the Mongols for years on end. "From these we were able to learn about everything: they told us most freely of all things without our having to question them, for they knew of our desire." Upon his return to Europe John acquired some measure of celebrity and was endlessly asked to regale audiences with tales of his journey. His account of his embassy found its way into the *Speculum historiale* of Vincent of Beauvais, a massively influential text within the literate echelons of medieval society.

The European mental image of the Mongols was thus enhanced. They were "broader between the eyes and the balls of their cheeks than men of other nations be," John reported. "They have flat and small noses, little eyes and eyelids standing straight upright." Their hair was long, their feet were short, and men and women seemed to wear alarmingly similar clothes.[105]

True, they drank too much. As William of Rubruck had also complained, both sexes were seemingly addicted to a pungent liquor which, when drunk, "leaves a taste of milk of almonds on the tongue, and it makes the inner man most joyful and also intoxicates weak heads, and greatly provokes urine." Sometimes they would "compete with one another in quaffing in a thoroughly distasteful and greedy fashion...And when they want to challenge anyone to drink, they take hold of him by the ears, and pull so as to distend his throat, and they clap and dance before him." True, "some of them speak filthy and immodest words." But they were also "more obedient than any other people in the world," and rarely fell to squabbling among themselves. There was hardly any fighting or theft, the women were chaste, and the Mongol tent, the yurt, was a marvel of compact engineering.[106]

On balance (and for its time the description *was* unusually balanced), "their manners are partly praiseworthy and partly detestable." Carpini's mixed response to Mongol society was shared by his counterpart William of Rubruck, who could certainly be rude. "The women there are astonishingly fat," he revealed, "and she who has the least nose is held the most beautiful. They disfigure themselves horribly by painting their faces." He had once been introduced to a Mongol leader, sitting on a couch "with a little guitar in his hand and his wife beside him." And such a wife: "It seemed to me that her whole nose had been cut off, for she was so snub-nosed that she seemed to have no nose at all. She had greased this part of her face with some black unguent, and also her eyebrows, so that she appeared most hideous to us."

Sometimes, however, Rubruck's descriptions were pristinely objective. Explaining the division of labor between the sexes, for instance, he calmly reported that "the men make bows and arrows, manufacture stirrups and bits, make saddles, do the carpentering on their dwellings and the carts. They take care of the horses, milk the mares, churn the mare's milk, and make the skins in which it is put. They also look after the camels and load them. Both sexes look after the sheep and goats, sometimes the men, other times the women, milking them." This was dull, but its dullness was its greatest virtue.[107]

Rubruck could also be impressed, whether by the best sausages he had ever tasted or by the undeniable magnificence of the Mongol court in the capital city of Karakorum:

> Mongke [Guyuk's successor as khan] had at Karakorum a great palace, situated next to the city walls, enclosed within a high wall like those which enclose monks' priories among us. There are there many buildings as long as barns, in which are stored his provisions and his treasures. In the entry of this great palace, Master William the Parisian had made for him a great silver tree, and at its roots are four lions of silver, each with a conduit through it, and all belching forth white mares' milk. Four conduits are led inside the tree to its tops, which are bent downward, and on each of these is also a gilded serpent, whose tail twines round the tree. And from one of these pipes flows wine, from another clarified mare's milk, from another bal, a drink made with honey, and from another rice mead, which is called terracina; and for each liquor there is a special silver bowl at the foot of the tree to receive it…the palace is like a church, with a middle nave, and two sides beyond two rows of pillars, the Chan sits in a high place to the north, sitting up there like a divinity.

It was a sight to rival anything that even Constantinople could offer. This was not a people who could simply be dismissed, and if they only remained in their homelands all would be well. They were, Carpini reported, "very rich in cattle, oxen, sheep and goats, and I think they have more horses and mares than all the world besides." The danger was that they would once more embark on missions of conquest. And given the Mongols' attitude toward the rest of humanity, John warned, that possibility could not be discounted. "Toward other people, the Tartars are most insolent, and they scorn and set nought by all other people, whether noble or ignoble." "They were of a disdainful nature and beyond all measure deceitful and treacherous. They speak fair in the beginning, but in the end sting like scorpions."[108]

—⚜—

John need not have worried. The Mongol threat to Europe was over, the ferocious horsemen would never again transgress her borders. By the last quarter of the thirteenth century, the Mongol Empire had divided into various spheres of influence—in the Mongolian homelands, China, the Golden Horde of Russia, and the Ilkhanate of Persia. Suddenly, European diplomacy moved from a posture of defense to one of mutual aggression. The once unthinkable prospect of civilized diplomatic relations with at least one offshoot of the Mongol empire—the Ilkhanate of Persia— was being proposed. It now fell to Rabban Sauma to enrich Asia's understanding of the West.

Rabban Sauma

> Let us leave these dogs to devour one another, that they may all be consumed and perish. And we, when we proceed against the enemies of Christ who remain, will slay them, and cleanse the face of the earth, so that all the world will be subject to the one Catholic Church, and there will be one shepherd and one flock.
> —Peter des Roches, bishop of Winchester, on the Mongol menace[109]

On a summer's day in 1287, a Chinese Christian monk sat on a rooftop in Naples, watching a naval battle unfold in the Bay of Sorrento. Rabban Sauma was five thousand miles from home. He had journeyed from a hermit's cave in the mountains above Peking and, through little more than happenstance, had become a trusted envoy of the Mongol khan of Persia. He had dined with a Byzantine emperor, and would soon be ministering the Eucharist to an English king and celebrating Mass with a pope. He would see Paris and Rome, Tuscany and Gascony. He would debate with scholars and cardinals and hatch plans to revive the crusades. He was the unlikeliest of ambassadors.

Born in northern China around the year 1260, Sauma had been a pious youth. There was even hope that he might become a priest of the Nestorian Church—Asia's ancient, enigmatic branch of Christianity. During the fifth century, Nestorius, a bishop of Constantinople, had posited a controversial theory about the two natures—human and divine—of Christ. His theory, that the two natures were always distinct and yet always linked on some metaphysical level, was deemed heretical in the West, and denounced at the Council of Ephesus in 431. His ideas had won supporters, however, and in the coming decades and centuries they sustained aspects of his theology, even sending missionaries as far as China in the east. It was this tradition that Sauma inherited.

Sauma had dutifully pursued his religious studies and embraced a life of chastity and humility, but at the age of twenty this seemly piety had given way to an all-consuming zeal. As he remembered it, "The divine fire was kindled in his heart, and it burned up the brambles of sin, cleansing his chaste soul." From that time on, "he esteemed dainty meats as things which had no existence, and he rejected wholly the drinks which make a man drunk." Sauma had decided to renounce the world and all its fleshly distractions. He also provided history with a peerlessly intimate account of a man's spiritual transformation. The corpus of medieval historical sources has nothing more fundamentally human to offer.

His parents were distraught. They remembered their struggle to conceive a child, and how they had "prayed to God continually not to deprive them of a son who would continue their race." At length, such prayers had been answered, but now their only son was preparing to abandon them. They begged Sauma to stay, "and with broken hearts made supplication to him, and brought before him promises of things of this world." Was their mourning sweet in his eyes? they asked him. "Is our affliction desired by you?" Sauma relented and agreed to remain in his parents' home, but after three more years his yearning to seek out the life of an ascetic was undimmed.

Sauma gave up his few possessions and took on the garb and tonsure of a monk. He shut himself in a cell for seven years and then, determined to "remove himself from the children of men," he trekked into the mountains. After finding "a certain place where there was a cave, and by the side of it a spring of water," he took up his solitary vigil.

Hundreds of miles to the east, in the city of Kawshang, a young Nestorian Christian named Mark heard stories of Sauma's reclusive life and resolved to seek him out. (Mark, as he was known in the European tradition; in the East he would more accurately be known as Mar Yahbh-Allaha.) After fifteen days' hard travel, he arrived at Sauma's cave and boldly announced that he, too, wished to become a monk. At first Sauma was unimpressed and urged Mark to return home to his parents, but Mark would not yield. Finally, Sauma agreed to take him into his cave. For the next three years the men prayed and fasted. They toiled together "in the cultivation of purity and holiness, comforted by God unto whom they had committed their souls."

One day Mark announced that "it would be exceedingly helpful to us if we were to leave this region and set out for the West."

They could visit the tombs of the holy martyrs and Catholic fathers and perhaps even reach Jerusalem. In that holiest of cities, so Mark imagined, "we might receive complete pardon for our offenses, and absolution for our sins of foolishness." Sauma was skeptical and tried to frighten Mark with stories of "the toil of the journey, the terror of the ways, and the tribulations that would beset him in a foreign country."

Mark would not be gainsaid, and since the two men had vowed never to part from each other, Sauma finally agreed to embark on the hazardous westward journey. Local Christians implored them to stay, warning them "how difficult it will be for you to travel over the roads," and predicting that, in all likelihood, they would never reach their goal. But Sauma and Mark had an eloquent answer. They had renounced the world, and "we consider ourselves to be dead men in respect of it." Adversity could not terrify such men. The monks and their brethren "kissed each other, and parted with bitter tears and distressful words."

An arduous journey lay ahead. Mark and Sauma travelled across China, through war-scarred provinces where the caravan roads had been severed, and through regions of "bare and barren desert." At times, rainwater provided their only sustenance. The two men would never reach Jerusalem. Instead, their lives would be transformed in Persia, itself a place newly turned upside down.

In 1258, Baghdad had fallen to the Mongols. The great Abbasid capital had suffered mightily. Mongol troops had swarmed in from all directions, thousands had perished, and the last Abbasid caliph had been strangled to death. The conqueror of Baghdad was Hulagu Khan, a grandson of Genghis Khan. The regime Hulagu established in Persia was far from the Mongol heartland in the Asian steppe, far less resilient than the Mongol provinces established to the north, on Europe's borders. It would endure for less than a century, but its role in the history of ambassadorial encounter, in the grander encounter between West and East, would be profound. When Sauma and Mark crossed the Persian frontier, Hulagu's successor, Arghun, had recently ascended to the throne of the Mongol Ilkhanate. He had an ambitious plan. He "intended to go into the countries of Palestine and Syria and to subjugate them and take possession of them," but realized that "if the Western kings, who are Christians, will not help me I shall not be able to fulfil my desire." Europe, so he rightly calculated, was still consumed with crusading zeal, still haunted by the dream of recovering Jerusalem. The khan had need of a "wise man, one who is suitable and is capable of undertaking an embassy, that we may send him to those kings."

Sauma and Mark had already been in Persia for some time when Arghun uttered these words. They had sojourned at a monastery, travelled widely, and garnered a local reputation as loyal servants of the church. When the Nestorian Church started searching for a new patriarch, the church's hierarchy was all too aware that "the steering poles of the government of the whole world were the Mongols." Mark was a man who had come from China, another land recently subjected to Mongol rule; a man who was "acquainted with their manners and customs, and their policy of government, and their language." He was the perfect candidate. With his election as patriarch, Mark was suddenly the most influential Christian in Persia. The khan, desperate to recruit a Christian ambassador to do his bidding in Europe, sought out Mark's counsel. The choice was obvious. Rabban Sauma—a Christian who knew something of Western languages—came before Arghun and simply declared: "I desire this embassy greatly, and I long to go." With letters, gold, and "thirty good riding animals," Sauma set out on the next stage of his remarkable journey.

His first destination was Constantinople, and as he approached its walls the emperor dispatched officials to escort Sauma into his presence with due "pomp and honour." The Byzantine empire was a polity in decline, but the city that had once been the diplomatic storm center of the world still had much to enchant an ambassador.

Sauma was given a mansion in which to lodge, and tours of the city's churches were arranged. As a Christian monk, he must have been awestruck by the abundance of holy relics still on display, despite the atrocities of 1204. He saw the hand of John the Baptist, parts of Mary Magdalene's body, the bowl in which Christ had turned water into wine, and the stone on which Peter had been sitting when the fateful cock crowed to announce his betrayal. Sauma was already demonstrating one of the most useful of ambassadorial attributes—a talent for flattery. "How are you after the workings of the sea and the fatigue of the road?" asked Emperor Andronicus II. "With the sight of a Christian king," Sauma fawningly replied, "fatigue has vanished and exhaustion has departed."

Heading west from Constantinople, Sauma and his companions witnessed an eruption of Mount Etna, and rode through the Italian countryside "marvelling because they found no land which was destitute of buildings." In Rome, cardinals were transfixed by news of those Christian priests who "have gone into the countries of the Mongols, and Turks, and Chinese, and have taught them the gospel." At Genoa, crowds rushed out to greet such unexpected visitors, and in Paris Sauma was staggered by the thirty thousand scholars of the university who studied not only theology but medicine, "geometry, arithmetic and the science of the planets and the stars." The French king even proffered an encouraging response to the notion of a joint military campaign in the Holy Land. "If it be indeed so that the Mongols, though they are not Christians, are going to fight against the Arabs for the capture of Jerusalem," Philip IV declared, "it is meet especially for us that we should fight with them."

At a meeting in Bordeaux, Edward I of England was similarly enthusiastic. He reminded Sauma that the kings of Europe "bear upon our bodies the sign of the cross" to remind them that Jerusalem was still in the hands of the infidel: "We have no subject of thought except this matter," he confessed. Firm commitments were not forthcoming, however, and on the road back to Rome Sauma began to wonder if the khan's great project was destined to be stillborn. "When I go back," he fretted, "what shall I say and what answer can I make to the Mongols, those men whose hearts are harder than flint?"

In fact, Ilkhan Arghun was delighted to welcome Rabban Sauma back to Persia. "We have made you suffer great fatigue," he told the monk, "for you are an old man." He was disappointed that the mission had failed, but pleased to see an old and trusted friend. "In future we shall not permit you to leave us...we will set up a church at the gate of our palace and you shall minister therein and recite prayers." Which was how Sauma lived out the rest of his days. When he died in 1294, his old friend Mark was inconsolable and "his weeping reached the heavens."

Sauma's mission had been a failure, as were all the others that followed in its wake. No treaties had been signed, no alliances had been forged. A Genoan named Buscarello de Ghizolfi would spend years vainly scuttling between Persia and Europe on diplomatic errands. An English mission would head to Persia in 1291, taking gifts of falcons for the Ilkhan. It returned with a leopard, fed daily on live mutton, and little else besides. But the history of the ambassadors is not merely one of diplomacy and statecraft. Upon his return, Sauma had presented Arghun with letters of blessing and talked fondly of the kings of Europe and "how they had welcomed him with love." He had "related the wonderful things which he had seen and the power of their kingdoms."[110]

9
THE NEW DIPLOMACY

Tamerlane

A T MIDDAY ON NOVEMBER 14, 1403, a ship sailed down the
Bosporus toward the Black Sea. Courtesy of a Genoese
seaman named Niccolò Socato, the Spanish ambassador
Ruy Gonzalo de Clavijo was finally crossing into Asia. The Black
Sea was unusually treacherous at this season, and by the next morning the ship had already lost its lateen sail, and the crew had taken
to their oars. Repairs were quickly made, however, and by sunset
Clavijo and his companions had dropped anchor at a Genoese-
owned island port. High winds all through the next day hampered
further progress. By midnight the gales had grown so ferocious that
the ship's boatswain suggested leaving the exposed harbor to find
more secure shelter behind a Genoese carrack stationed a little way
out to sea. It was a calamitous error of judgement.

"He had us to weigh anchor," Clavijo remembered, "and with
their oars our men tried to row us to where that ship was lying, but
by reason of the violence of the storm we failed to fetch up alongside her." Clavijo's ship, now wholly at the mercy of the elements,
dropped her anchors but, as "the storm still continued to increase
in fury, our anchors began to drag, and it was evident that surely
the galliot would be cast on to the rocks off the island." Merci-

fully, the anchors held, but the winds continued to rise, and Clavijo feared that "the danger of death was upon us."

> We all betook ourselves to prayer, beseeching our Lord God for mercy ... The waves of the sea now rose so high that they broke in over the bulwarks of our ship, the waters pouring out again on the other side, whereby the galliot began to fill. Then for a time we passengers and the ship's crew lost all hope: we could only place our trust in the mercy of our Lord God.

Suddenly the Genoese carrack that they had vainly tried to reach broke its moorings and rushed headlong toward Clavijo's ship. A collision was only narrowly avoided, and the carrack "drifted past us, borne toward the shore of the island, beam on. Long before daybreak she had gone to pieces so completely that no part of her wreck remained." Clavijo and his shipmates passed the next hours desperately baling out water. "We managed in the end to keep ourselves afloat until dawn broke, when the wind changed and it blew fair for crossing over to the Turkish coast."

The survivors from the Genoese carrack were amazed that Clavijo's ship had survived the night. "As they told us later, they had been sure when the galliot was seen by them to drift away from under the lee of the carrack, that we were about to perish. Expecting the worst they had turned to our Lord God in supplication and he had spared us from death."

Upon reaching the Turkish shore, the crew managed to unload all of the ambassador's belongings. The boatswain warned Clavijo that "though we were now safe ashore, it were very likely that the Turks, perceiving the case, would come and seize us prisoners, impounding our possessions to carry to their lord the sultan." Sure enough, a party of Turkish officers soon arrived, but they proved to be exemplary hosts. Clavijo asked if they might provide horses

to transport him and his possessions to another Genoese ship farther down the coast. They obliged, and the next day Clavijo requested passage back to Constantinople from the carrack's captain.
Captain Ambrose was delighted to transport so illustrious a guest
as a Spanish ambassador, "saying that for the service of his highness the king of Castille that we should regard this carrack as
though it were a Spanish ship and our own."

Clavijo knew exactly how lucky he had been.

> We clearly realised the miracle that our Lord God had vouch-
> safed in our behalf, in that he had mercifully saved our lives in
> that great storm, the like of which, for its fury, as the com-
> mander of the carrack and his ship-master told us, they had
> never seen before, though for twelve years past they had been
> sailors navigating the waters of the Black Sea.

Clavijo would be forced to winter in Constantinople. No more
boats would venture into the Black Sea until the next spring. This
was a nuisance, certainly, but the delay would force Clavijo to
make a much longer journey than he had at first planned, at the
end of which lay the city of Samarkand, the capital of the fabled
Mongol ruler Timur, or as the West would know him, Tamerlane.[III] The journey would be prompted by one of Tamerlane's
greatest military victories against the Ottoman Turks, the new and
fearsome threat on Europe's borders.

By the beginning of the fifteenth century the Ottoman Turks had
established themselves as the Byzantine Empire's most fearsome
adversary. In 1396 the Ottoman sultan Bayazid I had crushed
Christian forces at the battle of Nikopolis, and it now seemed

possible that Constantinople itself might fall. The Byzantine emperor Manuel II was obliged to embark on a mission to Europe to
beg for assistance, serving, so to speak, as his own ambassador. He
left Constantinople on December 10, 1399, and would not return
for three years. When he arrived in Venice, the doge, Andrea Contarini, sailed out into the lagoon to meet him—a sign of great respect. The emperor, lodged in a palace on the Grand Canal, then
set about regaling members of the Venetian Senate with pitiful
tales of his empire's plight. The Venetians listened patiently and
promised, in vague terms, to support his cause. He was treated just
as politely in Padua, Vicenza, Pavia, and Milan, the cities through
which he passed on the road to Paris. There, the French king
Charles VI also vowed to send an army to the East, as did Henry
IV of England when the emperor visited him in London.

They were empty promises, however, hastily made so as not to
humiliate a mendicant emperor. France, England, and Venice had
better things to do with their time and resources than rescue a mori-
bund Byzantine Empire. Manuel realized as much, and back in Paris
he distracted himself from affairs of state by composing poems and
theological treatises. Then, quite unexpectedly, glorious news arrived
from Constantinople. The fearsome sultan Bayazid had been defeated in battle. The Turkish army had lost fifteen thousand men
and the sultan himself had been captured. Who, though, were these
saviors of Byzantium? Ironically, they were the Mongols, partaking
of one last military adventure in the Near East.[112]

From the late thirteenth century, the great Mongol Empire had
begun to sink into decline. The empire established by Genghis
Khan and his progeny had been dependent on the potency and
charisma of talented individual rulers. In their absence unity evaporated, and rival khanates and dozens of tribal dynasties began to

compete for power and influence. In the middle years of the four-teenth century, however, another such ruler emerged. Tamerlane the Great pronounced himself lord of Samarkand in 1369. After con-solidating his hold over a confederation of Mongol tribes, he em-barked, after the fashion of the great thirteenth-century khans, on a mission of world conquest. He conquered Persia in 1380, and by the end of the century he had established dominion from Muscovy to northern India. He then turned west, overrunning Egypt, Geor-gia, and Syria, sacking Baghdad and Damascus in 1401, just before defeating the Turks at the Battle of Angora in July 1402.

Henry III, king of Castile, had sent intelligence-gathering en-voys to the Levant at Easter 1402. They had arrived just in time to witness Tamerlane's famous victory over the Turks. After the battle they introduced themselves to the Mongol leader and were graciously received. Tamerlane decided to send an ambassador back to Spain, accompanied by a cache of jewels and a party of Christian women rescued from the Turks. Impressed by news of Tamerlane's deeds, Henry III then dispatched his own official am-bassador—his chamberlain, and the man who would soon be fighting for survival on the Black Sea, Ruy Gonzalo de Clavijo.

The details of Clavijo's journey need not detain us for long. In the company of a friar named Alfonso Paez and the soldier Gomez de Salazar, Clavijo left Cadiz on May 21, 1403. They trav-elled to the island of Rhodes onboard a three-masted carrack, stopping off at Genoa and Gaeta, and then took a series of smaller vessels as far as Constantinople, arriving on October 24th. They had planned to catch up with Tamerlane in Georgia, but then their harrowing maritime misadventures had intervened.

Forced to remain in Constantinople for the entire winter, they did not cross the Black Sea until April 1404, by which time Tamerlane had returned to his capital city. The ambassador had already travelled 2,500 miles by sea. He would now have to embark on a 3,000-mile land journey. Clavijo's misfortune was to be history's blessing, however. He would provide Europe with a unique description, unmatched in its detail and accuracy, of the mighty city of Samarkand and of its redoubtable master, Tamerlane—a man who, over the coming centuries, would emerge as a cherished figure of romance and horror in the Western imagination.

Again, Clavijo's itinerary can be quickly summarized. The party travelled along the trade routes via Tabriz, an important commercial city in present-day northeastern Iran. Continuing through northern Persia they stopped off at Sultaniyah, where they met with Tamerlane's eldest son, and after passing through Tehran they skirted around the southern coast of the Caspian Sea. Heading farther east, they crossed the Oxus River, and then made a sharp northerly turn into today's Turkmenistan, finally reaching the vicinity of Samarkand, in present-day Uzbekistan, at the end of August 1404.

In comparison with those made by William of Rubruck or John of Plano Carpini, Clavijo's outward journey was unremarkable, largely because it was so efficient. Across his dominions, Tamerlane had established the *yam* system of post-horses and post-houses. "All along this route," Clavijo reported, "Tamerlane causes horses to be kept stationed ready for use...in one place there may be a hundred, in another two hundred horses, and this is the case right up to Samarkand." These animals were reserved for the emperor's messengers and the ambassadors of foreign nations who flooded in from across Asia, and if such people ever required additional horses then every Mongol citizen was expected to offer assistance. "The universal custom is that if any man riding his way, be he ever so great a lord or any merchant or private citizen, should meet an ambassador going to Tamerlane, or some messenger riding with despatches from his highness by post forthwith on demand he must set foot to ground and give him up his horse." If they refused, Clavijo revealed, they were likely to lose their heads.

All along this route, an ambassador would be offered lodging and food, even in otherwise unpopulated regions. Clavijo marvelled at such efficiency—Europe had nothing comparable—although he did notice that some overeager messengers sometimes abused the system. Tamerlane, aware that so many horses were dying from exhaustion, had decreed that no one should travel more than a specified distance in a day—ten or twelve of the leagues or stages into which the routes were divided. Despite this pronouncement, Clavijo reported that "it is scarcely to be believed…what a distance these riders can compass in a day and a night, for they ride their horses to death and exceeding the commands of Tamerlane will cover fifteen, nay even twenty of those great leagues…By the roadside many were the dead horses we saw during our journey, which had been thus ridden to death and the carcases abandoned: the number indeed a marvel to note."[113]

At his more leisurely pace, then, Clavijo had reached the outskirts of Samarkand. Here, within the city's walls, lay the kernel of his story.

Upon reaching the village of Kesh, only a few miles from the capital, Clavijo was informed that he would not be allowed to enter Samarkand until Tamerlane granted permission. Instead, he was escorted to a famous orchard in the nearby village of Meser. It was a pleasant enough place at which to await Tamerlane's invitation, "full of fruit trees of all kinds, save only limes and citron tress which we noticed to be lacking." Surrounded by streams and vineyards, deer and pheasants, a pallisaded enclosure dominated the center of the orchard. Atop a hill, it contained a dozen beautiful palaces, "magnificently ornamented in gold and blue."

The ambassador had already been made to wait for five days before a Mongol official finally came to apologize for the delay. He explained that Tamerlane was bidding farewell to another envoy and was, as yet, unable to allow Clavijo into the city. The official urged Clavijo "not to suffer annoyance on that account," and to appease the ambassador he "had sent us the wherewithal for a banquet that day." After enjoying a meal of mutton, horsemeat, and rice, Clavijo was presented with a hat, a golden robe, and two horses. Finally, on September 8th news came that he could enter the city, but Clavijo had not grown especially impatient with Tamerlane. "It is indeed ever his custom thus to delay and never give audience to any ambassadors who arrive except after a pause of five or six whole days, and the more important the embassy may be the longer is this same period of waiting." Clavijo had been made to wait eight days, and he was pleased about it.[114]

Clavijo was taken to an orchard on the city's outskirts. He was asked to hand over any presents he had brought for the emperor and, that done, "other attendants took charge of us, holding each [of us] under his arm-pits and led us forward." Passing by the large crowds that had gathered, and the mace-wielding imperial doorkeepers, Clavijo was ushered into Tamerlane's presence.

> He was seated under what might be called a portal, which was before the entrance of a most beautiful palace that appeared in the background. He was sitting on the ground, but on a raised

dais before which there was a fountain that threw up a column
of water into the air, and in the basin of the fountain there were
floating red apples. His highness had taken his place on what
appeared to be small mattresses stuffed thick and covered with
embroidered silk cloth, and he was leaning on his elbow against
some round cushions that were heaped up behind him. He was
dressed in a cloak of plain silk without any embroidery, and he
wore on his head a tall white hat, on the crown of which was
displayed a balas ruby.

Clavijo bowed three times before the emperor and was then invited
to advance. The officers who had been holding him under the
armpits now withdrew, not daring to approach any closer to their
monarch. Clavijo knelt down, but Tamerlane "commanded us to
rise and stand close up to him that he might the better see us, for
his sight was no longer good, indeed he was so infirm and old that
his eyelids were falling over his eyes and he could barely raise them
to see."

Tamerlane, withered by age, was not quite the world conqueror
Clavijo had expected. Seventy years old, almost blind, Tamerlane
spent much of his days drinking and playing chess, enjoying the
company of his latest (his eighth) wife. Unable even to ride a
horse, he would be carried around his city in a litter. But if the
body was weary, the spirit remained indomitable.

Tamerlane's notorious bad temper had certainly not mellowed.
One evening, Clavijo and his party were invited to a banquet. Unfortunately, their interpreter was missing, and by the time he was
located and the ambassador had rushed to the feast, the emperor
had already finished eating. He informed Clavijo that "on this occasion only would he overlook our not coming in time for, as his
highness asserted, he had arranged that feast especially for us, and
to display to us his court and his palace." Tamerlane did make sure
that the ambassador's party got fed that evening, sending them five

sheep and two jars of wine with which to prepare the meal. The interpreter fared less well. He was dragged before Tamerlane's officials and informed "that you were absent and to chastise you for the same we now order your nose to be pierced and a cord put through it by which you shall be led about the camp as a warning to all."[115]

Nor had age diminished Tamerlane's energies and ambitions. Every year, Clavijo reported, merchants would come to Samarkand from as far away as China and India. Embarrassingly, there was nowhere for them to properly exhibit their wares.

> Tamerlane therefore now gave orders that a street should be built to pass right through Samarkand, which should have shops opened on either side of it, in which every kind of merchandise should be sold. This new street was to go from one side of the city through to the other, traversing the heart of the township. The accomplishment of his order he laid on two of the great lords of the court, letting them know that if they failed in diligence—for the work was to go on continuously by day as by night—their heads would pay the penalty.

Unfortunately for the local residents, all domestic dwellings in the vicinity were simply to be torn down. "No heed was paid to the complaint of persons to whom the property here might belong. Those whose houses were demolished suddenly had to quit with no warning, carrying away with them their goods and chattels as best they might."

Work progressed well. Architects laid out a broad new street with shops on one side and a massive "high stone bench" on the other. Each shop was adorned with a domed glass roof, "and at intervals down the street were erected water fountains." Masons labored by day and night, and "the tumult was such that it seemed all the devils of hell were at work here." After only twenty days the whole street was completed, "a wonder indeed to behold."

The displaced residents were still seething with resentment, however. They recruited some of Tamerlane's favorite courtiers and asked them to plead their case. Finding the emperor playing chess one afternoon, "they ventured to tell him that since he of his good will had ordered all the houses belonging to those poor people to be laid low, it were but right that they should receive compensation." Tamerlane was furious at such audacity. Did they not realize that "all the land of the city of Samarkand was his private property"? Faced with an incandescent emperor, the courtiers were "completely abashed...but thankful that the order had not been given for them all to lose their heads." They quickly assured Tamerlane that "whatsoever his highness did must indeed be good," and the issue of compensation was never raised again.[116]

It was ruthless, Clavijo admitted, but it was also efficient and, frankly, the end justified the means. Tamerlane, however often he disregarded his subjects' rights, had managed to create the most vibrant of cities.

> Samarkand stands in a plain, and is surrounded by a rampart or wall of earth, with a very deep ditch. The city itself is rather larger than Seville, but lying outside are great numbers of houses which form extensive suburbs...The township is surrounded by orchards and vineyards [and] in between these orchards pass streets with open squares. These are all densely populated, and here all kinds of goods are on sale...Among the orchards outside Samarkand are found the most noble and beautiful houses, and here Tamerlane has his many palaces and pleasure grounds. Round and about the great men of the government also have their estates and country houses, each standing within its own orchard. So numerous are these gardens and vineyards surrounding Samarkand, that a traveller who approaches the city sees only a great mountainous height of trees, and the houses embowered among them remain invisible.

The streets of Samarkand were traversed by a network of water conduits, taking sustenance to the countless melon beds and cotton fields. Indeed, the soil of Samarkand was some of the most fertile Clavijo had known, producing vast quantities of wheat and fruit. All told, "the richness and abundance of this great capital and its district is indeed a wonder to behold." It was a hive of manufacturing, of silk-spinning factories, and spiceries, able to attract the "master-craftsmen of all nations." Weavers came (and were occasionally kidnapped) from Damascus, gunsmiths arrived from Turkey.

It was so vast a population, of perhaps 150,000 souls, "that lodging for them all could not be found within the city limits, nor in the streets and open spaces of the suburbs and villages outside." Some new arrivals were reduced to living in caves or beneath trees, but they could still enjoy the city's bustling atmosphere, wandering through "the open squares where butcher's meat was ready cooked, roasted or in stews," or the booths, kept open night and day, where pheasants and partridges, leathers and linens, rubies and diamonds, rhubarb and nutmeg stood ready for sale.

What every one of those 150,000 people fully realized was that Tamerlane was their master, and that he would brook no dissent. This was a ruler who beheaded butchers for selling their meat at exorbitant prices, who hanged corrupt politicians in the streets, and at the center of Samarkand stood his impregnable castle. Surrounded by deep ravines, no man dared to enter without express permission. Home to Tamerlane's vast collections of treasure, and to workshops busy turning out armor, bows, and arrows, it was a constant reminder of the emperor's plenitude. Those in need of further instruction in Tamerlane's power needed only to visit the plains outside the city, where fifty thousand Mongol warriors had pitched their tents.[117]

━━◆━━

There was a disappointing end to Clavijo's embassy. Tamerlane fell ill and, although he rallied, for a time there had been fears that his death might provoke an unseemly contest for succession. It was thought best that foreign ambassadors should not witness these potentially embarrassing scenes. Clavijo was provided with horses, and on November 21st, after a stay of three months, he left Samarkand forever. Once again, from a diplomatic perspective, nothing had really been achieved—Clavijo had not even secured a reply to his king's letter. But, once again, so much had been seen and experienced. As Clavijo himself explained in a preface to the account of his travels:

> This embassy being most arduous and sent to very distant countries it has appeared to me necessary and suitable that all places that we visited should be set down in writing when describing the countries that we passed through, with the happenings that befell us...For these things being thus written and recounted and made known, to the best of our ability in what follows, they shall not fall to oblivion and be lost.[118]

When Clavijo had reached the court of Tamerlane, his Mongol escort endured a moment of humiliation: "At his present appearance his friends laughed much for he was dressed by us in the manner and fashion of a gentleman of Spain." Such embarrassments and cultural misunderstandings were part of the texture of embassy, but so were the amazing sights and encounters. After all, during his long journey into Asia Clavijo had seen his first giraffe, a diplomatic gift being escorted to Tamerlane by a Persian ambassador:

This animal has a body as big as a horse but with an extremely
long neck. Its forelegs are very much longer than the hind legs,
and its hoofs are divided like those of cattle...when the beast
raised its head it was a wonder to see the length of the neck,
which was very thin and the head somewhat like that of a
deer...the belly is white but the rest of the body is of yellow
golden hue cross marked with broad white bands...the animal
reaches so high when it extends its neck that it can overtop any
wall, even one with six or seven coping stones in the height and
when it wishes to eat it can stretch up to the branches of any
high tree and only of green leaves is its food. To one who never
saw the giraffe before this beast is indeed a very wondrous sight
to behold.[119]

An embassy that brought news of a giraffe was something to be
cherished. And it brought so much more. The Renaissance would be
charmed and obsessed by the memory of Tamerlane, and the historical Tamerlane would morph into a dozen literary avatars. Thanks
to accounts like Clavijo's, Tamerlane's legend would, for a century
and more, encapsulate the promise and the peril of the East—cruel,
yet courageous; alien, yet familiar. The account of his journey—first
in manuscript copies and, with the advent of printing, in published
form—would be widely read. What Rubruck and Carpini had
achieved two centuries earlier, Clavijo had emulated. They did not
make the West mimic or adore the East, but they made the East
more tangible. Their stories were riddled with prejudice and snob-
bery, but they were quite the best stories Europe had.

Italy

And such is that book, as I discovered, written by an enemy of
the human race. In it are set out all the plans of the enemy and
the methods by which religion, piety and all types of virtue
could more easily be destroyed. For, although it bears the name
and style of a man, nevertheless, I had hardly begun to read the

book before I recognised that it was written by the hand of
Satan...Not to keep you in suspense any longer, the book is in-
scribed with the name of Machiavelli, a Florentine who is utterly unworthy to have so noble a city as his fatherland
—Reginald Pole on *The Prince*[120]

Clavijo's embassy marked the end of an era. In one sense, it
was innovative. Compared to the frustratingly spare accounts of
most medieval diplomatic missions, Clavijo's report was unfeasibly
detailed—a trend that would continue and one that makes early
modern ambassadors immediately more accessible than their predecessors. But Clavijo was also part of the tradition of epic ambassadorial adventure that had encompassed men like Chang Ch'ien,
Rabban Sauma, and John of Plano Carpini. Of course, there were
many spectacular journeys ahead, but during the fifteenth century
the goals and institutions of European diplomacy would undergo
a sea-change. A curious new political entity, known to history as
the nation-state, would appear, and toward the end of the century
the first rumblings of a religious revolution would be heard. Out
of such chaos, the modern diplomatic milieu would gradually
begin to emerge.

When pondering medieval Europe, it makes little sense to talk
of the nation of England or the nation of France. Though sometimes nominally united under a single monarch, in the modern
sense of the word they were not really nations at all. A king had
his, often substantial, royal demesne, in which he wielded something approaching full authority. Beyond its borders there were
rival nobles and a hodgepodge of ecclesiastical and municipal ju-
risdictions, all challenging the king's political dominance. At best
a king was primus inter pares, "first among equals."

During the later medieval period, however, such kings stream-
lined their financial institutions, enhanced their armies, and began

Of all diplomatic gifts, the elephant was perhaps the most impressive. An elephant sent from Louis IX of France to Henry III of England in the thirteenth century inspired this drawing in Matthew Paris's *Chronicle*.

Henry III's elephant was probably the first such animal seen in England since the time of the Roman invasions. Such an unlikely diplomatic gift was commemorated in this thirteenth-century misericord, still on display in Exeter Cathedral.

Diplomacy offered the opportunity to flatter rulers. In 1462 Florentine ambassadors presented Louis XI of France with this lavish biography of Charlemagne (himself a lynchpin of early medieval diplomacy). With such a gift, Florence was seeking to demonstrate its admiration for the French king's taste and erudition.

AD LODOVICŪ REGVM PRINCIPEM
DIVINO NVMINE CHRISTIANISSIMVꝶ
FRANCORVM REGEM DONATI ACC
AIOLI FLORENTINI IN VITAM :
CAROLI MAGNI PROHEMIVM INCIPIT

VM ORATORES OM
NIVM CHRISTIANO
rum priuatiq; etiam ho
mines undiq; ad te concur
rant Serenissime rex. q
felicitati tue gratulatu
ueniunt. ego etiam. qui pro tuis ac maiórum
tuorum non solum erga nostram rem. p. sed
etiam erga familiam meam singularibus me
ritis amplitudini tue plurimum debeo. non
alienum putaui aliquid regio nomine di
gnum ad hanc tantam celebritatem pro ui
ribus meis afferre. Verum cum cogitarem qd
nam esse posset. quod & maiestati tue gratum
esset futurum. & deuotionis ac obseruantie mee
erga amplitudinem tuam inditium pre se fer
ret: uenit in mentem caroli magni diuini ho

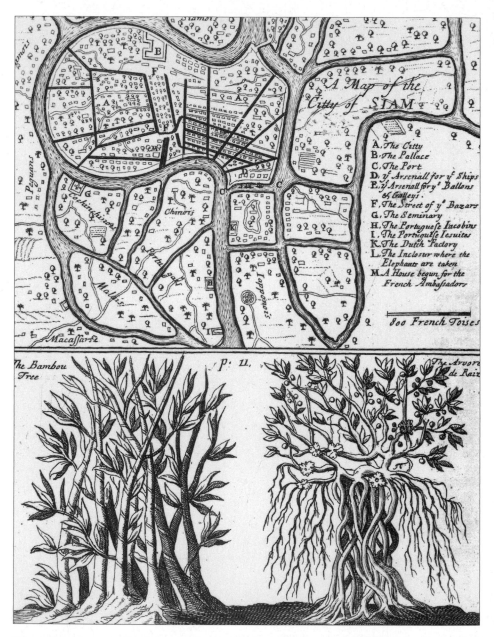

The following labels appear within the map:

A Map of the
Citty of SIAM

A. The Citty
B. The Pallace
C. The Port
D. y⁰ Arsenall for y⁰ Ships
E. y⁰ Arsenall for y⁰ Ballons
   & Galleys.
F. The Street of y⁰ Bazars
G. The Seminary
H. The Portugue∫e Iacobins
I. The Portugue∫e Iesuites
K. The Dutch Factory
L. The Inclosur where the
   Elephants are taken
M. A House begun for the
   French Ambassadors

800 French Toises

The Bambou Tree   p. 11.   The Arvore de Raiz

The crowning motivation of almost all diplomatic missions was the pursuit of political, military or economic advantage. However, such missions often provided a wealth of information about little-known corners of the world. This account (in English translation) of a French embassy to Siam in the late seventeenth century offered not only topographical detail (*above*) but also detailed drawings of Asian flora (*above and right*).

The Bananier.

The Jaquier.

The Tree w.ᵗʰ bears the Durions

Bunch of Banana's

The Potato: Tree

The Ananas.

The Mango-Tree.

The Coco Tree.

p. 172.

p. 172.

p. 172.

Sometimes unusual live specimens made it back to Europe. A British embassy to Asia in 1816 returned with an orang-utan from Borneo. The embassy's medical officer reported that the animal 'preferred coffee and tea, but would readily take wine and exemplified his attachment to spirits by stealing the captain's brandy bottle'.

Cultural comparison was everything in the business of embassy but, however assured of their superiority, Europeans were regularly impressed by the political, economic and artistic achievements of ancient Asian civilizations. Confronted with an elegant Tibetan mausoleum in the late eighteenth century, the British ambassador Samuel Turner was generous enough to insist that 'the architecture must not be criticized by scientific rules, for the different orders, as adopted in Europe, appear to be entirely unknown in Tibet'.

PHILOSOPHEMVR

From the fifteenth century, the 'resident' ambassador became a feature of the European diplomatic landscape. While 'extraordinary' or occasional ambassadors were still employed on especially momentous missions, the future lay with the careerist ambassador who dedicated much of his professional life to diplomatic service. Henry Wotton, a veteran of seventeenth-century missions to Savoy, Vienna, the Hague and Venice, encapsulated this trend.

to look askance at rival centers of influence. By concentrating his political power and humbling his rivals in battle, a king could extend his writ over wider distances. The classic example of such transformation is France. In the fourteenth century the royal demesne took in less than half of what we today define as France, and powers such as England and Burgundy controlled significant portions of French territory. Over the next hundred years, military might and accidents of death (which left many regions without rightful heirs), allowed the French kings to massively extend their influence. In the 1440s, Normandy and Gascony were seized from the English, Provence came under royal control in 1481, with Brittany following a decade later. During the sixteenth century a number of smaller fiefdoms were secured, and the nation of France came into existence.

The precursors of these newly unified nations had been the city-states of Renaissance Italy. In places like Florence, Naples, and Milan, the notion of a single, unchallenged dynastic ruler operating within a system of independent states began to blossom. It was an unusually cantankerous system, however, and fifteenth-century Italy was cursed with almost endemic warfare. There were endless treaties, endless breaches of treaties, endless political realignments. Then, toward the end of the century, Italy became a battleground for the great European dynasties, whether the land- and power-hungry Valois, or the Habsburgs, north of the Alps.

In such a world, the services of ambassadors were always in demand. Of course, there was more than one diplomatic method. Lorenzo de Medici, the absurdly talented son of Florence, perfectly embodied one of them. Lorenzo took the reins of Florentine power in 1469, at the age of twenty-one. By that date he was already an accomplished diplomatist. His success derived from his affability. He was not the most handsome of men, and his grating voice was an undoubted ambassadorial handicap. But he overcame such disadvantages through sheer force of personality. He was generous, spending fortunes on gifts and entertainments, and he was incurably honest.

In 1465, while only sixteen years of age, he had been dispatched to Pisa to meet with the king of Naples's son, Federigo of Aragon. Lorenzo charmed him beyond measure, discussing poetry and promising to send on a valuable collection of literary manuscripts. A few days later, Federigo visited Florence and caused an uproar when he refused to dismount from his horse in public, as Florentines expected all but the mightiest of princes to do. Lorenzo courteously remained by Federigo's side, shielding him from the taunts of the crowd. In a few short weeks Lorenzo had made a valuable friend. A few months later, the king of Naples sent Lorenzo a letter, affirming the abiding friendship between the two cities.

> Your magnificence, our most dear friend, we love you both for your own qualities and your family merits and heritage. But in the manly prudence and courage with which you have borne yourself in the new government, and in the demonstration you have so freely given of your powers, you have added to that love we bear you, so much as to make it an infinite increase. Therefore congratulate the magnificent Pietro on having so worthy a son; congratulate also the people of Florence in having so notable a defender of its liberties; and no less congratulate us, who have found a friend whose qualities will become greater with each day over the coming years.

Not that the whirligig of Italian politics often respected such promises. By the late 1470s, Florence was losing an expensive war with Naples, her former ally, and Rome, her perennial rival. The city was close to ruin, but once again the diplomatic skills of

Lorenzo de Medici came to the fore. A dramatic gesture was required, so Lorenzo decided to march directly into the enemy camp. He travelled to Naples to convince its king that Rome was an untrustworthy ally. If Florence was utterly defeated, he suggested, the pope would become dominant in northern Italy, and it would only be a matter of time until he turned his aggrandizing attentions to the south. After three months of intensive talks, King Ferrante was convinced.[121]

It was the boldest, and riskiest, diplomatic gambit that might be imagined, and it was entirely dependent on a person's character and reputation. However, the city-states of Italy had recently begun to experiment with a very different method of diplomatic encounter. Rather than sending out envoys, whether princes or bureaucrats, as and when they were deemed necessary, why not establish resident ambassadors at the courts of one's rivals? The advantages were immediately obvious. A steady stream of intelligence would flow in, and rather than simply reacting to unwelcome political developments, they could now be prevented. It was a diplomatic revolution.

Admittedly, the Gonzagas of Mantua and the Visconti of Milan had experimented with the strategy during the 1370s. Indeed, throughout history, there had been some scattered precursors of the resident ambassador. In ancient Greece, the office of the *proxenos* was a well-respected institution. A resident of, let us say, Athens, would be appointed to protect the rights of a particular foreign community within the city, advising Thebans when they became involved in legal proceedings, or offering hospitality to visiting Spartan dignitaries. It was a position of some dignity. After all, if Thebes chose you as her *proxenos* it meant that your political reputation had reached as far as Thebes. Less happily, *proxenoi*, the conspicuous advocates of foreign powers, did sometimes attract allegations of disloyalty.

There was also a medieval tradition of maintaining permanent representatives at the papal curia, and Venice regularly set up a *bailo* in Constantinople to protect Venetian merchants' interests. While not strictly an ambassador, the bailo, usually elected for a two-year term of office, did exercise some diplomatic functions, representing the doge during commercial negotiations and making sure that existing agreements were honored. In his large mansion, with his retinue of four sergeants, eight pages, a chef, two grooms, and a priest, he was undoubtedly the representative of the entire Venetian community, overseeing its finances and safeguarding its members' legal rights.

By virtue of its scale and sophistication, however, the Italian fifteenth-century experiment undoubtedly represented a watershed in the history of diplomacy. By the third quarter of the century, all of the major powers, from Milan to Florence, from Mantua to Venice, had permanent ambassadors at one another's courts. Nicodemo Tranchedini, often cited as the very first genuine resident ambassador, would serve as the Milanese representative in Florence throughout the 1440s and 1450s. Some cities even began setting up resident envoys further afield, with Milan establishing fixed missions in Hungary and at the court of the Holy Roman Emperor.[122]

Crucially, it was a practice that would spread out across Europe. Just as the powers north of the Alps adopted the new Italian notion of statehood, so they would shortly embrace the idea of resident ambassadors. Some were slower than others. Russia's first settled embassy would not arrive until 1688. The Turks would not seek permanent representation at a European court until 1793. But by the first decades of the sixteenth century, France, Spain, England, and the Holy Roman Empire had all embarked on the journey that would culminate in the diplomatic establishment we enjoy today.

With states came statecraft. The Italian cities espoused a pragmatic approach to diplomacy. If we recall the ancient philosophical debate between the realists and the idealists, then Florence and Milan were unashamed realists. One Florentine was perhaps more realistic than any of his contemporaries. Niccolo Machiavelli is often misrepresented, the nuance of his thought overlooked. It can hardly be denied, however, that he had a bleak view of human nature.

States were necessary because human beings were selfish and flawed. The Leviathan of government, to borrow a later philosopher's image, was needed to check humanity's baser instincts. History was Machiavelli's tutor, and by his calculation history was replete with examples of human avarice, overweening ambition, and idiocy. States, therefore, were inevitable, but a transcendent morality did not inform their actions. Morality was an artifice, a man-made invention. That which proved good for the state was labelled moral. Those things that sapped the state's resources or divided its people were deemed immoral.

In such a universe, the moral purpose of diplomacy was to promote a nation's self-interest. Sometimes this meant flattering one's peers, sometimes it meant slaughtering them in battle. Machiavelli was a diplomat himself, the veteran of missions to the French court, Rome, and Germany. His ideal ruler was Cesare

Borgia, an intelligent, ambitious, cruel leader who simply did whatever seemed best for his own career. Machiavelli represents only the most extreme incarnation of a political philosophy that pervaded fifteenth-century Italy. It was cynical, but it was also mature. Robbing diplomacy of any substantial ideological content made the work of ambassadors more efficient and, in extremis, markedly safer.

In 1495 Charles VIII of France occupied the kingdom of Naples. Venice, the pope, and the Holy Roman Emperor forged an alliance intent on driving him out of the Italian peninsula. They reached an agreement in Venice. During their deliberations, the French ambassador Philip de Commines was residing in the city. Even as France's enemies plotted against his king, Philip was still treated as the professional ambassador of an enemy state. He was ignored and humiliated by the extravagant celebrations of the new alliance, but he was not pilloried or persecuted as a moral enemy.

Shortly after the treaty was concluded, Commines remembered, "all the ambassadors of the league met together in boats upon the water (which in Venice is their chief recreation)…In this pomp they passed under my windows with their trumpets and other instruments of music." Such ambassadorial entertainments were now closed to Commines. Even the ambassadors of Milan, who had previously been especially friendly, "would take no manner of notice of me now." For three days Commines thought it best for his entourage to remain indoors, although the chances of any serious affront were still very meagre. The enemies of France set about celebrating their new alliance. "At night there were extraordinary fireworks upon the turrets, steeples and tops of the ambassadors' houses, multitudes of bonfires were lighted, and the cannon all around the city were fired."

On Palm Sunday the pope "ordered every prince who was a signatory and all their ambassadors" to carry an olive branch "in token of their alliance and peace." In Venice, a platform was erected that stretched from the doge's palace to the end of the Piazza San Marco. After mass was celebrated by the pope's nuncio, all the ambassadors marched together in stately procession, "all very splendidly dressed." "A great many pageants and mysteries were exhibited to the people," then "at a porphyry stone, where such things are usually done, proclamation was made and the alliance published."

This was all extremely humiliating for Commines, but not dangerous. In fact, he was even invited to a celebratory feast. Naturally, he declined, but the invitation marked the beginning of Commines's social rehabilitation. The league against France had now been publicly pronounced, and there was no longer a need to shun her ambassador. Commines remained in Venice for another month, "and was all the while as civilly entertained as before the publication of this alliance." Nevertheless, he clearly had to leave the city. He asked the doge's permission to return home, was given a passport, and was even escorted to Ferrara, a neutral safe haven, at the republic's own expense.[123]

Such civilized diplomacy was about to be disrupted. The culprit was religion.

There had always been divisions within the Christian commonwealth, and on occasion ambassadors were recruited to heal them.

Toward the end of 1378 three Italian cardinals, men high in dignity, reverend princes of the church, had received a letter that scolded them as they had never been scolded before. Pietro Corsini, Simone da Borzano, and Jacopo Orsini had recently pledged their support for Pope Clement VII—an unexceptional gesture, one might suppose, until one remembers that Clement was an impostor set up as a rival to Urban VI, the man elected as supreme pontiff six months earlier. When the previous pope, Gregory XI, had died, the ensuing election was swayed by popular riots demanding that the papal tiara should pass to an Italian. Thus Bartolommeo Prignano became Urban VI. Urban was pious and reformist—too reformist for some cardinals' tastes. His critics seized on the chaotic circumstances of his election, quit Rome, and elected Clement in his stead. For forty years Europe would be divided between the supporters of successive popes and antipopes. France, Scotland, and Spain sided with Clement; England, many of the Italian cities, and the Holy Roman Empire with Urban. Individual parishes, monasteries, and even families would be divided. The Great Schism, as this fracture has become known, would sap the energies and try the patience of the Christian commonwealth.

"Dearest brothers and fathers in Christ sweet Jesus," the letter began, "I write to you in his precious blood, desiring to see you return to the true light from the darkness and blindness into which you have fallen." They were traitors, limbs severed from the body that gave them life, men who had "assumed the task of devils." "What have you come to by not matching your dignity with virtue?" the letter asked. They were supposed to be the champions of the pope, not his betrayers. "You were the flowers put in to fill the garden with the scent of virtue. You were set up like pillars to give strength to this ship and guard Christ's vicar on earth." Instead, they had become embroiled in political maneuvering and

factionalism, victims of the "poison of self-love which has in-
fected the world....It has turned you from pillars to worse than
straw, from sweet-scented to stinking flowers that make the world
reek."

They had not sinned out of ignorance. They had taken part in
the election of the true pope, Urban, and had done him homage
at his coronation. Now they were claiming that they had only
elected him out of fear. It was a lie. They were motivated by ambition and self-interest.

They were "fools worthy of a thousand deaths...ungrateful,
cowardly and mercenary" ingrates who had turned their backs
"like mean paltry knights afraid of [their] own shadows." They
could still be saved, however. They should not "ignore the goad of
conscience that I know is continually stabbing at you." Their
flocks were praying for them to recant. "Yield at last to the tears
and sweat streaming from God's servants in such abundance that
you could wash from head to foot in them."[124]

Who would have the audacity to write such a letter? Not a
king, counsellor, or bishop, but a young woman from Siena. Born
in 1347, the daughter of a dyer, Catherine of Siena was an unusual
kind of saint. At an early age she rejected the world, making a vow
of chastity at seven years old, adopting a diet of boiled herbs, and
cutting off her hair when the issue of marriage was raised. "How
repulsive is our bodily life," she wrote, "with the stench we give out
from every part of our bodies." The body was "simply a sack of
excrement, food for worms, food for death." And yet, she was
strangely worldly, alert to (if critical of) the nuances of religious
and secular politics.

She joined the Sisters of Penance of St. Dominic in 1363 and
retreated to a life of penance and meditation, only ever speaking

to her confessor. Then one day she had a vision of Christ calling her beyond the threshold of her cell. She began tending the sick, visiting condemned prisoners and walking with them to the gallows, and healing rifts between squabbling families. She also, in her way, became that rarest of things—a medieval female ambassador. By the mid-1370s, her skills as a mediator, buttressed by her pious reputation, were in huge demand. In 1375 she was sent to Pisa and Lucca to try and prevent them from joining an anti-papal league.

This same league had alienated Florence from Rome, but when the pope dispatched Cardinal Robert of Geneva to the city with an army at his back, the Florentine government seemed to be convinced that reconciliation with the Holy See was prudent. They asked Catherine to serve as their envoy, dispatching her to Avignon in June 1376 to negotiate with the pope. They promised to delegate official ambassadors to ratify any agreements she reached, although these ambassadors were late in arriving and treated the papal court with disdain. It seemed as if Florence was less eager to make peace than previously. The pope, desperate to restore the peace of central Italy, was not to be deterred, however. In 1378 he sent her to Florence to try once more to secure reconciliation. Despite the turbulent time in the city—being threatened with violence on more than one occasion—Catherine finally achieved her goal, and the rift between Florence and the papacy was healed. Later, Catherine wrote to monarchs, whether the king of France or the queen of Hungary, urging them to join a crusade against the Turks. And with the arrival of the Great Schism, she set about chastising the disrupters of Christian unity. Ultimately, many years after she died, her strictures would be heeded.[125]

Ambassadorial saints were a rarity, but the Christian commonwealth was subject to some ailments that were immune even to *their* ministrations. Religion was useful, Machiavelli reasoned. Pious sentiment could check political corruption. It fostered unity. Even if a ruler was not dedicated to the dominant religious credo, he should still encourage it. But religious zeal had absolutely no role to play in the world of the ambassadors. Ideology of any variety was the enemy of efficient, measured diplomacy. It introduced higher allegiances and confessional enmities. It made for rash decisions.[126] Machiavelli was wrong about many things, but the sixteenth century would prove that his concerns about the deleterious influence religious passions could have on diplomacy were entirely justified. As we are about to see, the Protestant Reformation was about to queer the ambassadorial pitch. It was the last thing Europe needed. The work of diplomacy was already being disrupted and challenged in a dozen different ways, courtesy of an age of unprecedented discovery and exploration.

Renaissance

10
REFORMATION

An Age of Discovery

And surely this is a true testimony of great goodness intended, that our nation in such a Christian sort and manner refuses no hazardous danger to bring infidels to the knowledge of the omnipotent God. Yea, albeit great wealth and commodity may rise to us of their labours, yet the purpose of manifesting God's word and majesty among those that feed like monsters (and rather like dogs than men) does argue not only a blessed success, but persuades a prosperous and beneficial return.
—Thomas Churchyard, *A Prayse and Reporte of Master Martin Frobisher's Voyage*, 1578[127]

O N THE 9TH OF OCTOBER, 1577, an Inuit went duck hunting on the River Avon. He had been dragged to England from his home on Baffin Island by the fabled explorer Martin Frobisher. Less than a month after demonstrating his mastery of the kayak to the assembled citizenry of Bristol, with the mayor and aldermen in rapt attendance, he would die of pneumonia. A female Inuit who had shared his wretched journey across the Atlantic would perish a week later. A child survived a little longer and was sent up to London, but he too passed away before he could be presented to Queen Elizabeth I, along with rare flowers and high-grade gold ore, as a "token of possession" of the lands Frobisher had blithely claimed for the English crown.

All three would be buried in Christian churchyards—at St. Stephen's in Bristol, and at St. Olave's in London—although one of them would first endure an autopsy, to establish whether he truly was a human being. This final indignity sounded an echo to the moment during Frobisher's expedition when mischievous sailors had spied a deformed, elderly Inuit woman and, supposing her "to be either a devil or a witch...plucked off her buskins to see if she were cloven-footed."[128]

To Tudor England, the strange, icy lands of the North Atlantic were *meta incognita*, an "unknown goal," places of endless daylight reputedly inhabited by unicorns. They also held out the promise of a northwest passage through the American landmass, to the endless riches, the silks and spices, of Asia. This was the very dream that inspired Frobisher, the erstwhile Yorkshire cabin boy and privateer, to embark on his three voyages to the territories around Labrador and Hudson Bay. Having the inhabitants of such mysterious realms arrive in England in the autumn of 1577 offered a sensational, if sordid, opportunity for one part of the world to learn a little more about another. The "savage people" who "fed only upon raw flesh," who "wondered much at all our things," managed to captivate the European imagination. Paintings of Inuit abductees would be copied, circulated, and pored over across the continent. Stories would be told of their savagery and deceit; rumors would spread about their cannibalism. They would sometimes seem almost familiar, with complexions "not unlike the sun-burned country man, who labours daily in the sun for his living." More often, they seemed far beyond the prissy pale of European mores and manners—"they neither use table, stool nor tablecloth for comeliness."[129]

Sometimes natives were taken to learn more about their languages, sometimes because they proved to be excellent guides in uncharted lands, and sometimes in the hope of grooming interpreters. Barring a handful of infamous impostors, they furnished irrefutable proof that explorers had really been where they claimed, and they were apt to entice potential investors in future expeditions. It should never be forgotten how hard it was to drum up support for a sixteenth-century jaunt to the other side of the world. We live with the seemingly inevitable results of the Age of Discovery: Contemporaries lived with the prospect of financial embarrassment, or even ruin. To the Tudor mentality, sailing off toward Greenland was not dissimilar to postwar Americans shooting for the moon. There was precisely the same mixture of curiosity, one-upmanship, bravery, and vanity.

Those same natives were also prized, poked, and paraded as rare specimens of the exotic. Certainly, some came willingly, a few even flourished, and Europeans could claim no monopoly on the abduction of indigenous populations. Frobisher was part of a culture that approved, even lauded what he did, and does not deserve, single-handedly, to bear the weight of disapproval (however righteous it might be) that comes with hindsight. But all told, his was a clumsy, brutish mechanism of encounter: the counterpoint, in fact, to other, gentler ways of learning about the rest of the world, encapsulated by pilgrims, merchants, and, of course, ambassadors.

In one sense, however, an expedition like Frobisher's was flawless. It was inordinately difficult to achieve in terms of the distances travelled and the risks it entailed, but *culturally* it was easy and it was satisfying. It seemed to demonstrate European superiority, it added new lands to the British territorial portfolio, and, as Thomas Churchyard's quotation amply demonstrates, it could be justified as an act of daring maritime evangelism.

Had the entire Age of Discovery been made up of such adventures, it would have presented Europe with few significant intellectual challenges. Unfortunately—or perhaps mercifully—the sixteenth century was not, at heart, an age of empire and effortless colonialism. Aside from endeavors like the Spanish conquest of South America, the most that was usually achieved was the establishment of outposts and trading stations. The pursuit of profit, not land, was often the presiding motivation. Myths and geographical assumptions were routinely shattered, and new societies and civilizations were encountered—many of whose age and sophistication dented the notion of European cultural plenitude. The inhabitants of such places could not simply be bashed over the head and carried home. Subtler varieties of dialogue were called for, and the natural agents of such encounters were ambassadors.

With alarming frequency, these ambassadors would be ignored or treated with disdain, exploited by host societies for their scientific, linguistic, or military skills, or embroiled in internal political dramas that, on occasion, cost them their lives. To encounter Moghul India, Tokugawa Japan, Ming China, or the North American Iroquois Confederacy was often a humbling, even treacherous, experience.

―⊶⊷―

The great European Age of Discovery began in Portugal during the early fifteenth century. Expeditions reached out into the Atlantic—to Madeira, the Cape Verde Islands, and the Azores—and down the western coast of Africa. In May 1498, after rounding the continent's southern tip, Vasco da Gama dropped anchor off the coast of India, in search, so it was claimed, of Christians and spices. A century and more of evangelism and economic adventuring across Asia was thus inaugurated, and where the Portuguese went, the English and Dutch later followed. The Spanish, with explorers and conquistadores like Columbus, Cortez and Balboa in the vanguard, headed west, crowning conquests in the Caribbean with the seizure of Mexico and Peru and their vast deposits of gold and silver.

The French explorers Samuel de Champlain and Jacques Cartier, after the fashion of Martin Frobisher, focused on the northern reaches of the American continent, hoping to find a northwestern route to Asia. New France, as the territories in present-day Canada and the northern United States were known, was a vulnerable place. The settlements that grew up in the early seventeenth century—Montreal and Quebec chief among them— were surrounded on all sides by rival Indian tribes and federations. To the south and east of Lakes Erie and Ontario lay the homelands of the five-tribe Iroquois Confederacy. Farther north, the longstanding enemies of the Iroquois were to be found: the Algonquin of the lower St. Lawrence and, in a tiny area between Georgian Bay and Lake Simcoe, the 20,000 members of the Huron nation.

The Huron, Algonquin, and Iroquois had been fighting, on and off, for generations. It was a conflict into which the French were inevitably drawn. Very soon, the European arrivistes found themselves the allies of the Huron (key players in the lucrative fur trade) and the enemies of the Iroquois. Nonetheless, the French—especially the Jesuit missionaries who had begun arriving in America from 1611—arrogantly dreamed of civilizing and Christianizing these disparate tribal groups. This could never be fully accomplished in a state of perennial warfare.

In 1644 several Iroquois tribesmen were captured. As a gesture of goodwill, the governor of New France, Charles Huault de Montmagny, allowed two of them to return to their Mohawk brethren. The Mohawk (one of the constituents of the Iroquois Confederacy) were informed that the remaining two prisoners would also be freed, provided that the Iroquois made genuine efforts to reach a peace agreement with the French and their Indian allies.

So it was that in July 1645 a Mohawk chief and ambassador named Kiotsaton arrived at the fort at Three Rivers, eighty miles downriver from Quebec. As he approached the shore, Kiotsaton stood aloft in the bow of his boat and, "motioning with his hand for silence, he called out: 'Brothers, I have left my country to come and see you. At last I have reached your land. I was told, on my departure, that I was going to seek death, and that I would never again see my country. But I have willingly exposed myself for the good of peace. I come therefore to enter into the designs of the French, of the Hurons, and of the Algonquins. I come to make known to you the thoughts of all my country.'"[130]

The governor hurried down from Quebec and, on a scorching summer's day, negotiations got underway. Kiotsaton was a seasoned ambassador, possessed of an excellent memory, well versed in the metaphorical oratorical style of Native American diplomacy, and persuasive. "I am the mouth for the whole of my country," he began, "you listen to all the Iroquois in hearing my words. There is no evil in my heart; I have only good songs in my mouth. We have a multitude of war songs in our country; we have cast them all on the ground; we have no longer anything but songs of rejoicing."[131]

The various parties—French, Iroquois, Huron, and Algonquin, and a host of interpreters—were gathered together under cloth awnings. In the center of the assembly there was a large open space in which two posts, connected by a rope, had been erected. Kiotsaton had a number of points to make—a mixture of complaints, requests, and aspirations. As each argument was made he hung a wampum belt on the rope.

He opened with a diatribe against the way the freed Mohawk captives had been treated. When the Iroquois released prisoners, Kiotsaton reminded the governor, they had the good grace to escort them to their own territories. The French had shown no such concern, simply casting the two men out into the wilderness to find their own way home. The ambassador launched into a theatrical performance, acting out the difficulties the men had encountered on their journey. He showed them scrambling up rocky slopes, battling against rapids in their canoes, giving a performance that was "so natural that no actor in France could equal it."

After making a series of speeches recounting past losses, imploring the rivers to remain navigable and the clouds to scatter, Kiotsaton came to his central point. The tenth wampum belt was given "to bind us all very closely together. He took hold of a Frenchman, placed his arm within his, and with his other arm he clasped that of an Algonquin... 'Here,' he said, 'is the knot that binds us inseparably; nothing can part us.'"[132] The Iroquois seemed willing to reach an agreement.

Kiotsaton left the meeting in high spirits: "I go to spend what remains of the summer in my own country, in games and dances and rejoicing for the blessing of peace." Over the next months, many other tribal representatives visited Three Rivers to add their support to a peace treaty. After a final round of councils in September, as the great nineteenth-century historian of New France, Francis Parkman, put it, "there was a peace in this dark and blood-stained wilderness. The lynx, the panther and the wolf had made a covenant of love."[133]

Unfortunately, Kiotsaton was only one man, and the French were unsure if he represented the opinions of the entire Iroquois Confederacy—what were the views of the Oneida, the Onondaga, the Cayuga, and the Seneca? Ultimately, however, it was the Mohawk who had always been the principal Iroquois threat to French interests in the St. Lawrence Valley. It would be prudent for the French to send out ambassadors of their own to make sure the Mohawk honored the treaty. There was no better man for the job than a Jesuit named Isaac Jogues.

Jogues was an expert in the Mohawk dialect and had been to their territories before. It had not been a pleasant experience. Back in 1642 he had been captured by the Mohawk and endured a round of especially harrowing torture—his left thumb was cut off with a serrated shell, and he was tied to the ground and showered with hot coals. After several months' captivity he made his escape and returned to Europe. The Jesuit mission fields called him back, however, and after initial—and quite understandable—resistance he agreed to serve as the French ambassador to the Mohawk. He was maintaining the tradition of the clerical ambassador that had previously molded the careers of men like William of Rubruck and John of Plano Carpini.

Jogues set out from Three Rivers on May 16, 1646, in the company of two Algonquin emissaries and four Mohawk guides. Wary of antagonizing his hosts, Jogues exchanged his black Jesuit cassock for civilian clothes. He was now engaged in secular business, and saw little sense in reminding the Mohawk of the Jesuits' noisy, intrusive evangelism. His route took him past Lake Champlain and the Richelieu River, across Lake George, and on to the

Hudson. After resting at the Dutch-owned Fort Orange, on the site of present-day Albany, he continued on to a Mohawk settlement. A meeting was arranged, and Jogues passionately implored the assembled Indians to continue along the path of peace. They listened to him politely, assented to what he said, and exchanged gifts. The mission seemed to have been a success, the chances of a lasting peace much bolstered.

Unfortunately, the Iroquois had little interest in fulfilling the dreams of European diplomatists and colonists. They had ancient, conflicting agendas to pursue. The mood within the confederacy began to shift, and when Jogues reentered Mohawk territory in September he immediately realized that he was at risk. Some of the Mohawk still hoped for peace, many others yearned for a renewal of hostilities with their age-old tribal enemies. Jogues was unlucky enough to encounter a party of more hawkish Indians between Lake George and the Mohawk River. They took him captive.

Jogues, assuming he would return, had left a chest behind in the Mohawk settlement he had visited. It contained nothing more than beads, books, and vestments, but the local people began to regard it as a bad omen and a curse when the year's crops failed (actually the responsibility of a caterpillar plague) and famine and disease descended on the region. Jogues's captors were intent on revenge. They stripped off his clothes and led him into their town, where the priest was beaten with fists and sticks before having small strips of flesh cut from his arms and back. After a brief spell of recuperation, Jogues was, surprisingly, invited to a feast. He undoubtedly feared that some kind of trap was being set, but to refuse the invitation would be seen as a gross discourtesy. His fears were realized. Upon entering a Mohawk tent, he was struck in the back of the head with a hatchet. The blow was fatal, and the next morning Jogues's severed head, along with that of his travelling companion, Jean de Lalande, was displayed on the settlement's palisades.

There were few more harrowing reminders that, far from home and in complex, ancient political milieus, European ambassadors were sometimes hopelessly vulnerable. What European colonists hoped to achieve often counted for precious little. Mohawk whimsy and ageless Mohawk hatred of the tribes to the north were far more important than French colonial strategy. The French—bullish intruders, let it not be forgotten—assumed far too much. They assumed they could immediately transform a continent. In time, with the help of better weapons, drink, disease, and the equally presumptuous efforts of the English and the Dutch, they would succeed, and entire cultures would be destroyed. But in the autumn of 1646, as Isaac Jogues's demise bore witness, they were colonial dilettantes.

Europe did not possess a manifest destiny to transform the politics of the rest of the world. In the martyr's life of Isaac Jogues—and it is as a martyr that he is remembered—the certainties, protocols, and aspirations of European diplomacy and statecraft had proved utterly irrelevant.

———◆———

It was the same the world over. Sir Thomas Roe was no stranger to the new worlds opened up during the sixteenth century. He had been an investor in England's Virginia colonies and was the veteran of a gold-seeking expedition to Guiana. In 1614 the East India Company appointed him as their ambassador to the Indian court of the Moghul emperor Jahangir.

He arrived at Surat in September 1615, after a six-month sea voyage. He immediately saw one of the conventions of European diplomacy evaporate. The local governor ordered a search of all the Englishman's possessions. Roe lodged a protest and thought he had secured an immunity from search. In fact, the Indians began looking through Roe's luggage regardless, "whereon," Roe remembered, "I turned my horse and with all speed rode back to them, I confess too angry." He laid his hand on his sword and announced that he had been born free and would die so. For added emphasis, he denounced the Indians' earlier claims of friendship and, pointing to the pistols that hung from his saddle, explained that *they* were his true friends.[134]

Roe's histrionics won the day and the search was abandoned, but throughout his four-year embassy there was absolutely no doubt about who the senior partner was in the diplomatic encounter between England and India. Roe achieved a great deal—improving the lot of English merchants, though failing to secure a formal commercial treaty—but only because the emperor Jahangir happened to like him. When European ambassadors travelled to Moghul India, they were obliged to abide by Moghul court etiquette, to follow the court wherever it travelled, and to wait patiently for whatever favors and dispensations the Moghul emperor saw fit to grant. Quite often, he saw no need to grant any favors whatsoever.

In fact, the East was crammed with civilizations that had no reason to take Europeans especially seriously. China allowed a handful of westerners—Jesuit missionaries, for the most part—to visit the empire during the sixteenth and seventeenth centuries. They dreamed of winning the Chinese political elite over to Christianity. It was pure fantasy, but the Chinese tolerated their presence because they had scientific and scholarly skills that could be exploited. So it was that Jesuits helped the Chinese reform their calendar, worked in their astronomical observatories, designed cannons for them, mapped their empire, and at the Treaty of Nerchinsk in 1689, even served as their ambassadors.

At first, China's ancient rival, Japan, seemed much more amenable to western political and economic intrusion. For much of the sixteenth century the empire was riddled with civil war and lacked any effective central authority. These were good and profitable years for European priests and merchants. Toward the end of the century, however, a series of soldier-politicians, culminating in the first rulers of the Tokugawa shogunate, succeeded in restoring a measure of political harmony to the empire. Japan now looked askance at the inroads made by European interlopers in less well-governed times. By the late 1630s exclusion edicts were being passed that forbade any Spanish or Portuguese visitors from entering Japan. The Dutch were allowed to remain, although they were usually confined to the coastal city of Nagasaki. They also learned that a reinvigorated Japan was able to restore an ancient tradition of diplomacy that held most foreigners in low esteem.

Much like medieval Byzantium, Japan ranked the envoys of other nations in a strict hierarchy. One's place in this diplomatic scheme determined the degree of access one had to the shogun when visiting the royal court at Edo. Korea, for example, was a much-respected polity. Its ambassadors would be lodged at an important temple during their visits, at the shogun's expense. The entire ambassadorial entourage would be treated to fifteen-course banquets, hosted by some of the shogun's closest relatives.

The Dutch, by contrast, enjoyed no such entertainments. In fact, while Japan acknowledged the importance of the Dutch East India Company—the trading organization involved in Japanese commerce—it did not officially recognize the political existence of Holland. No letters could be sent between the Dutch and Japanese rulers; no bilateral treaties could be signed. When a Dutch envoy arrived at Edo, he was not received by the court, but merely viewed by the shogun and his family in a royal sitting room.

It was degrading, but it was the only possible way for the Dutch to maintain diplomatic relations with the leaders of Japan. In 1691, Engelbert Kaempfer provided an account of one such meeting.

> We were commanded to wait in [a] guard room, till we could be introduced to an audience…we were civilly received by two captains of the guard, who treated us with tea and tobacco… From thence we were conducted up two other staircases to the palace itself…Having waited here upwards of an hour, and the emperor having in the meanwhile seated himself in the hall of audience…our resident [was conducted] into the emperor's presence, leaving us behind. As soon as he came thither, they cried out "Hollanda Captain," which was the signal for him to draw near and make his obeisance. Accordingly, he crawled on his hands and knees to a place showed to him…and then kneeling he bowed his forehead quite down to the ground, and so crawled backwards like a crab, without uttering one single word. So mean and short a thing is the audience we have of this mighty monarch.

Further indignities were to follow, and a few days later Kaempfer and his countrymen endured a royal viewing, where they were obliged to "walk, to stand still, to compliment each other, to dance, to jump, to play the drunkard, to speak broken Japanese, to read Dutch, to paint, [and] to sing."[135]

Such treatment, much like the murder of Isaac Jogues, was a humiliating reminder that European ambassadors could not simply arrive in foreign countries and have foreign rulers agree to their demands. There were other diplomatic systems, other hierarchies, other worldviews and political landscapes in which Europeans had no privileged position. It was a difficult lesson to learn, and it provoked endless theorizing about the nature of international relations. It was more than enough for the western imagination to fathom.

But the sixteenth and seventeenth centuries were not just an age of discovery. They were also an age of religious revolution: a revolution that would provide its own share of challenges and disruptions to the world of European diplomacy.

On August 10, 1584, four Japanese teenagers arrived at the port of Lisbon. They had been sent as ambassadors by the leaders of the Jesuit missionary enterprise in the East. The four students of the Jesuits' school at Arima were to sport European clothes throughout much of their trip—it was important to show just how deeply they had imbibed western values. They were to be shown the principal sights, although their chaperones were instructed to keep them well away from any situations that might hint at the deep religious divisions that blighted the continent. They were to "learn or see only what is good, without knowing anything bad." Their trip is reminiscent of journeys to the Soviet Union during the Cold War, when ever-vigilant Intourist guides strove to portray Russia as either a communist paradise or, at the very least, as the contented, supremely cultured antithesis of the decadent West.[136]

The trouble was, by the late summer of 1584, the religious divisions of Europe—divisions that had fostered new military alliances, that had brought civil war to France, that had brought rebellion to the Netherlands—were inordinately difficult to conceal: something that ambassadors knew only too well.

The Field of the Cloth of Gold

It had demanded the exertions of three hundred masons, five hundred carpenters, and dozens of glaziers, tailors, and smiths. Linen had been rushed in from Holland; oak, pine, and walnut from the forests of the Auvergne. The silk tents and grandiose pavilions had all been erected, the yards upon yards of gold and silver cloth had been rolled out, and the wine-gushing fountains had been unveiled. An unexceptional field in northern France, between the villages of Ardres and Guines, just to the south of Calais, had been transformed into the playground of kings and ambassadors. For three weeks in the summer of 1520, Henry VIII of England and Francis I of France presided over a carnival of feasting and jousting, a riot of elegant, flirtatious living.

Their entire courts, perhaps as many as six thousand people, had accompanied them to the Field of the Cloth of Gold, the scene of the most opulent diplomatic encounter of the sixteenth century. They caroused together, but they also competed: Here was an opportunity for two nations—and nations is what they now were—to jockey for cultural primacy. Who had the best wine? Who was the more accomplished in the arts of chivalry? Whose women were prettiest, whose cuisine the most delectable, whose costumes were truly *comme il faut*? More was at stake than French and English pride, however. Fripperies aside, the meeting at the Field of the Cloth of Gold was also about the political destiny of Europe.

In 1514 Henry VIII's sister Mary had married the French king Louis XII, who promptly died—danced to death, some surmised, by his vivacious, much younger wife. His successor, Francis I, was torn, like any reputable Renaissance monarch, between seeking out martial glory and reaping the economic and social benefits of peacetime. For the time being, Francis plumped for peace, and in 1518 signed a treaty of friendship with England, his kingdom's oldest and most natural adversary.

The other two noteworthy rulers of western Europe at the beginning of the sixteenth century were the king of Spain and the Holy Roman Emperor. Alone, they posed no substantial threat to Anglo-French dominance. Together, they had the potential to overwhelm the political landscape. Charles Habsburg was already the king of Spain when France and England reached their accommodation in 1518. A year later, his grandfather Maximilian died, and Charles was elected as his successor as Holy Roman Emperor. He now ruled over Spain, the Netherlands, Naples, swathes of Germany, and the Habsburg homelands in Austria.

It was a ramshackle collection of dominions, and Charles V would never really succeed in imposing order and full authority over his empire. This was yet to be proved, however, and a king such as Francis I, hemmed in on all sides by Charles's principalities, shuddered at the prospect of Habsburg supremacy—a veritable universal monarchy—across the whole of Europe. Some variety of military engagement between France and the Habsburgs was inevitable, he knew, so the compact with England had to be strengthened, and Henry VIII had to be dissuaded from becoming a Habsburg ally. This was the goal of the meeting in 1520.

It failed. Henry ultimately chose to side with Charles V, and by 1522 English armies were fighting their way through France. But the Field of the Cloth of Gold, as glorious and as pointless an episode as might be imagined, was also witness to a diplomatic spectacle that, very soon, would be nothing more than a faded historical memory: the kings of France and England bowing their heads together in prayer.

On Saturday June 23rd, a richly decorated chapel was set up. Amid the gilt ornaments and golden candlesticks, seats were laid out, in strict order of precedence, for the ecclesiastical dignitaries of the two courts. Twelve French bishops would be catered to, along with three cardinals and a papal legate. England would be represented by eight bishops and the archbishop of Canterbury, with Cardinal Thomas Wolsey at their head.

Of course there was rivalry between the two groups: Many of the bishops were Englishmen or Frenchmen first and princes of the church a distant second. But, if only at the symbolic level, it was a potent reminder of a Christian unity that claimed to transcend the vagaries of dynastic politics. Services ran throughout the morning, culminating in a solemn mass at noon, with both monarchs in attendance. The choirs, organists, and musicians of the two royal chapels divided up the service, with the English singing the Gloria and the Sanctus, and the French taking the Kyrie, the Credo, and the Agnus Dei. Assisted by the dukes of Suffolk and Norfolk and the earl of Northumberland, Wolsey celebrated mass, the Bible was kissed by Francis and Henry, and after a rousing sermon the congregation took lunch together beneath a golden canopy.[137]

The unity of medieval Christendom was often disrupted, whether by rival popes or the latest heresiarch. There was anticlericalism, there always had been and always would be, but that did not necessarily make for a spiritual malaise. In the decades before the outbreak of the Protestant Reformation, European Christianity seemed to be in rude health—imperfect, conflicted, but robust. Ultimately, there was a shared devotional center and a belief, however attenuated, in the spiritual supremacy of the bishop of Rome. But this unity, so elegantly displayed at that service on the Field of the Cloth of Gold, was being destroyed. Barely three years earlier, Martin Luther had lodged his protest against the inadequacies of the papacy, and a revolution had begun.

It was a revolution that would transform and complicate the work of ambassadors. It would explode the efficient, albeit cynical world of fifteenth-century diplomacy, contaminating it with religious ideology and the skewed political decisions that went with it. French or Spanish envoys in London, and English envoys in Paris or Madrid would no longer simply be the representatives of dynastic rivals. Suddenly they were representatives of sworn confessional enemies, and they would sometimes be viewed, and treated, as the agents of Antichrist.

The Protestant Reformation appalled both of the kings who had supped and worshipped together on the Field of the Cloth of Gold. But while Francis remained a loyal, if headstrong, son of Rome, Henry would emerge as the unwitting, devoutly Catholic architect of a Protestant England. For those serving as ambassadors at the English court there were interesting years ahead.

The View from Venice

On the third day, I went to a park some thirty miles from London where the king was taking his pleasure in a small hunting lodge, built solely for the chase, in the midst of a forest. I saw the king twice and kissed his hand. He is glad to see foreigners, and especially Italians…He is tall of stature, very well formed, and of very handsome presence, beyond measure affable, and I never saw a prince better disposed than this one. He is also learned and accomplished, and most generous and kind, and were it not that he seeks to repudiate his wife after having lived with her for twenty-two years, he would be no less perfectly good and equally prudent. But this thing detracts greatly from his merits, as there is now living with him a young woman of noble birth, though many say of bad character, whose will is

law to him…he is expected to marry her, should the divorce take place, which it is supposed will not be effected, as the peers of the realm, both spiritual and temporal, and the people are opposed to it…Her majesty is prudent and good, and during these differences with the king she has evinced constancy and resolution, never being disheartened or depressed…[She] is not of tall stature, rather small. If not handsome, she is not ugly. She is a little fat, and always has a smile on her countenance.
—Mario Savorgnano on Henry VIII, Ann Boleyn, and Catherine of Aragon, August 1531[138]

Venetians did not know quite what to make of sixteenth-century England. Mario Savorgnano, an accomplished soldier and classical scholar (a typically Renaissance admixture of talents), regarded London as "a very rich, populous and mercantile city, but not beautiful." There were endless buildings, he admitted, but they were hideously ugly. The surrounding countryside was as delightful as it was fertile, though entirely incapable of sustaining vineyards—a failing that any right-thinking Italian would be unlikely to forgive.

The nation's menfolk had the virtue of being "more discreet in drinking than the Germans," but they were also markedly more idle. The women, by contrast, were seemingly beyond reproach: "They are all extremely handsome, nor did I ever see the like save at Augsburg." "It is customary," Savorgnano gleefully (and, one assumes, mischievously) reported, "after speaking once or twice to any lady, on meeting her in the street, to take her to a tavern (where all persons go without any reserve) or some other place, the husband not taking it amiss, but remaining obliged to you and always thanking you."[139]

Lodovico Falier, a Venetian ambassador to the Tudor court, had less time for such flirtatious pursuits, but he shared Savorgnano's ambivalence toward English society. The weather was rotten—"neither warm nor cold, but very damp." The country's national resources were partly impressive—an abundance of tin and silver, and sheep that produced the best wool in Europe—and partly disappointing: "The olive and the vine have been denied them," and all alcoholic drinks were derived from the less noble combination of malt and hops. England could boast twenty-two cathedral cities, two fabled universities, and a peerless legal system, but her population struck Falier as both confused and confusing. The Welshman was "sturdy, poor, adapted to war and sociable"; the Englishman was "mercantile, rich, affable and generous"; the Cornishman was "poor, rough and boorish." Unfortunately, divided by language, none of the three could understand a word the others were saying.

But even Falier could not quibble with the glamour of the monarchy, embodied by that finest of Renaissance princes, Henry Tudor. Falier was evenhanded in his description of the English queen, Catherine of Aragon: She was plump, of "modest countenance" and small stature, but was undoubtedly pious, fluent in several languages, and extremely popular with her people. When it came to describing Henry, however, Falier fell to gushing. "In this eighth Henry," he told his government back in Venice, "God combined such corporal and mental beauty, as not merely to surprise but to astound all men."

His face was not merely handsome, but angelic, and his corporal beauty was matched by his powers of oratory and his mastery of "every manly exercise…He sits the horse well, and manages him yet better; he jousts and wields his spear, throws his quoit, and draws the bow admirably." True, he had grown avaricious of late, but he remained deeply religious, usually hearing mass twice a day. All told, "who could fail to be struck with admiration on perceiving the lofty position of so glorious a prince to be in such accordance with his stature?"

After his election by the doge and Senate, Falier had embarked on his diplomatic mission in September 1528. He travelled overland via Savoy, Lyons, and Paris, and after relaying Venice's regards to Francis I, he left the French capital on December 10. A week later, an hour before sunset, he was met eight miles outside London by his predecessor, Marco Antonio Venier, and senior representatives of the Venetian community. A few miles farther on, he was greeted by members of Henry's Privy Council and the ambassadors of France, Milan, and Ferrara. They accompanied him to lodgings, close by the French ambassador's, which were to cost him 250 ducats to furnish and 100 ducats a month to rent. The permanent embassy building with which we are so familiar had no counterpart in sixteenth-century London.

Falier had received detailed instructions before setting out. His first task was to arrange audiences with the leading lights of the Tudor court, chief among them Cardinal Thomas Wolsey, archbishop of York and, for the time being, Henry's most trusted counsellor. A meeting was set for the 23rd, and after embracing the new ambassador and looking over his written credentials, Wolsey enjoyed, and promptly replied to, Falier's fawning Latin oration. Six days later, on the feast of St. Thomas Becket, the ambassador was woken at daybreak by a dean of the king's chapel, who escorted him by horse and barge to Greenwich Palace. Here, Falier was finally introduced to the king.

Beneath a canopy of golden cloth, a dagger lying by his side, Henry listened politely to the ambassador's words of greeting. It was at such moments that monarchs were expected to fill the representatives of other nations with awe, and Henry did not disappoint. "He wore a gown of gold brocade lined with very beautiful lynx skins," Falier recalled, "which apparel, combined with an excellently formed head and a very well proportioned body of tall stature, gave him an air of royal majesty, such as has not been witnessed in any other sovereign for many years." After another oration and a final inspection of Falier's credentials, the ambassador was led into a hall filled "with an infinite number of dukes, marquises, prelates, barons, lords and others." Dinner was eaten, mass was performed, and Falier returned to the city, making much better time on his homeward journey, courtesy of the flood tide.[140]

Falier was only the most recent addition to London's diplomatic community, joining representatives of the French and Spanish kings, the Holy Roman Emperor, several other Italian cities, and even a papal legate. Many of the tasks allotted to a Venetian ambassador would seem humdrum—negotiating with the syndics of the wool trade or lodging complaints when apprentices attacked Venetian merchants. But there were compensations. By all accounts, such men (however often they grumbled about the English climate, English beer, or English manners) enjoyed a pampered life.

A little before Falier's arrival, an ambassadorial secretary named Gasparo Spinelli had written to his brother Lodovico back in Venice. The previous night Spinelli had been a guest at a dinner given by Thomas Wolsey for the papal, French, and Venetian ambassadors. Spinelli confessed to feeling a little out of place, not least because the women at the banquet had been so intimidatingly gorgeous. After the performance of a Plautus comedy and orations praising the king, attention turned to the stage, where a lady of the court posed as the goddess Venus.

Six girls sat at her feet, "forming so graceful a group for her footstool that it looked as if she and they had really come down in person from heaven." At the sounding of a trumpet a cart came into view, carrying three "boys stark naked" and Venus's son, Cupid, who dragged in six old men, "clad in the pastoral fashion," at the end of a silver rope. He presented them to his mother, who commanded the six nymphs at her feet "to afford [them] all solace and requite them for their past pangs." The nymphs and the old men began to dance, and "on its termination the king and his favourites commenced another with the ladies there present." It was already daybreak, so Spinelli left for home, sated with revelry.

There was nothing unusual about such spectacular entertainments. A few months later, Spinelli was invited to a reception for the new French ambassador at Greenwich Palace. He "could never conceive anything so costly and well-designed as what was witnessed on that night." After watching a jousting display from the royal apartments, the assembled guests sat down to dinner, surrounded by "the most costly tapestry in England, representing the history of David." The king and his family sat at the head of the table, with the French, Venetian, and Milanese ambassadors ranged on either side, "each pairing with some great lady." After partaking of "viands of meat and fish," carried in on silver-gilt dishes, the guests were marshalled to another part of the palace. They entered a hall draped in silk with a ceiling decorated with a map of the world. Once again, Spinelli was dazzled by the women, "whose various styles of beauty and apparel enhanced by the brilliancy of the lights, caused me to think I was contemplating the choirs of angels."

A "very handsome youth...clad in sky-blue taffeta" addressed the king in the guise of Mercury. Henry, taking on the role of

Jupiter, was to decide whether love or prosperity was the more valuable possession. To help him reach a decision, the followers of Cupid and Justice staged a series of contests: Singers engaged in a choral battle, knights staged a choreographed sword fight. Then, at the back of the hall, a curtain suddenly fell to the ground, revealing the entrance to a cave. It was guarded by four gentlemen of the court decked with plumed hats and carrying torches. Inside, were "eight damsels of such rare beauty as to be supposed goddesses rather than human beings." Dressed in velvet caps and floating dresses, "decked with all the gems of the eighth sphere," they presented themselves to the king and began to dance. Love had triumphed in its debate with riches.

After a short pause, Henry, his nobles, and the French ambassador all entered the hall in masks, black satin hoods, and gowns. It was impossible to make out which of the men was the king until, at the end of the dancing, the costumes were removed. The guests returned to the supper hall to enjoy a rich selection of wines, and once again Spinelli could not understand where the time had disappeared to. "The sun, I believe, greatly hastened his course, having perhaps had a hint from Mercury of so rare a sight. So showing himself already on the horizon, warning being thus given of his presence, everyone thought it time to quit the royal chambers, returning to their own with such sleepy eyes that the daylight could not keep them open."[141]

Nothing could seem more idyllic or carefree than these ambassadorial entertainments. All was set fair at the English court. Until, that is, Henry VIII decided that he wanted a divorce. Falier, Spinelli, and their diplomatic colleagues would soon find themselves at the hub of European politics.

———

As early as 1529 Falier was witnessing Henry's mounting impatience with Rome over the issue of his marriage to Catherine of Aragon: "If the pope will not annul it," Henry boomed in March, "I will annul it myself." By June, Falier was watching Catherine "throwing herself on her knees before the king, [saying] aloud that she had lived for twenty years with his majesty as his lawful wife, keeping her faith to him, and that she did not deserve to be repudiated and thus put to shame." Henry was unmoved, convinced by the biblical texts that seemed to condemn the marriage he had made to his brother, Arthur's, widow in 1509. "If a man shall take his brother's wife," Leviticus warned, "it is an impurity. He has uncovered his brother's nakedness and they shall be childless." Henry began to suggest that the pope had not been entitled to dispense with this prohibition when the marriage had been arranged. Catherine had not provided Henry with a child since 1516, and the lack of a male heir had long been a cause of grave concern to the king: He "would no longer remain in mortal sin, as he had done during the last twenty years."[142]

It was complicated legal terrain, muddled by a rival text in Deuteronomy suggesting that it was a brother's duty to marry his brother's widow. It seems likely that, at any other time, the legal experts of Rome could have reached some compromise that would have both secured an annulment and preserved the papal prerogative to make dispensations—a prerogative that Henry's claims threatened to violate. At this particular moment, however, Roman politics were dominated by the emperor Charles V, and he was utterly opposed to the granting of an annulment, not least because Catherine was his aunt. Henry and Charles both dispatched their bishops and ambassadors across Europe, seeking support and scholarly advice.

Venice—which was not alone in this—was reluctant to take sides. As one English ambassador was informed, when requesting the counsel of legal scholars in May 1530, "considering the personages concerned therein, to whom it was desirable to avoid giving any offence," Venice preferred to keep its own counsel—"in so serious and uncommon a business an opinion given in favour of the one party must of necessity provoke great resentment in the other." The English grew furious at such procrastination, and by July the bishop of London was bellowing at the doge and Senate with "violent language," warning them not to make an enemy of Henry VIII. Ultimately, the Senate did allow legal scholars at the University of Padua to meditate on the rights and wrongs of Henry's proposed divorce, but they were only to speak to the imperial ambassador (not to the English) and to "keep the most profound silence as to this their permission."[143]

In the end, all the diplomatic errands and legal wrangling counted for nothing. Henry lived and died a devout Roman Catholic. He persecuted and, on occasion, executed Protestants with as much zeal as Francis I of France, cherishing his role as Defender of the Faith. He did not want a Reformation. What he did want was the annulment of his marriage to Catherine of Aragon. When the pope ultimately proved uncooperative, Henry determined to sever England's ties with the Holy See and establish a national church that would, at the very least, be more pliant.

A parliamentary campaign was staged in the early 1530s that effectively created an independent Church of England. The pope's jurisdiction was cast off. In 1533 the Act in Restraint of Appeals, preventing Catherine from challenging the annulment, entered the statute book and trumpeted English independence from papal authority: "By divers, sundry old authentic histories and chronicles it is manifestly declared and expressed that this realm of England is an empire, and so hath been accepted in the world." The English king had been "furnished by the goodness and sufferance of almighty God with plenary, whole and entire power" to dispense justice.[144]

By September 1532, the Venetian ambassador had reported seeing Anne Boleyn at Windsor, relishing her role as Henry's wife-elect, "her hair falling over her shoulders and completely covered with the most costly jewels."[145] By the next January, Catherine's marriage to Henry had been nullified, and Anne had replaced her as queen. The pope duly excommunicated Henry, and in 1534, through the Act of Supremacy, Henry duly assumed the title of supreme head of the Church of England.

⸻⸻

It was a political act, motivated by pride and, quite likely, infatuation with Anne Boleyn. The break with Rome had been about more than statecraft, however. It excited religious passions across British society. It opened the door of religious revolution to those with reformist sympathies—men like Thomas Cromwell, Henry's chief minister from 1532; Thomas Cranmer, his archbishop of Canterbury from 1533; and quite likely Anne Boleyn herself. By the end of Henry's reign, Catholic orthodoxies had been rattled, the monasteries had been suppressed, and the guardians of the boy-king Edward VI were poised to stage a liturgical and devotional coup to turn England into a radically Protestant nation.

When Carlo Cappello arrived in England in 1532 to replace Lodovico Farier as Venetian ambassador, all of this lay in the future. And yet, Cappello was struck by how many curious omens were being reported. In June 1532 two fish were caught in the Thames, one at Greenwich and one by the Tower of London. They were claimed to be thirty feet long and eleven feet wide, and "the people here in general consider this a prodigy foreboding future evil"—a sense of impending disaster that was only deepened by the appearance of a comet "in the form of a silver beard," and also that "within the last few days fourteen individuals, both men and women, have committed suicide by hanging or have drowned themselves."

There was an even more potent symbol of coming religious strife, however. On August 9th Cappello had set out for the house of the French ambassador, a property belonging to the king. When he arrived, servants were just finishing putting out a fire that had broken out in the chapel. A candle had been left burning after services, and "the chapel with all its furniture was consumed, as also the vestments used by the priest for the celebration of the mass."[146]

The English Reformation, despised and yet made possible by Henry VIII, carried forward by his children Edward VI and Elizabeth I, would disrupt European politics for generations. Ambassadors were not merely its witnesses, however. They were also its casualties. Not just in England, but in all the European countries ravaged by Reformation, they would be treated differently, and their rights, privileges, and immunities would come under new and closer scrutiny.

11
SCHISMS

Chapels

D ID A CATHOLIC AMBASSADOR IN PROTESTANT London have the right to practice a religion in the privacy of his embassy chapel, when that religion was deemed utterly illegal by the laws of the land? Perhaps surprisingly, given the otherwise venomous nature of Reformation politics, it was usually agreed that the ambassador did possess such a right: He had immunity from any anti-Catholic legislation. But he was expected to be discreet. The English government had expended huge amounts of energy and propagandist zeal in its efforts to undermine the dwindling Catholic community. Attendance at mass had been outlawed, and as the sixteenth century progressed, the refusal to participate in Anglican services attracted ever heftier fiscal, and ultimately custodial, penalties. Having a foreign ambassador brazenly indulge in Roman Catholic devotions was something to be frowned on, but a government would lose all patience when such an ambassador opened up his religious services to English citizens.

Such attempts to include English Catholics in an ambassador's personal immunity were deemed intolerable. In 1614 Elizabeth Moore, a widow, openly confessed "herself to be a popish recusant and that upon Sunday last was a seven-night…she was at the Spanish ambassador's house about nine or ten of the clock in the morning where she stayed an hour and…that she went into the chapel and said her devotions there." Many of London's Catholics had grown accustomed to being dragged before the ecclesiastical authorities to be accused of illegally attending services in embassy chapels. Few of them were quite as forthcoming as Elizabeth Moore. In the same month, the scrivener Thomas Davies had been spotted walking near the Barbican one Sunday morning with a "bough of hallowed palm in his hands"—a conspicuous clue that he had been to an embassy service. On the grounds that he could not be expected to incriminate himself—a prized early modern legal precept—Thomas refused to confirm or deny his attendance. Another scrivener, the Holborn resident George Matchet, did admit that he had been at the embassy between nine and eleven o'clock, but only "to speak with one Galloway about a house which he had to sell." Galloway, a vintner, followed the lead of Thomas Davies, and "being asked whether he heard mass there that day said he is not bound to accuse himself."[147]

Three years later it was reported that there was now "a daily resort of multitudes of English subjects of more than a hundred at once to mass at the French ambassador's in Durham House." A stern letter was dispatched to the bishop of Durham, the owner of the offending property.

> His majesty has been informed that there is a great liberty taken by diverse of his subjects, which report to the hearing of mass at Durham House, which as it is very scandalous to the church and of ill example to be suffered at any time…we cannot but take notice of it and do hereby pray and require your lordship to take this into your care. And although we would not that any disturbance or trouble be made within the house of the ambassador, yet such of this majesty's subjects as resort hither and shall be present at the mass we wish you to apprehend and to commit them to prison.

Similar instructions were sent to local justices of the peace, who were also urged not to do anything that breached the ambassador's personal immunity. Constables were to be posted on the coming Sunday, February 26, to apprehend any illegal visitors to the chapel, but they were not to trespass on the ambassador's property—they "should attend only without the walls and water stairs of Durham House on the water side" and outside the bishop of Durham's gate, on ground owned by the Lord of Salisbury.

The English government was eager to avoid a scene, but the French ambassador had other ideas. He was already furious that on the previous Friday two men had been apprehended in an ale house immediately after visiting the embassy chapel. He was unwilling to let Catholics be offended in such a way without at least making some protest. Early on Sunday morning he arrived home at Durham House "in a private manner to make a quarrel."

The English officers took up their positions shortly before mass was expected to end, but the servants of the French ambassador emerged from the embassy with swords in their hands "to carry the English papists by strong hand through the watch." As soon as the officers tried to seize the Catholics, a fight broke out, injuries were sustained on both sides, and Sir John Bath would have been killed by a rapier if its thrust had not been blocked by a gatepost.

News of the disturbance quickly spread, and crowds "came in heaps to Durham House gate with bills and clubs." They were only dissuaded from entering the ambassador's residence by the bishop of Durham himself, who was frantically trying to calm the situation. It was absolutely clear, however, that the French ambassador had sent out his armed servants as an act of provocation. The bishop demanded an audience.

This was quickly granted, but the ambassador was unrepentant. He said "that he wished his followers had killed the officers, and he was sorry they had not killed some of them, and that the king his majesty should require reason of the king of England for that which was done against the law of nations." He turned away, imperiously left the room, and his servants set about kicking the already-injured English officers who had escorted the bishop into the ambassador's presence.

The bishop could hardly believe the ambassador's audacity and ingratitude. When he had first arrived in London he had requested lodgings closer to Whitehall than his assigned billet at Hampton Court. The bishop had graciously invited him into Durham House, "crowding up himself and his whole family (being great) into the worst and beset rooms of the house leaving all the good and large rooms thereof...to the ambassador."[148]

No action was taken against the ambassador. Thanks to his immunity he was apparently above the law. But how could any nation tolerate such a state of affairs? Why was this curious concept of diplomatic immunity, which so often seemed to make fools out of governments, universally revered?

Immunities

> And it came to pass after this, that the king of the children of Ammon died and Ha-nun his son reigned in his stead.
> 2 Then said David, I will show kindness unto Ha-nun the son of Nahash, as his father showed kindness unto me. And David sent to comfort him by the hand of his servants for his father. And David's servants came into the land of the children of Ammon.
> 3 And the princes of the children of Ammon said unto Ha-nun their lord, Thinkest thou that David doth honour thy father, that he hath sent comforters unto thee? Hath not David *rather* sent his servants unto thee, to search the city, and to spy it out, and to overthrow it?

4 Wherefore Ha-nun took David's servants, and shaved off the one half of their beards, and cut off their garments in the middle, even to their buttocks, and sent them away.

5 When they told it unto David, he sent to meet them, because the men were greatly ashamed: and the king said, Tarry at Jericho until your beards be grown, and then return.

6 And when the children of Ammon saw that they stank before David, the children of Ammon sent and hired the Syrians of Beth-re-hob, and the Syrians of Zo-ba, twenty thousand footmen, and of King Ma-a-cah a thousand men, and of Ish-tob twelve thousand men.

7 And when David heard of it, he sent Jo-ab, and all the host of the mighty men.

—2 Samuel, 10:1–7

Renaissance envoys would be inundated with cautionary tales about the dangers of embassy. One writer told an especially harrowing story about the ambassadors of the Persian king Darius back in the fifth century. Darius had just defeated the kingdom of Thrace and, as Persian custom demanded, he dispatched messengers to demand tribute. The ambassadors were graciously received and a banquet was arranged in their honor. They were even provided with concubines, but the son of the Thracian king was outraged when they "handled and kissed them" far too lasciviously. He sent his father off to bed and set about wreaking his revenge.

Having promised the Persians they would be allowed "carnal company with which of these women every one should choose," he "sent forth these young dames to wash, and cleanse themselves for more delicacy to content the Persians." Unbeknown to the ambassadors, he dismissed the women "and forthwith brought in neat young men un-bearded, clad in the same apparel, and privily weaponed with daggers." As soon as the ambassadors "began to dally in amorous sort," the boys drew out their blades and slaughtered their victims.[149]

Not that early modern ambassadors had to consult the annals of ancient history to be convinced that diplomacy could be a hazardous pursuit.

To jump forward a few decades, in September 1653, Cromwell asked Bulstrode Whitelocke, a veteran of the parliamentary armies during the civil war, to serve as ambassador to the Swedish court. As Cromwell, whose execution of Charles I had scandalized western Europe, explained, "There is no prince or state in Christendom, with whom there is any probability for us to have a friendship, but only the Queen of Sweden. She has sent several times to us, but we have returned no embassy to her, only a letter by a young gentleman. She expects an ambassador from us, and if we send not a man of eminency to her, she would think herself slighted." Shared economic and strategic interests, and a common Protestant faith, made England and Sweden natural allies.

Whitelocke was terrified by the proposal, not least because the ambassadors of Oliver Cromwell had been enjoying unusually troubled times of late. One had been murdered during a visit to The Hague, and another, Anthony Ascham, had been killed by vengeful royalists in Madrid. As an added disincentive, Whitelocke's wife was pregnant and eager that her husband should remain at home. At a meeting on September 5th, Whitelocke did his utmost to reject Cromwell's invitation. "I return my humble thanks for the great honour done me in being judged worthy of so high a trust," Whitelocke began, "but I beg your excellency's consideration of my want of abilities, both of body and mind...and the season of the year: besides, there are some things relating to my private family." Moreover, Whitelocke added, "I want experience in foreign affairs and matters of state; in language and ceremony." To send such a man as himself would surely be an insult to the Swedish queen.

Cromwell was having none of it. "We know you have languages and have travelled and understand the interest of Christendom: and I have known you in the army, to endure hardships and to be healthful and strong, and of mettle and discretion, and parts most fit for this employment...really, no man is so fit as you are." Whitelocke persisted, suggesting that "I cannot subscribe to your favourable opinion of me" and reminding the lord protector of his wife's condition. Cromwell was prepared for this gambit: "I know my lady is a good woman, and a religious woman, and will be contented to suffer a little absence of her husband for the public good." Whitelocke asked if he might have a fortnight to think matters over: Cromwell said he could have a few days.

The two men met again on the 13th of the month, and after Whitelocke once more professed his lack of qualifications, Cromwell applied so much pressure that he left the soon-to-be ambassador with little room for maneuvering. "If you decline it," he warned, "the commonwealth would suffer extremely by it, your own profession perhaps might suffer likewise, and the Protestant interest would suffer by it." "I shall hold myself particularly obliged to you if you will undertake it," Cromwell promised, "and will stick as close to you as your skin is to your flesh." Declining the position was clearly no longer a sensible option: "I am resolved," Whitelocke announced, "to lay aside further considerations of wife, children, friends, torture and all objections and fears of dangers...by accepting this difficult and hazardous employment." It was always difficult to turn down Oliver Cromwell.

Whitelocke did not lose his life during his embassy, although he had been exposed to some name-calling: Crowds had apparently massed outside his lodgings and chanted unkind words about

"English dogs and king-killers." Upon his return in May 1654, he confessed that "I have endured many hardships for an old crazy carcass as mine is, but God was pleased to show much mercy to me." Negotiations with the Swedish government had gone well, and the best had been made of the cold Scandinavian winters.

> "I kept my people together and in action and recreation," he told Cromwell, "by having music in my house and encouraging that and the exercise of dancing, which held them by the ears and eyes and gave them diversion without any offence. And I caused the gentlemen to have disputations in Latin and declamation upon words which I gave them."

The puritanical Cromwell was doubtless unimpressed by the dancing, but the Latin exercises won his approval, and he praised the ambassador for making his house into "a little academy."[150]

From the earliest days of diplomacy, it was the fears—both real and imagined—of ambassadors like Whitelocke that forced societies to offer them protection. Diplomatic immunity is one of those concepts that permeate almost every phase of human history. It was rarely granted altruistically, out of some sense that killing, injuring, or inconveniencing ambassadors was morally reprehensible. It was a simple matter of pragmatism. If diplomacy was to flourish, its agents would have to be able to carry out their duties unmolested, secure in the knowledge that their lives and property were not at undue risk. This was a boon, a necessity even, for all concerned.

There was also the question of a ruler's dignity. The ambassador was his representative, and an attack on him was, by extension, an attack on the ruler. Potentates usually took this issue extremely seriously. In the seventeenth century, an Englishman in Morocco reported that an ambassador and his secretary had been "called to account by the [Moroccan] emperor, for a quarrel that happened between them on ship-board at their return from England." They had originally been sentenced to death, "the secretary for affrighting the ambassador (who then represented the emperor's person) and the ambassador for not executing the secretary at the same instant the affront was given." Happily, some of his counsellors had convinced the emperor to forgo the original penalty—being torn apart by wild horses—in favor of tying the men to a tree and whipping them.[151]

Respect for the code of diplomatic immunity was astonishingly widespread. Envoys to the Aztecs may have had to endure awful spectacles—seeing captured people being offered as sacrifices, for instance—but they were always guaranteed safe passage to and from the Aztec capital. In medieval Europe, complex legal arguments determined who might enjoy immunity in wartime. In theory, the privilege extended to priests, pilgrims, and peasants engaged in agricultural labor. Such rules of war were mostly honored in the breach, but one group whose immunity was genuinely regarded as inviolate were the heralds—men without whom the intricate mechanisms of medieval warfare would have crumbled. Almost outside of normal human society, French and English heralds, the members of an international chivalric organization, would gather together on a hilltop in 1415 and, in total security, watch the battle of Agincourt unfold beneath them.[152]

Offending the rules of diplomatic immunity could bring unwelcome consequences. Sometimes rulers were simply irritated when their envoys were mistreated. On July 21, 1708, the Russian ambassador to London, Andrei Matveev, was dragged from his coach by some bailiffs to whom he owed money. His footmen were attacked and Matveev spent several hours in prison. The rest of London's diplomatic community rallied to his defense and successfully demanded his release. Matveev's employer, Tsar Peter the Great, was furious. Brusquely, and very loudly, he informed the British ambassador in Moscow that he expected Matveev's assailants to be executed. His request was denied, but the British government did enact new legislation that reduced the chances of such an outrage being repeated.[153]

On other occasions, breaches of immunity were used as the pretext for full-scale military assaults. In 1218 several hundred Mongol merchants were killed and robbed in the Persian border city of Utrar. One of them managed to escape and rushed to Genghis Khan to report the incident. A furious Genghis dispatched three ambassadors to Persia to demand reparations, but the local governor they encountered seemed entirely unrepentant. In fact he murdered one of the envoys and shaved the beards of the other two—an especially humiliating punishment. The Mongols were passionate advocates of diplomatic immunity, and when news reached Genghis of his ambassadors' fates he immediately declared war.[154]

It was just as important to ensure that ambassadors did not abuse their own immunities. On November 21, 1653, a nineteen-year-old Portuguese nobleman named Don Pantaleone Sa visited the New Exchange on the Strand in London: "a public place at present much frequented by ladies and gentlemen of condition during the tedious hours of the night." Don Pantaleone was talking to his friends, in unflattering terms, about the English. A Colonel John Gerard overheard their chatter and, deeply insulted, drew his sword. Gerard received a minor wound and Pantaleone and his companions fled the scene. They had been offended by Gerard's actions, however, and planned to return to the New Exchange the next evening to confront him.

The Portuguese contingent, now much increased in size, arrived heavily armed. Their coaches concealed grenades and gunpowder and they had boats stationed on the Thames should a hasty getaway prove necessary. Colonel Gerard was nowhere to be seen, but Don Pantaleone and his servants were still determined to make mischief.

Harcourt Greenaway, a law student at Lincoln's Inn, was out shopping with his sister and his fiancée, hoping to "purchase fashionable articles for their approaching marriage." When the Portuguese began to discharge their weapons, Greenaway shepherded the two ladies into a nearby shop only to find himself in Don Pantaleone's line of fire. Greenaway was shot and killed. Don Pantaleone rushed to his brother's house. He expected to find refuge there because his brother was Joao Rodriguez Sa, the Portuguese ambassador.

The authorities were informed of events at the New Exchange, and troops surrounded the ambassador's house. Despite his initial protestations, the ambassador had no choice but to hand over his brother. Don Pantaleone was taken to the Tower of London, and in July 1654 was sentenced to death for committing murder. The ambassador had pleaded for his brother's life "on the ground that it is against the law of nations that one of his family should be tried by these laws," but the committee of judges rejected what was, as far as contemporary legal opinion was concerned, a specious argument. On July 10th Pantaleone Sa was beheaded on Tower Hill, and his brother left the country in disgrace.[155]

Diplomatic immunity was precious, but it did not protect the errant members of an ambassador's family any more than it extended to the mass-going Catholics of Elizabethan England. In an era of confessional strife, however, not even diplomatic immunity could protect an unpopular ambassador from mistreatment.

Don Alvaro de la Quadra

Of all the diplomats in sixteenth-century Europe, the Spanish ambassador to the court of Elizabeth I had perhaps the hardest furrow to plough. Nations that might have been expected to be natural rivals had become ideological adversaries. At the time of Elizabeth's accession, England was a nation in flux, made up of 8,600 parishes and between three and four million people, many of whom were puzzled by the much-discussed phenomenon called Reformation. For the past two decades, competing theologies had battled it out in the pulpit and statute book. With Elizabeth's arrival, some observers hoped that a moderate, resilient religious settlement might finally be achieved.

Venerable ecclesiastical structures, organized around bishops, would be retained, but some of the more palatable doctrinal lessons of Reformation would be heeded. By 1563, the Thirty-Nine Articles encapsulated England's doctrinal affiliations, and the journey between traditional and reformed ideas would be embarked on. Of course, such pragmatic compromises left many people deeply dissatisfied. England's dwindling Catholic population was disheartened by the definitive outlawing of the mass and the cautious embracing of Calvinistic ideas about grace and predestination.

As the reign progressed, disenchantment gave way to fear, as recusant legislation assaulted the consciences, liberties, and purses of any Catholics who declined to attend their local parish churches.

At the opposite end of the theological spectrum, meanwhile, radical Protestants were gratified that much had altered since Henry VIII's clumsy break with Rome, but they doubted if such change was really enough. Was it really acceptable, they asked themselves, that an avowedly reformed religion still retained so many reminders of the Catholic past—so many "dregs of popery"? Ministers were still wearing their lavish vestments, parishioners were still kneeling at communion and making the sign of the cross. As Elizabeth showed few signs of moving toward a more radical doctrinal position, they wondered whether "tarrying for the magistrate" was still a credible strategy.

The Protestantism that Elizabeth gradually imposed on England was, therefore, of a moderate, some said muddled, variety. It was Protestantism, nonetheless, and anathema to Spain, the champion of revitalized Catholic orthodoxy. A diplomatic presence was vital, particularly so that Spain could contribute to the debate and competition over who Elizabeth I should marry. But to be a Spanish ambassador in London was to be vulnerable and suspected. Few Spanish ambassadors were quite so shoddily treated as Don Alvaro de la Quadra, who took up his post in the Spring of 1559. The one thing that might be said in mitigation of the English government's behavior is that Quadra, at least in part, deserved it.

A Neapolitan nobleman, Quadra had enjoyed an illustrious career in the Spanish church, rising to the rank of bishop of Venosa, and then Aquila. In these early years of Elizabeth's reign, there was still much rumor and confusion about the religious settlement that would finally be reached, but Bishop Quadra feared the worst. As he arrived in England, the bishops who had served Elizabeth's Catholic predecessor, Mary I, were being ordered to remain in London. Soon they would face a choice between swearing allegiance to the new regime or losing their sees. Quadra also noted that England was quickly winning a reputation as a haven for persecuted Protestants, and he grumbled at the number of "Flemish heretics" pouring into the realm. He simply could not agree with the member of Parliament who had "compared the Queen to Moses, saying that she had been sent by God to lead the people out of bondage."[156]

It was clearly going to be a reign blighted by religious controversy. In February 1560 Quadra reported an undignified quarrel that had just erupted at court. Two noblemen had been heatedly discussing the issue of compulsory church attendance, and after exchanging "rough words [they] fell to fisticuffs and grabbing at each others beards." Elizabeth intervened, calling the men over to listen to her play music. The tensions in the country would not be so easily soothed. Even at this early stage, Quadra reported, the issue of Catholics' attendance at embassy chapels was already causing controversy. As he complained to one of his correspondents, the government had "ordered all the English people who were attending mass at the French ambassador's to be arrested. This was done with very little respect for the ambassador."[157]

But by Quadra's reckoning, respect for Catholic ambassadors was the scarcest of commodities within the Elizabethan regime. "Not a man dares to enter my house," Quadra complained, "because of the distrust that is publicly shown to all those who associate with me." In March 1562 news reached the ambassador that his English counterparts in Madrid were furious about "their trunks being broken open and everything examined, even their papers, and some of the people imprisoned." Quadra found it hard to be sympathetic. After all, he would endure far worse.[158]

One of the ambassador's regular correspondents was the Duchess of Parma, who resided in Flanders. The letters he sent her would usually take twelve days to arrive, but on one occasion, in the spring of 1562, his news was urgent enough to justify the employment of special couriers who could make the journey in three days. They had left London without incident and by nightfall had made it as far as the coastal town of Gravesend. When they set off the next morning they were followed by four horsemen who, two miles into the journey, accosted them and kept them under close guard for two days. Finally, the couriers were given back their possessions and sent on their way. Quadra was convinced that the English government had arranged the ambush and used the two days to send his confidential letters to London to be translated.

His suspicions seemed to be confirmed when he visited Elizabeth to lodge a formal protest. She blithely informed the ambassador that "if she suspected anything was being written from here against her interests she would, in such cases, not hesitate to stop the posts and examine what concerned her."[159] Quadra was flabbergasted, but even more outrageous insults to his dignity lay ahead.

On June 6, 1562, the ambassador sent alarming news to the duchess.

> The Queen's ministers have got hold of a servant of mine, who some years since was in Flanders on my affairs, and have squeezed out of him all the secrets he knew of what I was doing here, and not satisfied with this, they are trying to get him back into my house again (he having left in consequence of a quarrel of his own making) in order that they may be kept informed through him of all I may do with regard to English affairs.

The servant, Quadra's private secretary, Borghese Venturini, had sent the government two letters in which he denounced the ambassador's behavior, accusing him of gossiping about the queen's private life, encouraging the Spanish king to intervene militarily in

English affairs, and misrepresenting any number of government policies in his dispatches home. Simply resigning his position with Quadra would have been too suspicious, so Venturini "picked a quarrel with another of my servants, whom he mortally wounded and on the following day complaining of me he went and gave himself up to the palace people." The information he imparted was apparently so useful that the government was now trying to reinstall Venturini in the ambassador's household.

Quadra was hardly so naïve, however. He demanded that Venturini either be expelled from the realm or handed over to the ambassador's mercies. As Quadra confessed to another of his correspondents, the Duke of Alva, he was tempted to exact the harshest of revenges. He was only deterred from "taking his life by extraordinary means" by the realization that, as well as "being so foreign to my profession," it would probably only provoke even greater scandal and ill will.

Within a few days, apparently on the strength of Venturini's testimony, Quadra was scolded by the queen, accused of "always writing ill of her and her affairs." The ambassador's glib response was that his duty was to observe her behavior and draw his conclusion, whether good or bad. His conscience, he insisted, was quite clear. Next, Quadra was dragged before the lord chamberlain for another round of interrogation. He was accused of describing the queen as his mortal enemy. Quadra explained that he had not been referring to the queen's person, but to the government as a whole, and in that context, Quadra quipped, "I may have said it, and certainly with much truth." But had he not also claimed that the queen was promoting heresy in the Netherlands with the aim of undermining Spanish power there? Yes, he had said such a thing, Quadra admitted, since it was true. And as for spreading the rumors that Elizabeth had secretly married her lover, Robert Dudley, Quadra was hardly alone: "People were saying all over the town that the wedding had taken place." Quadra could not be expected to bear sole responsibility for gossip about the queen's intriguing love life.[160]

The ambassador's run-ins with the Elizabethan regime would continue. In January of the next year, "a man who had fired a harquebus at one of the servants of [a French nobleman] had sought refuge in my house." Quadra insisted that he did not know the man, that he had not invited him, and that he had immediately sent his servants to apprehend him. "During the four years I have been here," Quadra opined, "no criminal of any sort whatever has entered my house, nor have I had the slightest dispute with the officers of justice." But the English government, by Quadra's account, had gleefully "seized upon this pretext for turning me out of this house." An officer had been dispatched to inform Quadra that he was to hand over all the keys to his property. They were to be entrusted to a custodian who could then keep a detailed log of who visited the ambassador and at what times. The doors leading to the street, and down to the garden and river, would thus be under constant surveillance. It was a none-too-subtle attempt, Quadra surmised, to achieve "what they have long been hankering to do: namely to try to turn me out of the kingdom by ill treatment or, at all events, to disarm me from opposing them during this parliament."

Quadra had at first refused to surrender his keys, telling the officer that "for thirty years the ambassadors here had been allowed to reside in the royal houses. And they had invariably been accustomed to hold the keys of the houses wherein they lived." Undeterred, the government sent locksmiths the next day: Their purpose, "without any respect or consideration," was to "change the locks and keys on the doors and hand the new keys to the custodian."

Once again Quadra demanded an audience with the queen. She refused to meet with him, claiming to be too busy with affairs of state. The ambassador came before her Privy Council instead and demanded that they either provide him with keys of his own or find him a new residence. Once again, the government responded in the most aggressive terms, accusing Quadra of a litany of treacherous activities—his chapel was the resort of every papist in London; conspiracies against the queen had been hatched in his house; he had fomented rebellion in Ireland. Quadra ought to have been grateful that the council had acted against him with such restraint. Had they done nothing, "the populace would have committed violence toward me, and not a man of my household would have been left alive."

Quadra naturally reported the incident to his monarch, Philip II of Spain. He received a disappointing reply. "With any other prince," Philip explained, "we should have taken the matter up and duly resented it," but a different strategy had to "operate in the case of the queen." The well-being of every Catholic in the country depended on England and Spain maintaining at least a semblance of civilized relations. Quadra was ordered to put the incident behind him and adopt a conciliatory attitude.[161]

In truth, Quadra's forbearance was now all but exhausted. From the outset of his mission he had doubted whether it was possible to engage in mature diplomacy with a queen like Elizabeth I. As early as July 1558 he was claiming to "have lost all hope in the affairs of this woman. She is convinced of the soundness of her unstable power, and will only see her error when she is irrevocably lost. In religious matters she has been saturated ever since she was born in a bitter hatred to our faith, and her one object is to destroy it…Her language is so shifty that it is the most difficult thing in the world to negotiate with her. With her all is falsehood and vanity." Five months later he was musing on "what a pretty business it is to have to treat with this woman, who I think must have a hundred thousand devils in her body, notwithstanding that she is forever telling me that she yearns to be a nun and to pass her time in a cell praying."

In other words, there were always going to be tensions between Quadra and the regime, and the ambassador certainly deserved part of the blame for the breakdown in relations. More to the point, it is entirely possible that Quadra was guilty of everything the English government accused him of. Spanish ambassadors would prove themselves to be inveterate plotters and agitators against the regime throughout the sixteenth century. Quadra certainly took pains to set up an elaborate espionage system and was regularly briefed on developments at court. English ambassadors in Brussels, Antwerp, and Paris all gathered their own information that suggested Quadra was up to no good.

By the end of his mission, however, Quadra was more concerned with his personal financial difficulties than with preserving the fragile Anglo-Spanish relationship. Throughout his embassy he had grumbled endlessly about how much the honor of a diplomatic posting was costing him. "The emperor's ambassador has been my guest for six months," he complained in March 1560, and it was left to Quadra to "feed him and all those who come to visit him." Besides that, "not a day passes that I am not besieged by poor clergymen and students" who, having been turned out of their benefices and colleges, sought Quadra's financial assistance. Two years later, he was talking of the need to "sell and strip myself of my own property," but, he lamented, he had precious little property left.

"I have incurred these debts," he explained to Philip, "in matters so necessary and vital to the service of God and your majesty that it would have been a violation of my duties not to have incurred them." For all that, they had become a horrendous burden.

Quadra had endured enough, and in April of the next year he explained to Philip that "public affairs here and my own private troubles and necessities force me to beg your majesty to be pleased to allow me to leave this island. I am of but little use here and my residence is so costly and onerous that apart from my pecuniary estate, in which I am totally ruined, I am suffering much in health and all else."[162]

The plea came too late. Quadra died of the plague in August, 1563. Preparations were made to have his body sent back to Naples, but the ambassador's creditors seized the corpse, refusing to release it until Quadra's debts had been settled. It would remain unburied in England for a full year and a half. Even the lowliest of the ambassador's servants had their fiscal grievances. An Irish groom named Nicholas demanded the six crowns he was owed. Pedro the barber had "served in the chamber three years, and has received nothing." Jacques Namures, the cook, demanded thirteen crowns and four shillings, while a washerwoman called Isabel was owed a hefty twenty-nine crowns. The illusory grandeur of embassy was stripped away by the unfinished business Quadra left behind him. But if the internecine squabbles of Christendom had made the lives of European ambassadors more awkward, a more ancient, more fundamental religious divide—between Christianity and Islam—also played its part in complicating sixteenth-century diplomacy. Beyond the schisms of Europe, a mighty new Islamic power, Ottoman Turkey, had arisen.

12
"An Iliad of Miseries":
Europe and the Ottomans

The Abode of War

DURING ITS FIRST CENTURIES ISLAM did not hold diplomacy in any great esteem. There was boundless optimism, shored up by extraordinary territorial expansion, that one day the whole world would become Muslim. Until that came to pass, the earth was to be divided in two, between the House of Islam and the as-yet unconverted House of War. The struggle to enlighten the rest of humanity was known as jihad, and the person devoted to that most righteous of struggles was a mujahid. According to this stark, almost monolithic worldview, Islam was in a legal state of constant war with the rest of humanity, a war that would only end with the final Muslim victory. It was simply impossible for an Islamic leader to compact an enduring peace treaty with a non-Muslim power. All that was available were temporary truces, which could last no longer than ten years, and which could be abrogated by a Muslim state at a moment's notice.

Travel into the House of War was therefore hardly ever called for. Indeed, it fell into the category of actions that Islamic law deemed reprehensible, though not strictly forbidden. Crossing into the non-Muslim world to ransom hostages or to buy food in time of famine was broadly acceptable: Most other journeys were held to be disreputable.

This early Muslim worldview was a fiction, of course. It quickly became clear that Islam was not on the verge of converting the whole of humanity. What was more, the unity of the early Abbasid caliphate had begun to crumble. Rival Muslim states had established themselves in Spain, North Africa, and Egypt. The legal scholars of Islam were obliged to fashion a new code of international encounter, and some even went so far as positing the idea of an intermediary House of Truce, consisting of those states that had not converted to Islam but who recognized Muslim suzerainty and paid appropriate tribute to the caliph. In any event, political realities meant that stable borders had to be established and workable relations with non-Muslim powers inaugurated. The concept of the *aman* was introduced from the eighth century onwards: a promise of safe conduct for non-Muslims in Islamic lands, granted on condition that visitors carried no weapons and respected any religious observances they witnessed.[163]

In the early medieval world, the key dialogue between Islam and Christianity was conducted by Abbasid Baghdad and the Byzantine Empire. The two polities were in a near constant state of conflict, with Muslim raids into Anatolia an almost yearly occurrence. A remarkably civilized diplomatic apparatus developed in this seemingly unpromising environment. With every new military encounter, both sides would capture large numbers of hostages. Just as surely, ambassadors would meet at the borders between the two empires to exchange them.

In 845, for instance, the two sides met at the river Lamos. Bridges were erected, and the Byzantines sent over three thousand Muslim men and five hundred women and children. Parity was everything on such occasions, however, and when the Muslims sent a smaller number of prisoners across the river, the Byzantine ambassadors protested. Abbasid officials were quickly sent to scour the markets of Baghdad for Byzantine slaves, and the requisite number was finally achieved by releasing a number of Byzantine women from the caliph's harem.[164]

Byzantium and Baghdad were enemies, but diplomacy allowed them to behave decorously towards each other. Indeed, it sometimes granted them the opportunity to lavish extraordinary attention on each other's ambassadors. In 917 two Byzantine envoys, John Radinos and Michael Toxaras, travelled to Baghdad to negotiate a temporary pause in hostilities and to organize the routine exchange of prisoners. It took them two months to reach Takrit, 125 miles north of Baghdad. They were detained there for eight weeks, but when they arrived in the capital on June 25, their irritation turned to delight.

They were led to the caliph's compound through troop-lined avenues, with the ships on the river Tagus all wonderfully decorated in the background. They were taken on a tour of no less than twenty-three palaces: the palace of the tree, with its spellbinding automata; the palace of the hundred lions, where wild beasts set to "sniffing them and eating from their hands"; and the palace of paradise, where eunuchs served the ambassadors with ice water and sherbet. Thirty-eight thousand wall hangings, twenty-two thousand elegant carpets, and endless trays of jewels had been put on display to impress the visitors. Finally, they entered the presence of the caliph Muktadir. He sat atop an ebony throne, surrounded by precious stones, the largest of which was of "such a size that its sheen eclipsed the daylight."[165]

These were troubled years for Baghdad. The economy was weak, theological quarrels simmered away, and within two years a disgruntled citizenry would be in open revolt, burning down prisons and looting shops—the first of some eighteen popular uprisings between 921 and 932. But the Abbasid caliph had no intention of betraying such anxieties to his enemy's ambassadors. As ever, diplomacy offered an opportunity for ostentatious subterfuge.

Indeed, as unique as it was, the encounter between Islam and the West was sometimes reassuringly familiar. There were diplomatic gifts in abundance: Harun's elephant, of course, but also the slaves, partridges, cranes, ravens, and starlings that the emperor Michael VI received while negotiating a frontier armistice in the 1050s. Maintaining ambassadorial dignity was also a constant concern.[166] In the ninth century Viking invaders had made substantial territorial gains in northern Spain. The emir of Córdoba dispatched an ambassador named al-Ghazal (the gazelle) to their court, and two days after arriving he was granted an audience with the king. Al-Ghazal had been sure to inform his hosts that he had no intention of kneeling before an infidel monarch, but the Vikings had laid a trap. The doorway into the king's chamber was so low that a person could seemingly only enter it on his knees. Al-Ghazal was not to so easily browbeaten, however. "He sat on the ground, stretched forth his two legs and dragged himself through on his rear, and when he had passed through this doorway he stood erect." He came before the king and, without the vaguest hint of fear or diffidence, calmly read out his message: "Peace be with you, O king, and with those whom your assembly hall contains. May you not cease to enjoy power, long life and nobility which leads you to the greatness of this world and the next."[167]

It was an impressive display, a timeless example of an ambassador striving, in straitened circumstances, to retain his honor and composure. What such virtuosity could not conceal, however, was the tension and animosity that sometimes blighted Islam's relationship with the West.

—◀▭◖◗▭▶—

Diplomacy did bring its share of cultural blessings to the Muslim world, whether the Byzantine mosaic craftsmen and glass experts who helped to embellish the mosques of Cordoba and Damascus, or the ambassadors who carried scores of Greek scientific texts back to Baghdad.[168] But throughout the medieval period, Christianity was infinitely more interested in (and fearful of) Islam than Islam was interested in the West. Asia could provide silks, spices, ceramics, and medicines, while Africa supplied slaves and gold. Beyond the occasional artisan and manuscript, Europe had little to offer the Muslim world. Islamic scholars showed hardly any interest in European languages, history, or geography. While European diplomats were happy to enter Islamic lands, when reciprocal ambassadors had to be sent to Christian countries it was thought far preferable to employ a non-Muslim, often a Jewish, agent.

Islamic disregard for the minutiae of Western political life died hard. At the time of the French Revolution, the Austrian ambassador in Istanbul arranged for his translator to complain about the Frenchmen who were wandering around Istanbul with tricolor cockades in their hats—that damnable symbol of a regicidal regime. "May God punish these Frenchmen as they deserve," the translator told the Ottoman official. "They have caused us much sorrow. For heaven's sake, if only you would have these cockades stripped off their heads." The reply was more than blasé:

"My friend, we have told you many times that the Ottoman empire is a Muslim state. No one among us pays any attention to these badges of theirs. We recognize the merchants of friendly states as guests. They wear what headgear they wish on their heads and attach what badges they please. And if they put baskets of grapes on their heads, it is not the business of the Sublime Porte to ask them why they do so."[169]

And if Muslims were reluctant to engage with western Europe, one could hardly blame them. The Christian north of Spain was happy to import Córdoba leather, Toledo steel, and even the Andalusian linen it used for its altar clothes.[170] Christian women in Sicily would avidly seek out Muslim perfume and jewelry. Beyond such superficial encounters, however, medieval Europe despised Islam, the religion that had been bold enough to seize Jerusalem, the very cradle of the Christian faith.

It was impossible for a Muslim traveller to properly observe his faith in the West—there were no mosques, no dispensers of Halal meat—and if he *tried* to do so the ecclesiastical authorities were very likely to pounce. The contrast with the Muslim world was striking. True, Christians and Jews in a medieval Muslim state would pay additional taxes, and there would always be pressure on them to convert to Islam. But as followers of two religions "of the book" that Islam respected—Christ and Moses being held as genuine, if now superseded prophets—they were entitled to practice their faith unmolested. The intolerant West offered no such dispensations, expending most of its energies in cultivating stereotypes of Islamic barbarity, cruelty, and prurience.

All told, restricting diplomatic contact between Islam and medieval Christendom to a bare minimum was probably a wise strategy. With the coming of the fourteenth century, however, an Islamic power rose up in Anatolia that Europe was unable to ignore.

Harborne, Busbecq, and the Turks

> They are, and have been ever, the most inhumane of all other barbarians. Their manner of living is for the most part uncivil and vicious. For their vices they are all pagans and infidels, sodomites and liars. They are a very scornful people and their pride is so great as it is not possible to be described.
> —Anthony Nixon, on the Turks, 1602[171]

> The king of the Turks, who rules over a great part of Europe, safeguards the rites of religion as well as any prince in the world. Yet, he constrains no one, but on the contrary permits everyone to live as his conscience dictates. What is more, even in his seraglio at Pera he permits the practice of four diverse religions, that of the Jews, the Christians according to the Roman rite, and according to the Greek rite, and that of Islam.
> —Jean Bodin, on the Turks, 1576[172]

When the Mongol armies abandoned Anatolia during the thirteenth century, a number of rival Turkish states began competing for supremacy. The Ottomans, with their base at Sogut, barely two hundred miles south of Constantinople, would emerge victorious. By the end of the fourteenth century, Ottoman armies had seized Gallipoli (their first European foothold) and Adrianople (their new capital in Bulgaria, two hundred miles west of Constantinople). They had defeated the Serbs and Bosnians at the battle of Kosovo (1389) and now held dominion in the Balkans, as far as the Danube, and across most of Anatolia. The early fifteenth century would bring its setbacks (notably, defeat at the hands of the Mongol leader Tamerlane), but a resurgent Ottoman state soon recommenced its phenomenal territorial expansion, and in 1453 seized the ancient Byzantine capital of Constantinople.

Europe was offered some respite at the beginning of the sixteenth century as the Ottomans dedicated themselves to overrunning the Middle East, securing Damascus in 1516 and Cairo a year later. With the arrival of the great sultan Suleiman (reigned 1520–1566), however, the onslaught was resumed. Belgrade fell in August 1521, and in 1522 Ottoman naval supremacy was efficiently demonstrated by the capture of Rhodes. Hungary was invaded in 1526, and three years later Ottoman troops reached the gates of Vienna. This was to prove the farthest limit of their adventuring. The inclemency of European winters meant that Ottoman armies only fought for half the year, and their campaigns in Europe always involved a long march from camps in Anatolia. Supply lines could only stretch so far, and Ottoman armies could only march finite distances.

This was small comfort to western Europe. The Turks had effortlessly taken over a vast swathe of the continent. Their expansionism had stalled, and in the coming decades they would even suffer bruising military defeats, most famously at the naval battle of Lepanto in 1571. But by the late sixteenth century, the Ottoman Empire was at its greatest extent, ranging from Hungary to Mesopotamia, from Tunis to the Crimea.

It was a disaster, wrote the historian Richard Knolles in 1603: "The long and still declining state of the Christian commonwealth with the utter ruin and subversion of the Empire of the east and many other most glorious kingdoms and provinces of the Christians" could never be "sufficiently lamented." Islam was to blame. Its prophet, Muhammad, had been "born in an unhappy hour, to the great destruction of mankind"; his "gross and blasphemous doctrine [was] first fantasised by himself in Arabia and so by him obtruded unto the world." The Ottomans had "from a small beginning become the greatest terror of the world."[173]

Diplomacy could not falter in the face of such an adversary, however. The nations of western Europe quickly realized that there might even be an advantage in negotiating with the Ottoman interlopers. Many Protestants, for instance, relished the Turkish advance. It distracted the emperor Charles V and prevented him from turning his full attention to stamping out the Lutheran Reformation—a task he was desperate to accomplish. Some Balkan Christians even suggested that compared to the unflinching intolerance of Rome, their new Ottoman overlords were decidedly enlightened, continuing the Islamic tradition of ensuring religious freedom for "people of the book." As the Balkan proverb put it, "better the turban of the Turk than the tiara of the pope."

The Venetians had also been eager to exploit the new political realities of eastern Europe. Almost as soon as Constantinople had fallen in 1453, Venice sent an emissary to Sultan Mehmed II to negotiate the continuation of valuable trading privileges in the city and across the Ottoman Empire. To the scandal of the rest of Europe, some Venetians found it remarkably easy to acculturate to the Ottoman world. Andrea Gritti, a future doge, spent years on diplomatic duty in Istanbul before returning with five sons (four of them the children of the Turkish concubine he had lived with during his stay in the city) and an abiding admiration for Ottoman culture.[174]

The French, dynastic enemies of the Habsburgs, saw the Ottomans as a potential ally in that difficult struggle. When Francis I was captured by Charles V at the battle of Pavia in 1525, his mother, Louise of Savoy dispatched an ambassador to Istanbul in the hope of negotiating an alliance. The mission was unsuccessful, but talks continued, and by 1542 French and Turkish fleets were fighting alongside each other in an attempt to seize Milan from the Habsburgs. After the joint siege and sack of Nice, the French even allowed the Ottoman fleet to winter in Toulon harbor.

As for the English, they were no more likely than the Venetians to allow cultural or religious antipathy to stand in the way of economic progress. In 1575, the Turks granted Richard Staper and Edward Osbourne permission to trade within the empire. Conscious that the rights of merchants would have to be closely guarded, Elizabeth I dispatched her envoy William Harborne to Istanbul three years later.

After a twelve-week journey to the Ottoman capital, Harborne quickly set about securing privileges for the English trading community. They were to be guaranteed freedom of movement across the Ottomans' dominions. If they died while visiting the empire, local authorities were to respect all conditions of their wills, and if they were enslaved they were to be released as soon as they announced themselves to be Englishmen. Factories and consulates were to be set up at Aleppo, Tunis, Tripoli, and Damascus, and any disputes between English and Turkish subjects were to be adjudicated by an English consul.

Unfortunately, as soon as Harborne left Istanbul the French ambassador (jealous of such a raft of privileges) succeeded in having the agreement annulled. It became obvious that a permanent English ambassador, rather than a temporary envoy, was required, and so Harborne returned to the city in 1583. With his new rank came the predictable round of diplomatic ritual. Upon his arrival he visited the sultan and his high admiral, presenting them with gifts of "three fair mastiffs in coats of red cloth, three spaniels, two bloodhounds, one common hunting dog [and] two greyhounds." The three men then shared a drink of rose water, sugar, and spices, and Harborne embarked on six years of commendable ambassadorial service. At every opportunity he encouraged the sultan to wage war against Philip II of Spain, England's most hated enemy, and rushed to the defense of any embattled English merchant.

Harborne's arrival had distressed the ambassadors of the other European powers. The Venetian Senate sent explicit instructions to the republic's ambassador, urging him to work with his French counterpart to prevent the Englishman's accreditation. The diplomacy of Istanbul would always be blighted by rivalry. Early in the next century, the French, Venetian, and English ambassadors all conspired to stop a new Dutch envoy from receiving official recognition, even resorting to bribing Turkish officials. "[The] French envoy…went to the length of offering ten thousand sequins to upset the negotiations and although the English ambassador…at first took no steps…when it far advanced he endeavored to join with France, and on his side also offered to spend a similar sum for that same purpose."[175]

Harborne had survived similar machinations, and managed to renegotiate the trade treaty soon after his arrival at court. Its terms were soon put to the test. An English ship, the *Jesus*, had been illegally seized by the Ottoman authorities in Tunis. It had been engaged in entirely legitimate activities—transporting oil—but just before departure one of the crew had smuggled a friend onboard. This friend apparently owed money to local creditors, and as the ship headed out to sea the Turks opened fire. The ship was boarded, her cargo seized, and the crew imprisoned. With the swiftest justice it was determined that the captain and the stowaway should be hanged and the rest of the ship's complement sold off as galley slaves.

News of this outrage only reached England when one of the captives managed to send a letter to his father in Tavistock. He immediately sent news to the queen, who in turn instructed Harborne to lodge a protest with the Ottoman government. This Harborne did, and also dispatched a furious letter to the governor of Tripoli, the official responsible for the seizure of the *Jesus*. "You shall answer in another world to god alone, and this world to the [sultan] for this heinous crime committed by you against so many poor souls, which by your cruelty are in part dead and in part detained by you in most miserable captivity." All of the surviving English sailors were immediately released.

Despite such conspicuous successes, the Levant Company, the organization that oversaw trade in the empire and also paid Harborne's wages, decided that a permanent ambassadorial presence in Istanbul was too expensive. This presumably amused Harborne, who had spent much of the last six years complaining, much like Bishop Quadra earlier in the century, that service as an ambassador was bringing him close to personal financial ruin.

He returned to England with detailed accounts. He had spent nearly £5000 on housekeeping, £1372 on servants' wages, £1028 on ambassadorial apparel, £1442 on gifts, £1203 on buying back captives, and a dozen other things besides. He claimed that his salary only represented a fraction of his total expenditure. But if Harborne was bitter, he had at least done much to enhance England's reputation in Istanbul. As the writer Thomas Nashe put it in 1598, "The mercurial-breasted Mr Harborne hath echoing noised the name of our island and of Yarmouth so tritonly, that not an infant of the cur-tailed, skin-clipping pagans but talk of London as frequently as of their prophet's tomb at Mecca."[176]

Europe had learned the value of negotiating with the Turks. As in all eras, such negotiations often called for flattery. In 1541 the Habsburgs had sent Suleiman an appropriately handsome gift: "a high-standing cup of gold after the German fashion, curiously set with rich stones and a wonderful globe of silver of most rare and curious device, daily expressing the hourly passing of the time, the motions of the planets the change of the face of the moon."[177] Not to be outdone, the English would also shower the Ottomans with extravagant presents. When a new sultan came to power in 1595, Elizabeth I dispatched a special ambassador to relay her congratulations. He brought with him the most intricate of musical organs.

The organ's maker, Thomas Dallam, accompanied the embassy, which was just as well because upon arriving in Istanbul the instrument was unpacked and found to be in parlous condition. The pipes were all broken and the costly decoration ruined. Dallam spent a month restoring the organ before unveiling it during an audience with the sultan.

> First the clock struck twelve, then the chime of sixteen bells went off and played a song of four parts. That being done, two personages which stood upon the corners of the second story holding two silver trumpets in their hands did lift them to their heads and sound a tantara…in the top of the organ, being sixteen feet high, did stand a holly bush full of blackbirds and thrushes which at the end of the music did sing and shake their wings.

The sultan was entranced and asked for an encore. He was now transfixed by the self-depressing keys. Was it possible, he asked Dallam, for the organ to be played manually? It was, Dallam replied, and he would gladly have given a demonstration, but the sultan "sat so near the place where I should play that I could not come at it but I must needs turn my back towards him and touch his knee with my breeches which no man, on pain of death, might do." Amazingly, the sultan allowed Dallam to proceed and at the end of his performance filled his hand with gold coins. This might have been the Christian meeting the pagan barbarian, the Muslim encountering the infidel, but it was also astonishingly polite. If only for a moment, hatred, mistrust, and imperial hauteur had melted away.[178]

But if the Turks could be talked to and flattered, could they possibly be admired? Richard Knolles may have believed the Turks to be "the greatest terror of the world," but he could not deny their extraordinary achievements. "At this present," he wrote, "if you consider the beginning, progress and perpetual felicity of this Ottoman empire, there is in this world nothing more admirable nor strange…nothing more magnificent or glorious…nothing more dreadful or dangerous."[179] Such ambivalence toward the Ottomans—the acknowledgement of both the glory and the danger—permeated European culture. And as might be expected, it was often best articulated by ambassadors.

The Habsburg homelands represented the frontline in the engagement with the Ottomans. Hungary had been lost in 1526, her king, Lewis, perishing on the battlefield at Mohacs. Buda fell in September, and the Hungarian nobility elected Zapolyai, the voivod of Transylvania, as their new monarch. Habsburg interests in central Europe were overseen by Ferdinand, the brother of Charles V. Unhappy with Zapolyai's election, Ferdinand marched into Hungary, defeated his rival, and pronounced himself the rightful monarch. Zapolyai immediately appealed to the Ottoman sultan, who believed himself, by right of conquest, to be the arbiter of Hungarian affairs. Furious at Ferdinand's invasion, he sent his own armies northward and, as we have seen, they reached Vienna in 1529. The city did not fall, but the terrified Habsburgs had little choice but to recognize Ottoman suzerainty in Hungary. The

Turkish menace was to be met not with force of arms but with diplomacy.

Between 1555 and 1562 Ogier Ghiselin de Busbecq made four journeys from Vienna to Istanbul as the ambassador of the Holy Roman Emperor. His accounts of these memorable embassies epitomized the muddled European attitudes toward Turkish culture.

As soon as Busbecq crossed into Hungary in the winter of 1555, he was met by a Turkish escort of 150 horsemen. "It was a very pleasant spectacle to a man unaccustomed to see such sights," he remembered. With their oddly painted bucklers, bejewelled sword handles, and plumed helmets, they made Busbecq feel welcome, entertaining him in what he described as a "military manner." He met with the local governor and, given that it was December, marvelled at the sound of frogs croaking in a pond kept unseasonably warm by "sulphurous exhalations." Busbecq was troubled by the lack of decent beds, and resented having to sleep on "shaggy rugs of tapestry," but that minor complaint aside, it had been a gentle enough introduction to the Ottoman Empire.

Busbecq moved on to Buda, where the governor and his family courteously came out of the city to meet him. He soon had his first glimpse of the fabled janissaries, the empire's elite fighting corps. They had a fearful reputation but Busbecq found them more peculiar than intimidating. They visited him two by two, and after bowing "ran hastily to me and touched either my garment or my hand as if they would have kissed it," and then "forced upon me a bundle or nosegay of hyacinths or narcissus."

Indeed, the ambassador, being such a curiosity, was blessed with many visitors during his stay in Buda. Many Turks "supped with me," probably because they were so "mightily taken with the delicious sweetness of my wine." One evening, after drinking too much, Busbecq excused himself from dinner and asked his guests to leave. They obliged, but were apparently disappointed "because they had not had their full swig at the goblet." They sent Busbecq a message, asking if they might be allowed some more wine and the loan of some silver cups, "for they were willing, by my leave, to sit at it all night in some corner of the house." The ambassador happily obliged, and the Turks drank deeply until they all passed out.

This confused Busbecq. He had understood Muslims to be fiercely opposed to the drinking of alcohol. One of his visitors explained to him that, especially among the young, drunkenness was seen as merely a venial sin and, besides, they could "expect no less punishment after death for drinking a little wine than if they drank ever so much." Later, in Istanbul, Busbecq would see a man utter a hideous noise every time he was about to take a drink: "He did it," Busbecq was informed, "to, as it were, warn his soul to retire into some secret corner of his body or else wholly to emigrate and pass out of it." Guilt might thus be avoided.

Buda had once been a mighty city, Busbecq revealed, "anciently adorned with many stately palaces." Its natural beauty had endured—"It lies in a pleasant place, and in a very fruitful country. It is extended all along the brow of a hill, so that on one side it borders on rising ground, abounding with choice vineyards." But the ancient palaces had crumbled and now provided homes for weasels and mice. The Turks had little interest in renovating the ruins, however. It was an Islamic trait, Busbecq explained, "not to covet magnificent buildings," since this was a "sin of a proud lofty and aspiring mind."

A meeting with the Turkish ruler of the city on December 7th went badly. The ambassador had "sweetened him with some presents," but his complaints about the ravages of Turkish soldiers over the border in Habsburg territory went unanswered. The ambassador's next destination was Belgrade. He sailed down the Danube, which was both quicker (five days rather than twelve) and safer than travelling by land.

From there he passed into Serbia. He was satisfied with the food he received—platters "full of barley boiled to a jelly with a little piece of flesh"—but less enamored of the sleeping arrangements. He was usually expected to bed down in dormitories with his escorts, but "I did greatly abhor this sort of lodging because the eyes of all the Turks were continually upon us." Whenever possible Busbecq sought out the home of a local Christian, however humble, and pleaded for a night's shelter.

The bewitching sights continued. In Sofia he marvelled at the women, whose tall hats made them resemble "Clytemnestra or some Hecuba or other from the flourishing time of Troy." At the Bulgarian seashore in Selimbria, cooled by a Thracian breeze that brought "an incredible sweetness of air," he gathered cockles and saw dolphins sporting in the water.

Some Turkish characteristics had begun to annoy him. He was constantly expected to bribe people for information or the granting of the most basic favors. Such largesse was apparently necessary because "the Turks are so ill-natured and such under-valuers of all nations but their own, that without this open-handedness there were no living among them." Other things he found utterly fascinating. In some of the inns where he had stayed he had noticed tiny pieces of paper tucked into small cracks in the walls. He was informed that this was done out of the Islamic reverence for paper—a material on which it was possible to write the prophet's name and, therefore, not something to be rashly discarded. "I remember," Busbecq continued, "that my Turkish guides were once very angry with my servants for making use of paper to clean their posteriors."

On January 20, 1556, the ambassador finally arrived in Istanbul. He presented his gifts, visited various officials, and was even granted permission to visit the city's great mosque—ordinarily, Christians were forbidden from entering, lest they pollute so important a Muslim place of worship. Busbecq was utterly seduced by the city. "It seemed to me to be naturally placed as fit to be the mistress of the world; it stands in Europe and has Asia in view." The seafood—mackerel, tuna, and swordfish—was exquisite. The orchards would have made "pleasant homes for nymphs." "There is no place in the world," Busbecq concluded, "more pleasantly seated to the eye, nor more convenient for trades." Which made it all the more tragic that "the mother and nurse of all good arts and sciences" had fallen to the infidel a century earlier.

After several weeks Busbecq was invited to visit Suleiman the Magnificent in Cappadocia. The ruler of the Ottoman world greeted him with a "sour and frowning look" and a bow and arrow by his side. He possessed, Busbecq admitted, "a certain majesty mixed with severity in his countenance." The ambassador approached the throne, although in the wake of a recent assassination attempt his arms were tightly held to his sides by two servants. He made his speech of greeting and quietly withdrew.

The sultan was unimpressed. He had no real cause to heed the requests of the Habsburgs. Busbecq received nothing more than a temporary truce and two oversized embroidered vests that "were so heavy that I could hardly stand under them." He was not even honored with a farewell dinner, and he left the encampment mumbling about the sultan's overindulgence in wine.

He reached Istanbul on June 24th, and after spending a few days recuperating in the city's bathhouses set out for Vienna. Despite the sultan's cool reception, Busbecq had been charmed by the Ottoman Empire. It was filled with more variety than he had ever imagined. Not that the darker side of the Turkish invasions could long be forgotten. As he left Istanbul, he saw wagonloads of boys and girls from Hungary being driven into the city, destined for a life of slavery. "I could not forbear weeping and bemoaning the unhappy state of poor Christendom."

The Ottoman Empire, far more than any earlier Islamic state, engaged with western Europe. While it did not establish resident embassies until the late eighteenth century, it did tolerate, and even encourage, the expansion of the western diplomatic community in Istanbul. It also sent its own envoys far and wide. To Christendom, the Ottoman empire seemed as cruel as it was magnificent. Such was the paradox that all sixteenth-century Europeans had to fathom. But at least Busbecq had seen it for himself. When he reached Vienna, he noticed that "many persons who refused to accompany me to Istanbul, whether for fear or I know not what motive besides, wished they had gone along with me, now they saw me return in safety." But Busbecq had a quotation from Plautus especially prepared for such people: "If you will eat the kernel you must take the pains to break the nut. He does himself wrong that thinks to reap part of the fruit but takes no part of the pains"— a motto for inquisitive ambassadors everywhere.[180]

Toward the Enlightenment

13
WOTTON VERSUS SHERLEY

Continuums?

> In the midst of the most cruel and ridiculous confusion, I am
> now set down to give you a very imperfect sketch of the mad-
> dest people that the maddest times were ever plagued with...
> This, this is liberty! Genuine British liberty! This instant about
> two thousand liberty boys are swearing and swaggering by with
> large sticks.
> —Ignatius Sancho to John Spink, June 6, 1780[181]

THE ANIMOSITIES OF REFORMATION were resilient. By the
1770s, England's Roman Catholic population was small,
vulnerable, and rudderless. If Catholics had ever posed a
meaningful threat to Protestant cultural or political dominance,
that threat had surely vanished. And yet, any efforts to alleviate the
sufferings of the persecuted Catholic minority were still likely to
be met with rabid popular opposition. In 1778 Parliament passed
a Roman Catholic Relief Act. The sons and daughters of Rome
would now be entitled to buy and inherit land without restrictions,
and their priests and bishops would no longer be subject to in-
discriminate arrest. It was a severely limited variety of relief, and
dozens of discriminatory measures remained firmly entrenched in
the statute book. Nonetheless, many contemporaries still regarded

it as being woefully indulgent to the papist menace. The fear of Catholic resurgence was deeply embedded, and perhaps still lingers to some degree, in the British psyche.

Dozens of Protestant associations were established to lobby for the act's repeal. Lord George Gordon had managed to prevent the act becoming operative in Scotland, and he returned to England as a Protestant hero. Seeing an opportunity to turn burgeoning anti-Catholic sentiment against his great political rival, Lord North, Gordon accepted an invitation to become president of the London Protestant Association. He set up a petition in the foyer of his home that called for the immediate striking down of the Relief Act, and it quickly attracted thousands upon thousands of signatures.

At ten o'clock on the morning of June 2, 1780, large crowds gathered at St. George's Field, south of the River Thames, on the spot where Waterloo Station now stands. They carefully stitched together the unwieldy sheets of the petition, raised it aloft, and began their slow march toward Westminster. They were orderly at first, crossing the river and moving toward Cheapside in tidy columns. Very soon, however, less disciplined elements— prostitutes, beggars, criminals, and drunks—began swelling their ranks. As the crowds moved along Fleet Street and into the Strand, they grew ever noisier and alarmingly unruly. A dignified protest, a calm and collected presentation of the petition, was descending into chaos. By the time the marchers reached the Houses of Parliament, they had become little more than a mischievous mob.

The crowds set about harassing members of the House of Lords as they arrived for the day's parliamentary session. Those deemed unsympathetic to the petitioners' cause were simply turned away from the House. All others were made to shout out "No Popery!" and to put a blue cockade, the petitioners' emblem, in their hats. When the unpopular lord chancellor arrived, he was pulled from his coach, struck on the head, and pelted with mud. Others had the windows of their carriages smashed, their snuff boxes stolen, and the wigs pulled from their heads; still others were kicked or showered in excrement.

The more sober petitioners, appalled by such excess, started leaving for home, but this still left fourteen thousand Londoners pounding on the doors of the House, chanting anti-Catholic slogans. It was at this most opportune of moments that Lord George Gordon, the petitioner's great champion, rose in the chamber. The petition was brought forward and Gordon demanded an immediate debate on the repeal of the Relief Act. His motion was denied, discussion would have to wait until the next week, and the crowds outside were enraged. They now required victims, and with something approaching inevitability, they turned to those obnoxious symbols of Catholic intrusion—the chapels of London's Roman Catholic ambassadors.

Just before midnight a mob armed with tools and torches marched toward Lincoln's Inn Fields. They gathered outside the house of the Sardinian ambassador on Duke Street and set about dismantling his chapel. Valuable silver lamps were spirited away, all the chapel's stained glass was smashed, the vestments ripped to shreds, and a huge bonfire of pews and ornaments was set alight. By the time troops arrived to quell the riot, the chapel was engulfed in flames, and by dawn it was burned to the ground. Aside from a handful of token arrests, the arsonists succeeded in fleeing the scene. Across town, another group of protestors had turned their attention to the residence of the Bavarian ambassador on Warwick Street. A German blacksmith braved the mob and managed to rescue a handful of mass books and some church furnishings, but the rest of the chapel was ransacked and despoiled. As added recompense for their vandalistic troubles, the looters also found large amounts of tea and other contraband goods in the ambassador's house: For years, as was common knowledge, the Bavarian ambassador had proved himself a resourceful black marketeer.[182]

From his grocery shop on Charles Street, Ignatius Sancho had seen the day's frenzied events unfold. Sancho was a phenomenon. Born aboard a slave ship, he had transformed himself from an indentured butler to the English aristocracy into a respected entrepreneur and darling of the London literary establishment, and had been the first black man to vote in a British general election. The events of that infamous June day appalled him, and, one assumes that with an indignant sense of irony he set about denouncing the "worse than Negro barbarity of the populace."

The riots would continue for several days. The prisoners of Newgate would be set free, a fire at a Holborn distillery would kill hundreds—firemen mistakenly doused the flames with alcohol instead of water. The city's Irish population would be bullied and beaten by the angry mob, many of their houses razed to the ground. The Gordon riots were about more than religion: They were also the clumsy social protest of a disaffected, disenfranchised populace. But religion had a huge role to play.

Sancho remembered watching the Sardinian ambassador offer the rioters five hundred guineas "to save a painting of our Saviour from the flames, and one thousand guineas not to destroy an exceeding fine organ." They replied that "they would burn *him* if they could get at him, and destroyed the picture and organ directly."[183]

————

It was as if the previous two hundred years had never happened. The chapels of Roman Catholic ambassadors were as unpopular with eighteenth-century Protestant Londoners as they had been at the height of Reformation—the most potent reminder of confessional enmity. Unwelcome ambassadors were still the symbols of ingrained cultural difference and distrust.

⚬

On September 26, 1792, a fleet of three ships and seven hundred men embarked for China. At their head was the fifty-five-year-old Irishman and ambassador Lord George Macartney, veteran of successful embassies to Catherine the Great of Russia—as intransigent a monarch as the eighteenth century could provide. His crew contained an unusual mix of botanists and priests, musicians and translators, and his cargo was made up of the finest British manufactures. It was hoped that Wedgwood porcelain, the Birmingham steel blades of Thomas Gill, and a rich assortment of clocks, paintings, and hot-air balloons would dazzle the Chinese imperial court. They might even convince that government to take the West seriously, after centuries of disdain.

There was trade in the East, in tea, silk, and porcelain, and it was wonderfully profitable; but the English (like all other Europeans) were only allowed to pursue it within the limits of the port of Canton. And so this embassy had been dispatched to gain new privileges and greater access for English merchants, and to convince the emperor to allow a permanent English ambassador to reside in Peking. It was a bold and, to be evenhanded, a timely and entirely justified diplomatic gambit.

After a ten-month journey, via Rio de Janeiro, Java, and Vietnam, the fleet arrived at the coastal port of Dengzhou in Shandong province. Macartney and his entourage travelled by land and river toward Peking, all the while being treated with the courtesy and hospitality that envoys to China almost always enjoyed. As soon as they had arrived on Chinese soil, the emperor had sent much-needed provisions—hundreds of ducks, sheep, and chickens; ten chests of tea; and two thousand melons. They arrived at the capital on August 21st, but were informed that their meeting with the emperor would take place 120 miles to the north, at the imperial summer residence.

Macartney had already grown concerned about the imperial court's closely defined ritual. The English saw themselves as potential trading partners; to the Chinese they could only be conceived as bearers of tribute to the Son of Heaven. All envoys who came before the emperor were required to make the kowtow, a ceremony whereby a person knelt down three times and knocked his head nine times against the floor. Macartney would not countenance performing such a humiliating gesture. He was the representative of an English king, he informed the Chinese officials, and would do no more than go down on one knee before the emperor and kiss his hand. If such homage was enough for an English king, it was surely enough for a Chinese emperor. The motive of the entire embassy, after all, was to inaugurate profitable commerce between equals.

The Chinese were staggered by Macartney's revelation, but they endeavored to seek a compromise. The ambassador would be allowed to forgo the kowtow and bend one knee, although there was no question of a western barbarian kissing the emperor's hand. So it was, at seven o'clock on the morning of September 14, 1793, that the imperial court assembled in the Garden of Ten Thousand Trees. The Qianlong emperor was carried in aloft on a throne, and every person in attendance—hundreds of ministers, mandarins, soldiers, and other ambassadors—fell prostrate to the floor. Everyone, that is, except Macartney and his party. Ushered into the emperor's presence, the ambassador climbed the steps to the imperial throne, fell on one knee, and presented some enamelled watches and a letter from King George III in a gilt box. The emperor responded politely, offered Macartney a jade scepter, and listened to his bullish trade proposals.

The Chinese court had been deeply offended, however. Macartney, in an attempt to maintain his and his monarch's dignity, had ruined all hope of a diplomatic triumph—not that such a triumph had ever been especially likely. "As your ambassador can see for himself," the emperor glibly informed George III, "we possess all things. I set no value on strange or ingenious objects and have no use for your country's manufactures." There were to be no new trading privileges, no new ports opened up to English merchants, no resident English ambassadors.[184]

It was as if the previous two thousand years had never happened. Ambassadors were still the vessels of cultural rivalry and misunderstanding, the men who allowed competing worldviews to collide.

There had been Native American ambassadors in England before. In 1710, four Mohawk chiefs, representatives of the redoubtable Iroquois Confederacy, had travelled to London to request the dispatch of Christian missionaries and military assistance to oppose the French. They presented Queen Anne with Bibles and communion plate, and in their dashing red cloaks they held London society transfixed. They attended cockfights, watched a performance of *Macbeth* at the Haymarket Theatre, and had their portraits painted, rather crudely, by the Dutch artist Jan Verelst. But fifty years later, an even more spectacular party of Native American ambassadors arrived, totally unexpectedly, in Plymouth harbor.

England and the Cherokee Nation had recently fought an ill-tempered war. When a Cherokee named Ostenaca arrived unexpectedly in England aboard the HMS *Revenge* on June 16, 1762, his mission was to pledge his people's friendship to the English crown, and to consign recent unpleasantries to the past. He had been escorted to England by the naval officer Henry Timberlake. The ambassador and his two tribal companions took a coach to London, stopping off at Exeter to view the cathedral, and by June 24 they were happily ensconced in their Suffolk Street lodgings. One of their first ports of call was a tailor's shop in the Haymarket. Fitted with vibrantly colored clothes "in the mode of their own country," they were soon to be seen strolling through Kensington Gardens.

The baffled English government arranged tours of the Tower of London, St. Paul's, and the Houses of Parliament, and the lord mayor mounted a banquet in their honor at the Mansion House. Dinner invitations and inquisitive visitors began to flood in. The novelist Oliver Goldsmith was sure to pay his regards, although he regretted it after being kissed on the cheeks by Ostenaca and covered with the Cherokee's lurid face paint.

The Cherokees' visit came at a pivotal moment in Europe's discussions about the indigenous people of the Americas. Debates raged about whether men such as Ostenaca were noble savages, possessed of an idyllic, elevated, natural lifestyle, or brutish barbarians in desperate need of the cultural ministrations of Western civilization. The Cherokee embassy helped Londoners make up their minds, and there was barely a journalistic hack in the entire city who did not scribble down his conclusions about the significance of their visit.

The attentions lavished on the three Cherokees soon became oppressive, however. Newspapers began to advertise their every coming and going, giving the public advanced notice of where the men would be on any particular night. Publicans and theater-owners made tidy profits by raising their admission prices whenever the Indians were expected to visit their establishments. The embassy began to take on an unsavory, exploitative aspect—perhaps a distant echo of those Inuit that Martin Frobisher had obliged to go fishing on the River Avon two hundred years earlier. Large crowds would rush at Ostenaca and his companions wherever they went, sometimes even bursting unannounced into their lodgings. Poets began writing, in predictably stereotypical terms, about Indian scalping and sexual depravity.

The quality and significance of the embassy ought not to be diminished, however. The blend of fascination and repulsion, courtesy and exploitation, was typical.[185]

It was as if the last three millennia had never happened. Ambassadors were still providing a way for distant civilizations to meet and compare one another. It was Priscus at the court of Attila, Megasthenes in India, Rabban Sauma in Rome, Iosip Nepea in London, all over again.

It might seem that nothing much had changed. Ambassadors were still serving the same cultural purposes, still representing their nations, still provoking rows and insults, still serving in the vanguard of encounter. From the outset, indeed, this book has insisted that, elegant and convenient as such a theory might be, there is no obvious sense of progress in the history of the ambassadors. Transference there certainly was. Byzantine ideas about the ceremonial aspects of diplomacy had been emulated across Europe. Even the great Ottoman sultan Suleiman moved away from meeting visitors cross-legged on the floor and began sitting on a jewel-encrusted throne with crown and scepter in hand. That empire's notion of an organized, codified approach to foreign affairs was taken up first by the city-states of Italy and passed from there to the courts of Renaissance Europe. Greek heralds styled themselves as the sons of Hermes, and it was an identity readily adopted by generations of future ambassadors. An ambassador whose immunities had been challenged in the seventeenth century was usually able to cite, chapter and verse, instances of an ambassador whose immunities had been challenged a thousand years earlier. But wrangling about whether ancient Greece was better at diplomacy than ancient India or fourteenth-century Venice is probably—no, is assuredly—a futile pursuit.

But a lack of progress does not preclude a lack of change. These three stories from the eighteenth century are certainly reminiscent of other, older ambassadorial adventures. Much of the business and responsibility of embassy had endured for centuries. But the ambassadors of eighteenth-century Europe found themselves inhabiting a diplomatic world that was profoundly different from anything their predecessors had known. Therein lies the paradox: On one level, nothing had changed; on another, everything was in flux. A catastrophic, one might say idiotic, war in the first decades of the seventeenth century had bequeathed a peace settlement that elucidated a radical realignment in the political landscape of Europe. New theories had been proposed about the nature of international relations. And for better or worse, diplomacy was becoming ever more professional and bureaucratic in response.

It is impossible to decide if this was of benefit to the human race. Those of us in the West who live in the shadow of the 1648 Treaty of Westphalia and the elegant Natural Law theory of men like Hugo Grotius (about both of which, much more to come) usually assume that it was. Cozy notions of sovereignty, the community of nations, and inalienable human rights certainly hold sway in the West. To gainsay them is deemed heretical, and is quite possibly an intellectual mistake. That they are contingent, historical accidents can hardly be denied, however. They might be wondrous, they might be debilitating, but they are not inevitable. It is sobering, at the very least, to realize that the inhabitants of nine-tenths, perhaps even ninety-nine-hundredths, of human history would simply not have understood or respected what such notions even meant.

The remainder of the book asks, in its circuitous way, how we, in the West, adopted such assumptions. How did the orthodoxies of modern diplomacy get their start? The theorizing is harder, and comes last. The emergence of the modern professional diplomatic mentality is easier to trace, and comes first.

Where we last left it, Europe had discovered the resident ambassador. He would endure, making a choice between the ambassadorial adventurer and the ambassadorial careerist inescapable. The careerist, as any modern capital city bears witness, was triumphant, but at the end of the sixteenth century there was still time, and an ounce of hope, for the errant envoy. We will soon meet Henry Wotton, the precursor of the new ambassador. But ahead of that comes Anthony Sherley, Wotton's friend or, at least, his esteemed acquaintance. The more worthy Wotton won the day, but the colorful Sherley, for no good reason, or perhaps every good reason, was adored.

Ambassador Errant: Anthony Sherley

> *Sophy:* What powers do wrap me in amazement thus?
>   Methinks this Christian's more than mortal.
>   Sure he conceals himself! Within my thoughts
>   Never was man so deeply registered.
>   But God or Christian, or whate'er he be,
>   I wish to be no other but as he.
>   —*The Travels of the Three English Brothers,* I.i, 75–80[186]

In 1601, William Parry offered some blunt advice to the "homebred vulgars" who ridiculed the exotic stories of early modern travellers. Yes, of course some people resorted to exaggeration or outright deceit when recounting their journeys, but only because those journeys had been unutterably dull. "Diverse there are (entitling themselves travellers for crossing the narrow seas to the neighbor parts of Picardy peradventure, or the Low Countries) [who] from thence take authority to utter lies in England at their return." But for those who had travelled farther and seen astonishing sights, such deceptions were superfluous. Sadly, the majority of people refused to believe anything outside of their own "oracular experience," and dismissed good, honest travellers as fraudsters, their revelations as fantasies.

Such was the human condition, Parry mused. Men could only fathom what they themselves had seen, heard, or touched. When confronted with something new and challenging they sank into denial. They could hardly be blamed. "How would a man, from his birth confined in a dungeon or lightless cave, be brought to conceive or believe the glory and great magnificence of the visible, celestial and terrestrial globes?" Even if such a person were "suddenly transferred to the top of some mountain or lofty turret" how would he be able to understand and truly accept the "resplendent and crystalline heavens over-canopying the earth?"

Nevertheless, Parry urged his readers to try their very hardest when appraising the picaresque deeds of one of his former travelling companions and the subject of his 1601 book, *A New and Larger Discourse of the Travels of Anthony Sherley.* Sherley lived one of the most chaotic lives of the Renaissance, by turns a soldier, a privateer and, of course, an ambassador. "To write of the fashions and dispositions of the Germans and Italians," Parry explained, "were a matter not worth my pains because it is so well known to all men that knows, or have read or have heard anything." The life of Sherley allowed Parry, and a bevy of other adoring biographers, to turn to "matters more marvellous."[187]

Sherley enjoyed a respectable, if mundane early life, following the well-trodden gentry path from his Sussex birthplace to Oxford and the Inner Temple. The law hardly suited his temperament, however, and Sherley was soon indulging in more glamorous pursuits, fighting with notable bravery in the Netherlands and serving on diplomatic errands to Henry IV's France. Always eager to enhance his reputation, Sherley accepted the conspicuous honor of entry into the Order of St. Michael during one trip to Paris. Unfortunately he had not received the English government's permission, and upon his return to London he was rewarded with a spell in the Fleet Prison.

Exiled from court after his release, Sherley next experimented with married life, but when this proved intolerable he decided to turn pirate, joining a privateering expedition to the Portuguese-controlled Gulf of Guinea. It was a financial disaster, and after returning to London an impecunious Sherley gratefully accepted the earl of Essex's proposal to assist the beleaguered Cesare d'Este, the ruler of Ferrara, in his territorial war with the pope. In fact, by the time Sherley arrived in Italy, hostilities had come to an end. Undiscouraged, Sherley headed for Venice and it was there, in 1598, that the idea of a journey to Persia was first proposed. Whether the idea came from the earl of Essex or whether it was of Sherley's own devising, we will likely never know. One thing is clear, however: Sherley headed east in the pursuit of riches and prestige. He would find nothing of the first, and only a dubious variety of the second.

In the company of his brother Robert and William Parry, Sherley sought passage to the Middle East. After coming to blows with a party of Italians who had openly slandered the name of Elizabeth I, the three friends found berths on a dilapidated Greek-owned ship. After twelve perilous days, mostly taken up with keeping the vessel afloat, they reached Cyprus. Here, the Italians they had recently encountered had mischievously informed the Turkish rulers of the island that the Englishmen were either spies or pirates. Narrowly avoiding arrest, Anthony and his brother made for the safer haven of Aleppo, where they were well received and entertained by the sizeable English community. Finally, after trekking across Arabia, they came to the great kingdom of Persia. Sherley and his travelling companions were delighted, and not a little surprised, by what they found there. The people were generous, courteous, and hospitable, Parry recalled, and "upon our first entrance we thought we had been imparadised."

The travellers made for the capital, only to learn that Shah Abbas I was away on a military campaign. Safavid Persia was well accustomed to receiving ambassadors. During Sherley's stay an envoy arrived from as far away as Lahore in pursuit of a marriage between his ruler's granddaughter and the shah's eldest son. To sweeten the proposal, he offered enough money to fund three thousand soldiers for seven years. The sophisticated Persian bureaucracy even had specialized officers, including the *mehmendar bashi,* or "presenter of ambassadors," to cater to the needs of visiting envoys—providing them with lodgings and stipends and serving as their guide. Sherley did not fit such a system. He was an aberration and an adventurer, and he might very easily have been ignored. Luckily, he was deemed suitably exotic, and when news came of the shah's return, Sherley was allowed to meet him on his approach to the city. He was confronted with an eloquent reminder of Persian military prowess—the heads of 1200 enemy soldiers mounted on pikes, and a vanquished king and his sons being dragged along in chains.

To the sound of kettle drums and trumpets, Sherley and the shah discussed the Englishman's journey and homeland, and the shah seemed genuinely interested in Sherley's grand military idea. Would it not be possible, Sherley suggested, for Persia and the rulers of Europe to form an alliance against their common enemy, the Ottoman Turks of Istanbul? Over the coming weeks, the shah's affection for Sherley blossomed. The two men conversed almost every day. On one occasion, by Parry's account, the shah even summoned Sherley to his chamber at midnight, so eager was he for his new friend's counsel.

Sherley and his companions seem to have been genuinely impressed by Persia. It was a Muslim nation, so it was always to be suspected and derided to some degree, but it was afforded far more sympathy than Ottoman Turkey. The Persians, Parry opined, were excellent hunters and hawkers, and their bazaars were richly stocked with spices, medicines, and gems. Their insistence on eating on the floor was irritating, however, and their religious beliefs were patently wayward. They accepted Jesus as a prophet but insisted that "because God never had a wife, therefore Christ cannot possibly be his son." Most of all, however, the Englishmen noticed, and were grateful, that the Persians treated "all strangers with great kindness and civility."

Looking back a decade and more later, Sherley would offer the most generous portrait of the shah: He was "excellently well-shaped, of a most well-proportioned stature, strong, and active... his furniture of mind infinitely royal, wise, valiant, liberal, temperate, merciful, and an exceeding lover of justice."[188] Given what happened next, it served Sherley's interests to portray the Persian ruler as a man of wisdom and discretion. After Sherley had spent several indulgent weeks at the Persian court, the shah suddenly announced his extraordinary proposal. He would consider joining Europe in a consortium against the Turks, and he would immediately send an envoy to the courts of Christendom to negotiate the terms.

The shah had likely always aimed at such an alliance. Indeed, negotiations with Russia toward an anti-Turkish military campaign had been underway since the late 1580s. Sherley's timing was, nonetheless, exquisite. During his stay, a Turkish ambassador had visited the Persian court and behaved appallingly. He had boasted of Ottoman superiority and made exorbitant territorial demands. The shah, Sherley recalled, had responded with great dignity: "Without anything moving from his accustomed gravity," he had tempered "the justice of his indignation with the true magnanimity of his mind." Much like that Byzantine emperor who met that ill-mannered crusader with noble disdain, the shah quietly set about deflating the Turkish envoy's self-love. The might of the Ottoman emperor "might breed wonder and terror in those who were not capable of greatness," but it impressed a Persian king not one jot.

Irked by such insolence, the shah was more determined than ever to seek alliances with the European powers. His choice of ambassador was less predictable. Anthony Sherley was to do his bidding: "Because you have been the mover and persuader of this business, you also shall be the actor of it."[189]

To ensure that the rulers of Europe treated his ambassador appropriately, the shah provided Sherley with fulsome credentials:

> All you princes that believe in Jesus Christ, know you that [Sherley] has made friendship between you and me; which desire we had also heretofore granted, but there was none that came to make the way, and to remove the veil that was between us and you, but only this gentleman...the entertainment which [he] had had with me is that daily, while he has been in these parts, we have eaten together of one dish, and drunk of one cup, like two brethren. Therefore when this gentleman comes unto you Christian princes, you shall credit him as my own person.[190]

In case Sherley should grow weary of his duties during his journey, the shah insisted that his brother Robert remain behind as a hostage. This was quickly agreed to, and in the company of a Persian fellow-ambassador, Hasain Ali Beg Bayat, and an Augustinian monk from Portugal named Nicolo de Mello, Sherley embarked in May 1599. By most accounts, the monk was to prove something of a liability. Parry, with transparent anticlerical venom, reported that upon Mello's arrival in the Persian capital, he gratefully accepted rooms in Sherley's mansion and immediately hired himself a whore—a practice he kept up nightly, with an occasional foray into sodomy, for the remainder of his stay. On the long journey across the Caspian Sea and into Russia, he apparently regaled Sherley with sordid tales of seduction in the confessional, and by the time the ambassadors arrived in Moscow six months later, the two men had grown to detest each other.

It hardly made for a unified diplomatic front, and the sight of two envoys trading insults and accusations did little to impress the Russian court. Finally, his "blood already boiled with the excess of his choler's heat," Sherley, "to suppress his heat, gave the fat friar a sound box on the face," knocking him down "as if he had been struck with a thunderbolt."[191] The tsar had no intention of negotiating with such absurd ambassadors, especially after Sherley began complaining about having to walk behind the Persian ambassador during official engagements—Sherley was an Englishman and the shah's trusted envoy, he insisted, and deserved precedence.

The Russian stage of their mission now in tatters, Sherley and his Persian counterpart travelled on to Prague in November 1600, trying and failing to recruit the support of the emperor Rudolf, and from there they went on to Rome. The two ambassadors spent most of their time arguing, swapping accusations of theft and espionage, and campaigning to secure better lodgings than the other.

It had been a diplomatic fiasco, and Sherley knew as much. In truth, the Western powers had learned to accept the reality of Ottoman power in the Near East: Indeed, they had learned to exploit its economic advantages. The prospects for some latter-day crusade were always meagre. What Sherley did help foster, however, was Persian curiosity about the West. Over the next years and decades, Persian embassies would travel to Portugal, Holland, and France, ostensibly seeking military alliances but also hoping to foster joint ventures in the silk trade.

Abandoning his brother Robert to his fate, Sherley gave up on the embassy and, from March 1602, offered his services as a spy in Venice. When this won him too much notoriety, he returned to Prague and accepted the emperor's offer of a position as an envoy to Morocco. Here, he lived far beyond his means and did his utmost to offend the court in Marrakech. Invited to a banquet, Sherley rode into the emperor's palace on horseback and refused to dismount, despite the loud protests of the assembled courtiers.

Riddled with debt, and with such crass breaches of etiquette behind him, Sherley next headed for Spain. Occasional flirtations with piracy failed to alleviate his financial woes, however, and the Spanish king, Philip III, resolved, out of pity for a man so fallen in dignity, to grant Sherley a small annual pension of 3000 ducats. Over the next years, his name occasionally cropped up in the writings of travellers and diplomats. In 1619, an English ambassador in Madrid met an Anthony Sherley who was "as full of vanity as ever he was, making himself believe that he shall one day be a great prince, when for the present he wants shoes to wear."[192]

The remarkable thing about Sherley is not what he achieved, but the reception of his story in England. For all the upheavals that the diplomatic profession had undergone during the sixteenth century, there was still a healthy appetite for romantic, exotic ambassadorial tales.

William Parry published his account of Sherley's Persian adventure, and Sherley, adding wordsmith to his long list of accomplishments, would soon provide his own. In 1607 Anthony Nixon added to the chorus of adulation with *The Three English Brothers*—"His fame and renown," Nixon wrote adoringly of Sherley, "is known and made glorious to the world by his honourable plots and employments against the enemies of Christendom."[193] In the summer of that year, the Anthony Sherley story took to the London stage. Deriving their tale largely from Nixon's book, the playwrights John Day, William Rowley, and George Wilkins mounted successful performances of *The Travels of the Three English Brothers*. The mastermind behind both Nixon's book and the play was probably Thomas Sherley, who was eager to sustain the public's interest in his two beleaguered brothers, both of whom, lest it be forgotten, were still stranded far from home.

The play is not a masterpiece of the English stage, but it has much to tell about the English worldview. In a sense, it *is* the English worldview of the early seventeenth century. The idea of a noble Englishman impressing an Islamic ruler so much that he was willing to entrust him with a delicate diplomatic mission flattered English pride. It provided a counterblast to the prevailing political reality of the Age of Discovery, whereby foreign potentates either ignored English ambassadors or, at best, treated them with disdain. As ever, the history of the ambassadors was not simply about tangible diplomatic achievements. It was also about the use cultures made of ambassadorial myths to assert their superiority.[194]

And yet, as gratifying as all this must have been, there is something of the relic about Anthony Sherley, whether in his historical or fictional incarnation. There would always be quixotic ambassadors, but the world, for good or ill, had moved on. The future of diplomacy now lay with men like Henry Wotton.

Henry Wotton

> A noble Englishman, a youth adorned with all the virtues, who
> has lived many years abroad in order that, returning home at
> length, he might truly recall the account of Ulysses, that he had
> seen the cities of many men, and known their minds. Wherever
> he comes, therefore, his first care is to meet with those from
> whose company he may depart a better and a wiser man.
> —Isaac Casaubon, on the young Henry Wotton[195]

In October 1637, the sixty-nine-year-old Sir Henry Wotton
composed his will. He had led a more demure life than Anthony
Sherley, but one that was no less uncommon.

> In the name of God, Almighty and All-merciful, I Henry Wot-
> ton, Provost of his majesty's college by Eton, being mindful of
> mine own mortality, which the sin of our first parents did bring
> upon all flesh, do by this last will and testament thus dispose of
> the poor things which I shall leave in this world. My soul I be-
> queath to the immortal God my Maker, Father of our Lord
> Jesus Christ, my blessed Redeemer and Mediator...My body I
> bequeath to the earth: if I shall end my transitory days at or
> near Eton, to be buried in the chapel of the said college, as the
> fellows shall dispose thereof, with whom I have lived (my God
> knows) in all loving affection. Or if I shall die nearer Bocton
> Malherbe in the County of Kent, then I wish to be laid in that
> parish church, as near as may be to the sepulchre of my good
> father, expecting a joyful resurrection with him in the day of
> Christ.[196]

It was the last testament of a good Protestant, free from any mention of the Virgin Mary or the intercession of the saints. Wotton
was confident that he was included among the elect destined to
reign in heaven, but this was none of his own doing. He had not
earned his salvation through good works, it had simply been
granted to him, as was predestined to happen, by God's "mere

grace." But then, Henry Wotton had lived his entire life, and fashioned his diplomacy, as a good Protestant should.

He had also travelled. To Charles I, "my most dear sovereign and master of incomparable goodness," he left portraits of four Venetian doges, "in whose time I was there employed, with their names written on the back-side, which hang in my ordinary dining room." Charles was also to receive "a table of the Venetian college, where ambassadors had their audience" and "the picture of a duke of Venice, hanging over against the door, done either by Titian or some other principal hand long before my time." Wotton beseeched Charles that "the said pieces may remain in some corner of any of his houses, for a poor memorial of his most humble vassal."

Henry Rich, Earl of Holland, was to receive a crystal that Wotton had bought in the Alps. John Bargrave, a dean of Canterbury, was left a viola da gamba, "which has been twice in Italy, in which country I first contracted with him an unremovable affection." Sir Francis Windebank was promised "the *Four Seasons* of old Bassano, to hang near the eye of his parlour, which I bought at Venice, where I first entered into his most worthy acquaintance." Wotton was disposing of the precious souvenirs collected over the course of an illustrious, if turbulent, diplomatic career.[197]

Fresh from Oxford in 1589, he had played the law student in Heidelberg and the tourist in Frankfurt and Vienna. His mastery of the German language was almost total, or so he boasted, and this served him well as he entered Italy in the winter of 1591. Elizabethan Englishmen, perhaps like any other generation of Englishmen, were ambivalent about Italy. One could hardly ignore its cultural riches or classical pedigree, but it was also a nest of papists.

William Cecil, Elizabeth I's chief minister, had advised fathers: "Suffer not thy sons to pass the Alps, for they shall learn nothing there but pride, blasphemy and atheism."[198] "What is an Englishman Italianated?" Roger Ascham had asked. "He that by living and travelling...brings home into England...the religion, the learning, the policy, the experience, the manners of Italy."[199] In the next century, Sir Thomas Roe—an ambassador who travelled as far as Constantinople and Moghul India—encouraged his friend Sir Francis Fare to study Italian history and to take in the sights of Florence and Genoa, but also cautioned that he would "see many gods there served, but you must pass like an Israelite and bow to none...Let none of these specious paintings deceive you and, if you doubt, fly only to the oracle, God's book."[200] One travel writer complained that all that an English visitor was likely to get from a trip to Italy was an empty purse and an upset stomach, but in 1616 James I expressed graver concerns. Young men were witnessing the Catholics' rites, being "corrupted with their doctrine," and "poisoned with their positions." They were returning "into their countries both averse to religion and ill-affected to our state and government."[201]

These were trepidations that Henry Wotton undoubtedly shared, but he was nonetheless determined to see Italy for himself, especially the den of papist iniquity that was Rome. It had always been possible for English Protestants to visit the Holy City. They would present themselves to Cardinal William Allen, the unofficial overseer of English affairs in the city, and be given a few closely monitored days to visit their fill of churches, monuments, and galleries. They would be treated courteously but their freedom of movement would often be curtailed. This would not do for Henry Wotton. He wanted to witness the evils of Catholicism, the shady workings of Roman politics, at first hand, without lets or hindrances. This was where his fluency in German became extremely useful.

He posed as a native German student and made his way to the city with a German noble with whom, despite his religion, Wotton "entered into a very intrinsical familiarity." In fact, the German was magnificently lacking in piety and "given much to women." This suited Wotton perfectly. A man so distracted by his own vices was less likely to notice that his travelling companion was an impostor.

Nor did Wotton opt for an inconspicuous entry into Rome. Sneaking into the city would only raise suspicions. Instead, he donned extravagant clothes, "with a mighty blue feather in a black hat." He was pointed at in the street, which was discomfiting, but no one ever imagined that he was an Englishman. Englishmen simply did not wear such dandyish costumes.

It all allowed Wotton to engage in a reconnaissance mission of which he was inordinately proud. As he wrote to his friend Edward Zouche:

> No man containing himself within his allegiance to her majesty has seen more concerning the points of Rome than I have done. The Whore of Babylon I have seen mounted on her chair, going on the ground, reading, speaking, attired and disrobed by cardinals...Certain other private points, which are not to be committed unto letter (because I know not the event of a piece of paper) I will defer until the rendering of myself unto your honour's sight and service.

Wotton was already proving himself a cunning gatherer of intelligence, a talent that would serve him well in his coming ambassadorial career. He offered a useful pen portrait of the pope and accounts of recent papal legislation dealing with everything from the punishment of bandits, to the treatment of Jews, to the devaluation of the Bolognese currency. As for Rome, the pope had at least made life harder for whores: "All dishonest women of open profession are prohibited to wear any sort of silk or gold, either in suits or lace, [or] to turn up or curl their hair after the manner of Rome." Not that this softened Wotton's conclusion about the city. The place was beautiful, but ravaged by sin and heresy: "Her delights on earth are sweet and her judgements in heaven heavy."[202]

The next few years were filled with adventures that even Anthony Sherley would have relished. Wotton entered the service of the earl of Essex (who had also sponsored some of Sherley's adventures), joining him on his anti-Spanish expeditions to Cadiz and the Azores. He also followed the earl to Ireland in 1599, where he took part in negotiations with the Irish rebels led by the earl of Tyrone. A treaty was secured but its terms appalled Elizabeth I. Essex, who would soon foment a rebellion of his own, fell from favor and Wotton thought it an opportune moment to leave his service. He once more made for the continent, stopping off at Lucca and Pisa before reaching Florence in the spring of 1601. It was here that Wotton met Anthony Sherley. As chaotic as his mission was, Sherley at least did history one service by introducing Wotton to the grand duke of Tuscany, the man who would launch his ambassadorial career.

The grand duke, Ferdinand, had learned of a plot to assassinate James VI of Scotland. He asked Wotton to travel to Dumbarton as his envoy. He was to carry warnings and a trunk of medicines and antidotes if such warnings came too late. Once again, Wotton took on a disguise, this time posing as "Ottavio Baldi," an Italian merchant. He travelled via Germany and Denmark and reached the

Scottish coast in the first week of September. He rushed to James's court and introduced himself as an Italian merchant bearing tidings from Tuscany. James agreed to meet with him that evening and Wotton, still retaining his disguise, addressed the monarch in fluent Italian. He then approached James and whispered in his ear "in his own language, that he was an Englishman, beseeching him for a more private conference." James agreed, and that evening Wotton explained the real reason for his visit to a grateful monarch.[203]

James was an excellent ally to have made. In less than two years, with the passing of Elizabeth I, he would be crowned as James I of England. Upon hearing the news of his accession, Wotton wrote to Robert Cecil inquiring whether "it may now please your honour to receive a poor traveller into the public obligation?"[204] James was delighted to offer his patronage to Henry Wotton. A seasoned traveller and an accomplished linguist with influential contacts across Europe, he had the makings of an ideal ambassador. He was offered positions in France and Spain, but Wotton chose a posting in Venice, the city that would serve as the fulcrum of his diplomatic career.

<hr />

When Wotton left for Venice on July 19, 1604, he was accompanied by a typical seventeenth-century ambassadorial retinue. A chief secretary, responsible for arranging the ambassador's diary and keeping a register of his activities, was joined by two assistant secretaries, whose time would mostly be taken up with translating documents. A steward, charged with housekeeping and maintaining the mission's accounts, a chaplain, and a physician made up the suite. The upkeep of the household was the ambassador's sole responsibility. He received a per diem wage of £3 6s. 8d., as well as allowances for travel, relocation, and special expenses. In theory, this salary was sufficient to maintain an embassy abroad. In reality, James I's government was often sluggish in releasing payment—a failing that Wotton, like generations of earlier diplomats, endlessly remarked on.

When an ambassador first arrived in Venice, as Wotton did on September 3, he did so without any great pomp. He was expected to quietly enter the city, announce his presence, and await the pleasure of the Venetian government. After two days he would be taken by gondola to the island of Santo Spirito out in the lagoon, where he would be met by a party of senators. The more senators who deigned to attend, the more important an ambassador was deemed to be. The senators and the ambassador would then row back to Venice and, on the next day, an initial audience with the doge would be arranged.[205]

In theory, political power in Venice resided with the Senate. In reality it belonged to the Collegio—a body made up of the doge and the twenty-five most influential senators, who met in the ducal palace. It was here, and only here, that ambassadors would go about their business. A man like Wotton would visit the Collegio, sit by the doge's side, and make his requests and arguments. Minutes would be taken, the doge would consult with his counsellors, and decisions would be reached and related in due course. In theory, the ambassador was to have no other diplomatic conversations with influential Venetians, although, naturally, such rules were unofficially breached from time to time. Any astute ambassador also needed to gather his own information, and Wotton established a thriving network of informants across Venice and as far afield as Rome, Turin, and Milan. Nor was he above robbing the posts or inserting agents into Jesuit communities. As he explained in one letter home in which he requested additional funds, "The invisible part of my expense will exceed the apparent: for I find knaves dearer than honest men, and in this country fully as necessary."[206]

In a mirror image of the duties of a Catholic ambassador in Protestant England, part of Wotton's remit was to protect English travellers from the lures of Catholicism—"the restraint of his majesty's subjects abroad," as he put it, "from that foul contagion." He also genuinely believed that he might be able to turn Venice into a Protestant republic. It was a ludicrous idea, but one that Wotton pursued with considerable panache.[207]

Relations between Rome and Venice had always been tense. Venice prized her independence and resented papal interference, even in spiritual matters. In recent years Rome had been scandalized when Venice taxed local clergy without seeking papal permission, and had roundly criticized new laws that required the granting of governmental approval before any new churches or monasteries could be built. Rome lost all patience when, in 1605, Venice arrested two priests and refused to hand them over to the ecclesiastical authorities.

Rome's protests went ignored, and on April 17, 1606, the pope issued a bull of interdict and excommunication. It was now illegal for Roman Catholics to so much as take communion within the republic's borders. The doge simply told his people to ignore the papal ruling and continue with their devotions as normal. The ambassadors of Rome and Venice withdrew from their respective postings, and the Jesuit order was banished from Venetian soil.

Many Catholics were confronted with an awkward crisis of conscience, a choice between loyalty to their spiritual or their temporal rulers. The Benedictines in the city hit on an elegant solution. They found, Wotton reported, "a notable way to delude the pope's authority not yet daring to deny it…they have caused a chest to be made without a lock, fast nailed on all sides, and in the top thereof a hole, into which they throw all letters that are directed to their convent without exception, lest they might receive some prohibition from their general, and so mean to save their consciences by way of ignorance."[208]

Wotton suffered from no such qualms and was plainly delighted with the brewing conflict. As a respected diplomat, he was in an ideal position to further alienate Venice from the Holy See. Whenever his counsel was sought in the Collegio, he urged the doge to strike out for Venetian independence. He also seemed to have found an ally in Paolo Sarpi, recently appointed as the Republic's official theologian and the author of virulently antipapal and anti-Jesuit tracts. By June 8, 1606, Wotton was fully expecting war to break out between Venice and the papacy, and it was at this crucial moment that he showed more initiative than his masters back in London might have wanted.

Without consulting the English government, he began to suggest to the doge and his council that if Venice took up arms against Rome, James I of England, Henry IV of France, and a number of German Protestant states would probably rally to his cause. Wotton had plainly overstepped the bounds of his authority, and upon hearing of his overtures London told him to desist. In fact, his plans of a grand alliance had already begun to falter with the arrival of the French ambassador Cardinal de Joyeuse. France had no more intention than had England of fighting the pope, and Henry IV had dispatched an envoy to mediate between Venice and Rome. If an accommodation could be reached it would bestow considerable prestige on the French.

The cardinal's arrival clearly irked Wotton—it "has over-thrown my reason" he reported on February 16, 1607. He was intensely jealous of the new ambassador's reception: Sixty senators had gone out to meet him in the lagoon, "in their best robes, with the barges of the prince, whereas other ambassadors are commonly received in gondolas." A new star in Venice's diplomatic firmament not only wrecked Wotton's plans to steal the city away from the Roman Catholic fold, it also lessened his personal standing.

Joyeuse was successful in his campaign to reconcile Rome and Venice. In fact, Wotton's unauthorized promise of English military help had actually strengthened the Venetian's bargaining position, and they emerged with a very satisfactory outcome: There would be no changes in the laws that Rome had criticized, and the Jesuit order would not be allowed to return.

For all that, it had been an embarrassing few months for Wotton. Nonetheless, he continued to dream of the conversion of Venice, hatching plans to establish Protestant ceremonies and asking for Protestant books to be shipped into the republic from England. He continued, probably erroneously, to insist that Paolo Sarpi was, at heart, sympathetic to the Protestant cause, and in September 1607 even sent his portrait to the king, hoping it would give "some pleasure unto his majesty to behold a sound Protestant as yet in the habit of a friar."[209]

But Wotton had hopelessly misread the religious climate. Venice was, and would remain, a Catholic bastion. It was a lesson that Wotton neglected to learn. In 1609 James I published a book defending the oath of allegiance, which was now to be taken by all English subjects. In the wake of the Gunpowder Plot, it was envisaged as a way of testing Catholic loyalty. *A Premonition to All Most Mighty Monarchs, Kings, Free Princes and States of Christendom* caused something of a stir.

"The principal subject of discourse at present through Italy," Wotton reported on July 23, "is our good master's excellent work." James had sent copies of the book around Europe, and it had received mixed reviews, not least because within its pages he referred to the pope as the Antichrist. But if it had been refused entry into Spain, Wotton calculated, "here no doubt it will be kissed."

It was a ludicrously naïve assumption. Wotton reported that the doge was "a little confined within his chamber by a humour fallen down into one of his legs," but the ambassador eagerly looked forward to presenting him with a copy of James's book. But how was a Catholic ruler expected to react to a tract in which his church's spiritual leader was mocked and slandered. There were clues all across Italy. The grand duke of Tuscany had ordered the book burned; the duke of Savoy had not even allowed it to cross his borders.

On July 25, Wotton presented the doge with his copy, beautifully adorned with a gold and crimson binding. The doge was in an impossible position. He did not want to offend the king of England, so he "kissed the book with a very cheerful and ingenuous countenance," and told Wotton to thank his master for taking the trouble to send it. But as soon as Wotton had left, the doge gave orders for the book to be locked away—forever—in the palace chancery.

Wotton simply did not appreciate the colossal error of judgement he had made. Even two weeks later he was still reporting that people all over Venice were asking for copies of the book, telling James that "I think on my conscience if one of your majesty's best ships were laden therewith and sent to this port we should find means to vent them." Within a fortnight, however, Wotton's optimism was utterly shattered.

The doge, inevitably, had no intention of allowing the circulation of such a book within his city. "It may please his majesty to be informed," Wotton wrote home on the twenty-eighth, "that, since the acceptance of his book here in that kind manner (which I have formerly advertised), there hath order been given to all booksellers of this town, out of the office of the inquisition, to consign immediately to the general inquisitor all the copies that have or shall come to their hands."

The ambassador assumed that the papal nuncio was responsible for the outrage, though of course it had been the doge's own doing. Wotton perceived the banning of the book as a rank insult to James I's honor and dignity, and on September 11th he said as much to the doge and his council. "I told them...that if the king of Great Britain, my master, were the most inconsiderable prince of Europe, yet did the love which he bore this state merit more respect than I found in so just a complaint as I had made. That to suffer his book now to be forbidden was a greater affront than not to have received it...I demanded of them either the personal chastisement of the inquisitor for so presumptuous an act...or otherwise some equivalent public demonstration of their respect toward his majesty."

When no apology was forthcoming, Wotton resigned his office and stormed away from the ducal palace. It was a gross overreaction, but Venice was still eager to maintain good relations with England. A special ambassador was sent to London to reassert the republic's affection for James I and, in its turn, the English government scolded Wotton for behaving so petulantly. Wotton apologized to James, "beseeching your majesty to forgive the immoderation of my proceeding," and then made his peace with the republic, assuring the doge that with the dispatch of a special ambassador to London, English honor had been satisfied.[210]

For several months Wotton continued in his duties as a respected, if now somewhat damaged ambassador, but it was clear that his recall to London would likely please all concerned. In the spring of 1610, he departed, though not before reporting the arrival of Galileo Galilei on the Italian scientific stage—or, as Wotton described him, "the mathematical professor at Padua who by the help of an optical instrument (which both enlarges and approximates the object) invented first in Flanders and bettered by himself has discovered four new planets rolling about the sphere of Jupiter, besides many other unknown fixed stars."[211]

After a brief mission to Savoy, Wotton returned to Whitehall and life as a courtier. Several years earlier he had visited Augsburg and, always eager to flaunt his learning, had composed a proverb for his host's commonplace book. "An ambassador," he quipped, "is an honest man sent to lie abroad for his country." In the original English it was a witty enough idea—the word "lie" carrying the double meaning of *residing* abroad and *being untruthful* abroad. Unfortunately—and it was a piece of extraordinarily bad luck—when James came to hear of the aphorism, it had been translated into Latin. "Legatus est vir bonus peregre missus ad mentiendem rei publicae causa." Here, there was no double meaning, all the playfulness had disappeared, and it looked as if Wotton had been making a cold, cynical comment about the mendacity of English ambassadors.[212]

Wotton tried to explain but James was furious, and several months of official disfavor ensued. His ambassadorial career did begin to revive as the decade progressed. First he was sent to The Hague to contribute to, frankly, tedious territorial negotiations over lands on the border between Holland and the Empire. Finally, in July 1616, Wotton was summoned back to Venice.

It was not a successful mission, and by May 1618 he was begging to be recalled. Venice was not quite done with Henry

Wotton, however, and—with some reluctance—he made one last embassy to the city in 1621. From the outset, Wotton felt isolated and undervalued. Upon his arrival only eighteen or nineteen senators came out to meet him in the lagoon—he was accustomed to seeing sixty. The doge offered a halfhearted explanation: Presumably each senator had assumed that all of his colleagues would go to greet such an esteemed ambassador and had not thought it necessary to join the delegation himself. Wotton politely accepted this tenuous theory but he was not impressed. With the petulance that was now becoming characteristic, he simply refused to visit the doge and his council for a full nine months.

Indeed, this incident touched on an issue that obsessed Wotton and every one of his ambassadorial counterparts. The diplomat, if he was to be successful, had to be respected. He must, at all costs, preserve his dignity and his standing. When anyone, whether his host or his fellow ambassadors, undermined him, he had a duty to protest. As in so many earlier eras, debates about ambassadorial dignity and precedence dominated—one might say distracted—seventeenth-century diplomacy, and deserves a closer look.

In July 1618 Wotton's steward, Edward Leete was attacked. Leete had been sent to proffer dinner invitations to two English noblemen. He had been returning home, alone and unarmed, in a borrowed gondola. As he approached the city arsenal he was spotted by the captain of the watch, "a ruffian-like fellow," who was a shipwright by day. Being a master of this vital profession, "of so singular use to the state," the government was "now and then contented to wink at his mad humours." With his friends, the shipwright dragged Leete out of his gondola, threw him into a filthy room in the arsenal, and kept him under lock and key until the next morning. The shipwright returned to release Leete and boldly announced that "if he had not the night before said he did belong to the ambassador of the king of England he would have let him go."

On hearing this sorry tale, Wotton was furious. An attack on his steward was an attack on his own dignity. He rushed to the Council of Ten, the governmental body responsible for criminal affairs, and demanded the shipwright's arrest. Within hours the culprit "was snatched up in the open place of St. Mark's and thence carried to close prison." Deciding on a suitable punishment was less straightforward. Wotton was adamant and demanded "sentence against him proportional to his offence, both for violating the immunity of my family and especially for his opprobrious words whereby the king's honour was touched and scandal put upon our nation."

The Council referred the matter to the Senate, but Wotton would brook no procrastination. He warned the government that "I could appear no more in the seat of ambassadors (which is at the right hand of the duke) after such an indignity and violation without some public judgement to satisfy the world." Thus harried, the Senate sentenced the shipwright to perpetual imprisonment, *senza luce*, "never to be freed without my assent and desire." Wotton, who could now afford to be magnanimous, "did instantly deliver him, as not delighting in his misery."[213]

It was not only assaults on his immediate entourage that damaged an ambassador's reputation, however. On July 7, 1618, seven English ships dropped anchor off the Dalmatian coast. Upon coming ashore they met with another English crew who boasted about their unusually high wages. The new arrivals, who were being paid much less, decided to mutiny and refused to return to their ships until their wages were increased. The captains of the crews were unable to placate the angry sailors, although some lower-ranking officers were making progress. It was at this point that the Venetian captain Piero Barbarigo entered the fray.

He summarily ordered the arrest of all the sailors, carrying them in chains to his ships. The next day he put the officers on trial and had eight of them hanged, during which he "very inhumanly lay upon his pavilion laughing at that cruel spectacle." Mutiny was a serious matter, Wotton admitted to the doge, but it hardly deserved such brutal and unusual punishment—especially when the mutineers were Englishmen. "It is surely," Wotton wrote home, "in all circumstances a most inhuman piece of justice and worthy, in my poor opinion, to be there expostulated with the Venetian ambassador at the council-table...especially the point of the general's looking on, and feeding his eyes with the blood of our men, which would scant have become any of Caligula's generals."[214]

Ultimately, of course, it was insults to his own person and character that most concerned an ambassador. "I was taking the air in my gondola," Wotton wrote on December 31, 1609, "and being told of a galley newly come in wherein was an English slave unjustly detained, I thought it by duty and charity in me to understand his case." Upon his reaching the galley, a Spanish-bred Greek brought out the slave and struck him down "with a great cudgel before my face and beside, for my approaching so near, [gave] me very uncivil language with some menacement." Once again Wotton demanded retribution, and the sailor was sentenced to life imprisonment.[215]

Some slights were far more subtle, however. Ambassadors had always been obsessed with precedence, with not being made to look inferior to their peers. We might remember Liudprand of Cremona's anger at being given a worse seat at dinner than a Bulgarian ambassador in tenth-century Constantinople. Or we might remember Anthony Sherley competing with his Persian colleague for better lodgings in seventeenth-century Rome.

Most polities established a hierarchy of ambassadors, granting certain privileges to some, preferential treatment to others. When relations between such polities soured, privileges might be stripped away. In fourteenth-century Constantinople the representatives of Genoa and Pisa were invited to dine with the emperor on Sundays: The representative of Venice, a city fallen out of favor, was not.[216] The issues over which ambassadors competed were sometimes faintly ludicrous. Should one ambassador meet another at the foot or at the top of the stairs? How many horses should a particular ambassador be allowed in his equipage? Should one ambassador hold the door for another ambassador or shake him by the hand?

Such petty squabbles could be infuriating, as Wotton knew only too well. During his mission to The Hague in 1614, he had grown increasingly impatient with the delegates wrangling over seating and speaking order.

> Thus after some little debatement about the persons and qualifications, we are met together with one intent (according to the outward appearance) in this town. But to bring us here altogether in the same room, in the qualities that we bear, there is no possible means devisable by the conceit of man, considering the sundry disputes concerning [precedence] which distract this body. For neither will Brandenburg give place to Neubourg, being the heir apparent of an electoral house, nor Neubourg to him, being (since the death of his father) an absolute prince.

The [Dutch] States will likewise by no means give way to the
Archdukes, and Monsieur Schonberg hath also acquainted me
(to my no small wonder) that they disputed the precedence
with the elector [Palatine] his master or, to speak more properly, with the duke of Zweibrucken, his master's representative
at the time of the baptism of my Lady Elizabeth's child, which
doth make the said Schonberg now abstain from all intermeet-
ings of the state deputies here, save at their known lodgings, lest
he should call this point again into question, which cannot be
touched without much indignity.[217]

It was confusing and it was absurd.

There was, in theory, a set hierarchy of diplomatic representatives. In theory, then, if all ambassadors abided by this scheme then
rows over precedence could be avoided. Louis XIV of France, of
course, had little respect for theories. Notionally, the representatives
of the Holy Roman Empire were the highest-ranked secular ambassadors (ministers of the Holy See often enjoyed special status).
The Holy Roman Emperor, after all, was the descendant of
Charlemagne. The Holy Roman Emperor was, in reality, a withered, impotent ruler, and Louis XIV—Europe's most powerful
ruler—had no intention of allowing *his* ambassadors to be sub-
servient to the empire's.

When the Turkish grand vizier received the imperial ambassador with conspicuous honors in 1687, the French ambassador demanded equal treatment. When the grand vizier refused, the
ambassador, knowing the mind of his king, threw down his documents in disgust. The vizier later claimed he had been struck, the
ambassador spent some time in jail, and the outright severing of
relations between the two nations was only narrowly averted.[218]

Louis was no more willing to give place to the ambassadors of
Spain. An important, and potentially disruptive, diplomatic event

was the arrival of a new ambassador in a city. There were many celebrations and ceremonies and just as many opportunities to row about precedence. The centerpiece of the new ambassador's induction was a grandiose carriage ride through the city's streets. It was common practice for other ambassadors to avoid the ceremony, thus preventing disputes about where each envoy's carriage ought to be in the line of procession.

In 1661, when a new Swedish ambassador was about to arrive in London, Louis deliberately ordered his ambassador to take part in the ceremony and to make sure of securing pole position in the procession. Lest any arguments be provoked, the ambassador was to attend the ceremony with five hundred armed men. Not to be outdone, the Spanish king gave his ambassador in London identical orders, only he was to employ the services of two thousand soldiers. The outcome was inevitable. The two ambassadors battled it out for the head of the procession, shots were fired, and a number of lives were lost.[219]

Diplomatic relations between France and Spain were broken off and Louis dispatched a final envoy to Madrid to demand an apology. Such was France's political and military dominance at this period that, ultimately, Spain had little choice but to capitulate. An envoy was sent to Versailles and in front of the assembled diplomatic corps was made to read out loud a humiliating promise that Spain would from now on "abstain from competition with [Louis's] ambassadors and ministers in all public ceremonies that [Spain's] ambassadors and ministers might attend."

Ambassadors were the representatives of kings, and preserving their dignity was simply one more way for those kings to compete. It was the diplomatic equivalent of having more mistresses or better musicians at one's court, or building Potsdam to rival Versailles.

Sometimes, however, the individual egos of ambassadors certainly became involved. Wotton remembered an incident in Vienna, when the newly arrived ambassador from Parma was visited first by his counterpart from France, and next by his counterpart from Spain. Etiquette demanded that visits should be returned in the order in which they were given, so in this instance the minister from Parma ought to have visited his French colleague first. Instead, his first visit was to the Spanish ambassador, on the grounds that their two rulers were blood related. It seems an infinitesimally minor incident, but the French ambassador was outraged. "Concealing his passion," he ordered a servant to invite Parma's ambassador to pay his overdue visit, "and gave precise order to his gentleman, first to let him descend from his coach and then to shut the gate against him." The Parmesan ambassador was left standing in the street, "flaming like a furnace," as the avenged French ambassador gleefully told Wotton.[220]

In the last years of his final Venetian embassy, Wotton had more urgent problems with which to contend. His career would end with a moment of humiliation. Antonio Foscarini had been the Venetian ambassador to London between 1611 and 1615. Some years after his return to Venice, his enemies accused him of holding secret, conspiratorial meetings with foreign ambassadors. The charges were false, but this was not discovered until after Foscarini had been tried and sentenced to death. Wotton remembered the sight of Foscarini hanging by one leg from the gallows, "from break of day until sunset, with all imaginable circumstances of infamy, his very face having been bruised with dragging on the ground: though some did consider that for a kind of favour rather than disgrace, that he might be the less known."[221]

Wotton would soon have a very personal interest in Foscarini's downfall. Rumors, again almost certainly unfounded, began to circulate that Foscarini had held his illicit meetings in the home of the English noblewoman Alethea Talbot, the countess of Arundel. Wotton received word that the Venetian government was planning to ask the countess to leave the republic. At the time, she was residing at her villa outside the city, and Wotton immediately sent a message that she should remain where she was and, under no circumstances, to put herself at risk by entering Venice.

It was terrible advice. First, Wotton had no irrefutable evidence that the government planned to move against the countess. Second, even if the government was so minded, it behooved the countess to act with courage rather than cowardice and confront her accusers. Anything else would be a tacit admission of guilt. This was precisely what Alethea Talbot told Henry Wotton, after she arrived, against all his advice, at his mansion in the city. She demanded that he accompany her to the doge's palace. The next morning, the doge and his council received the countess with great courtesy, promising her that there was no question of her being asked to leave Venice.

The countess was not satisfied, however: something that the doge fully realized. Formal resolutions proclaiming her innocence were produced; she was even sent costly confectioneries; and, finally, was invited back to the Collegio to hear the Senate's resolution read aloud. It was an embarrassing meeting for Henry Wotton, since he had been required to provide his own account of recent events. He had to reveal, in other words, that it was he who had advised the countess to remain outside the city. All in attendance realized what a gross error of judgement this had been, and Wotton's attempts to justify his actions fell on deaf ears.[222]

It was an inglorious end to a worthy, if sometimes joyless, diplomatic career. For the next months Wotton went gingerly about his duties, and heard with great sadness of the death of Paolo Sarpi, the man he had once thought might lead Venice toward Protestantism. In the spring of 1623 he asked for leave to return home, and after waiting to see the election of a new doge, he bade farewell to the Venetian government on September 13. The doge (a former ambassador himself) thanked Wotton for his service and promised to uphold the long, loving friendship between the republic and the English king, "of whose wisdom and splendour and royal integrity...he had himself been a witness." The speech struck Wotton as sincere and it impressed him: It was "uttered so seriously that he seemed to fetch it out of his bowels." Venice, a city Wotton had both loved and hated, was in safe hands.[223]

Wotton returned to England, indulging his passion for art and taking up a position as provost of Eton College. His diplomatic career had been flawed, but it had also been emblematic of the dedicated ambassador who could now make an entire career out of foreign service to his nation. In the years of Wotton's happy retirement, such ambassadors would face the most difficult of challenges: ending a thirty-year's war and recasting the political identity of Europe.

1648 and All That

In the name of the most holy and individual trinity: Be it known to all, and every one whom it may concern, or to whom in any manner it may belong, that for many years past, discords

and civil divisions being stirred up in the Roman Empire, which
increased to such a degree, that not only all Germany, but also
the neighbouring kingdoms, and France particularly, have been
involved in the disorders of a long and cruel war.
—The Treaty of Westphalia, 1648[224]

Before his final mission to Venice, Wotton had spent some
time in Vienna. He had been there before, during his first tour of
the continent, and he had found it to be an insalubrious city.
"Walking in the streets at night," he wrote in November 1590, "is
as dangerous as in the wantonest town in Italy," although there was
some compensation in that the cost of living was remarkably low:
a boon for any cash-strapped student.[225] In 1620 he returned to
the city in much grander style, as the ambassador of an English
king. He had been charged with an unenviable task—the preven-
tion of a war whose likely participants had no interest in peace.

In the wake of Reformation, the Holy Roman Empire, fatally
divided along confessional lines, had stumbled on a compromise—the Peace of Augsburg of 1555. Henceforth, the ruler of
each German principality (of which there were hundreds) would
be able to determine whether his people worshipped as Lutherans
or as Catholics: "the religion of the prince," as the new legal prin-
ciple declared, "is the religion of his people." Like all compromises, it infuriated as many as it delighted. First, it infuriated
Calvinists, whose religion was not granted official recognition
within the settlement's terms. Most of all it infuriated the Habsburgs, occupants of the empire's throne for generations and a family determined, one day at least, to reclaim the whole of Germany
for the Roman Catholic Church.

For the moment, the Habsburgs, headed by Emperor Charles
V, had been forced to tolerate a Protestant presence within their

dominions. A similar state of affairs pertained to their territories in central Europe. In places like Bohemia and Moravia, Lutherans, Calvinists, and Utraquists (the followers of the doctrines of Jan Hus) had secured some limited freedoms to practice their religions.

From the second decade of the seventeenth century, however, the Habsburgs in Vienna had begun a campaign to stamp out these freedoms and the unseemly religious diversity that came with them. Since that campaign constituted an assault on both their consciences and their political autonomy, the nobility of Bohemia were having none of it. On May 23, 1618, they made their feelings clear by throwing three Habsburg representatives out of a window in Hradshin Castle. The famous "defenestration of Prague" unleashed a conflict that would rage, without respite, for thirty years, at the cost of tens of thousands of lives.

At first, the Habsburg emperor, Matthias, believed armed conflict with Bohemia might be averted. His adviser, Cardinal Khlesl, sent out emissaries to negotiate. Matthias's son and heir presumptive, Ferdinand, was more hawkish and, with the connivance of the Spanish ambassador in Vienna, pushed for a more militant response to Bohemian disloyalty. He arranged to have the conciliatory Cardinal Khlesl arrested and, in February 1619, after the death of Matthias, Ferdinand was himself elected Holy Roman Emperor. He could now pursue whatever policy he so chose.

The Bohemians realized that, vulnerable and isolated as they undoubtedly were, they needed a champion. Such a man seemed to present himself in the person of the German prince Frederick V, Elector Palatine, and the son-in-law of James I of England. Frederick sent ambassadors to Prague, suggesting that he would be able to deliver the military assistance of his father-in-law as well as the conglomeration of German Lutheran states known as the Protestant Union. All he asked in return was the crown of Bohemia.

His proposal was accepted, and he was crowned in November 1619. Unfortunately, his promises had been, at the very least, inflated. The Protestant Union offered Frederick money, but no troops. James I had no intention of fighting the Habsburgs—on the contrary, he had hopes of securing a marriage treaty with the Spanish branch of the family for his son Charles. Such negotiations would ultimately come to nought, and the principal negotiator, the duke of Buckingham, would return from Madrid in September 1623 with little more than "twelve Spanish genets, four Barbary horses, four mares and ten foals covered with mantels of crimson velvet."[226] In 1619, however, James still hoped to win a Spanish bride for his son, and to placate the Habsburgs, he dispatched ambassadors—including the Vienna-bound Henry Wotton—to try to calm the increasingly tense political situation.

The Emperor Ferdinand had no desire to avoid a war, however. He had been busy with his own diplomacy, recruiting powerful allies such as Maximilian of Bavaria, who held sway over the Catholic League—the confessional counterpart, made up of various German provinces and principalities, of the Protestant Union. He also secured promises of troops and subsidies from his Habsburg cousin, Philip IV of Spain. Ferdinand's diplomacy, in other words, had been highly skilled while Frederick's had been naïve, rooted in promises he had no way of keeping.

Ferdinand struck and he struck mightily, crushing the Bohemians and their few allies at the Battle of the White Mountain in November 1620. News of the victory, Wotton reported from Vienna, "filled all this court and town with jollity."[227] Bohemia and its chief ally, Moravia, submitted once more to Habsburg rule. It had been a doubly disastrous campaign for Frederick of the Palatinate, since Spanish armies had taken the opportunity to overrun his possessions in the Rhineland. Spain now held a continuous swathe of territories, through which its armies could march un-opposed, from Italy to Belgium. It had been a Habsburg victory par excellence. But therein lay the dilemma. The Habsburgs, from the perspective of their dynastic rivals, had proved themselves *too* powerful.

At first there were hopes that a lasting peace might be achieved. Frederick had fled the battlefield in 1620 and found refuge in the West. His father-in-law, James I, with the assistance of the Span-ish, pleaded with him to reach an agreement with the Habsburgs. If he gave up his claim to the Bohemian throne—which was now something of a dead letter anyway—he would be allowed to re-tain at least some of his German possessions. To this end, James arranged a grand diplomatic congress in Brussels in 1622. It was a futile gesture. Frederick had no interest in reaching an accom-modation, and with Habsburg armies continuing to run rough-shod over more and more German principalities, the other great powers began to realize that the Habsburg threat would have to be contained.

By 1624 the need for a grand anti-Habsburg alliance had been accepted by England, France, and the Dutch Republic. They had approached the Swedish king Gustavus Adolphus as a potential leader of the anti-Habsburg assault, but he had asked for too much in return. Instead, they turned to Christian IV of Denmark who, courtesy of his territories in northern Germany, could claim a legitimate interest in the internal workings of the empire.

Depressingly, as soon as Christian arrived in Germany he was crushed in battle by the great general Albrecht von Wallenstein. The Habsburg ascendancy continued, and the government in Vi-enna began to exploit it. An edict of restitution was issued that re-stored all lands seized from the Catholic Church since the Peace of

Augsburg in 1555. The religious dimension of the war thus came into even sharper focus.

The Habsburgs, already possessed of a land army of one hundred thousand troops, now determined to build a mighty navy with which they could dominate the Baltic Sea. It was this development that brought Sweden, now facing a direct threat to its sphere of influence, into the war. So as not to be distracted, Sweden signed a peace treaty with its longtime adversary, the king of Poland—the Peace of Attmark, mediated by French and English diplomats. Then, backed by French money, Sweden launched an invasion of northern Germany in July 1630. A famous victory was won at Breitenfeld, and much of southwestern Germany was brought under Swedish control. An inconclusive battle followed at Lutzen, during which Gustavus Adolphus lost his life, and in its wake Habsburg forces began to regain some of the ground they had recently lost.

The hostilities would follow this oscillating pattern for another dozen years, and the details need not concern us. With the entry of France and Sweden into the war, however, it was clear that the Habsburg's unchallenged takeover of central Europe had been averted. By the early 1640s a bloody sort of stalemate had developed, and the prospect of an interminable, pointless struggle had begun to emerge. It was time to make peace.

The Thirty Years War had always been a curious mixture of military engagements and diplomacy. Each summer troops would join battle, and each winter, since the weather made battle impossible, ambassadors would scuttle around the continent, sometimes pursuing new allies, sometimes making halfhearted attempts to end the conflict. As the war approached its conclusion, this curious pattern continued.

Final negotiations were begun four years before hostilities ended. At two separate locations in Westphalia—Osnabruck and Munster—the opposing sides gradually approached a settlement. The progress was infuriatingly slow. The French did not even submit their first serious draft of demands until June 1645, but once these and the Habsburg's counterproposals were in play, serious discussions could get underway.

The details of the resulting Treaty of Westphalia, crafted, in large part, by the new breed of career diplomatists, is convoluted and confusing. The more important resolutions included the establishment of freedom of religion in Germany; Sweden securing financial compensation and control of various German territories; France being granted rights over Alsace; and, crucially, the dismantling of much of the imperial governmental machinery. It was such machinery that had allowed the Habsburgs of Vienna to intervene in the internal politics of Germany for generations. Henceforth, ancient oaths of allegiance, imperial rights to raise taxes, to dispense justice, to impose religious orthodoxy, and to guide foreign affairs within Germany were struck down.

Such supranational interference—and here was the epochal moment—was now deemed obsolete. Something was born in Westphalia in 1648. The overall vision of Westphalia was optimistic, hopelessly so:

> That there shall be a Christian and universal peace, and a perpetual, true, and sincere amity. That this peace and amity be observed and cultivated with such a sincerity and zeal, that each party shall endeavour to procure the benefit, honour and advantage of the

other. That thus on all sides they may see this peace and friendship in the Roman Empire, and the Kingdom of France flourish, by entertaining a good and faithful neighbourhood.

But the genius was in the detail.

And to prevent for the future any differences arising in the politic state, all and every one of the electors, princes and states of the [Holy] Roman Empire, are so established and confirmed in their ancient rights, prerogatives, liberties, privileges, free exercise of territorial right, as well ecclesiastical as political lordships... by virtue of this present transaction: that they never can or ought to be molested therein by any whomsoever upon any manner of pretence.

"That they never can or ought to be molested": The states of Germany, in other words, had *sovereignty*—the right to make their own decisions without interference from any quarter, whether a Habsburg emperor, a dynastic rival or a Roman Catholic pope.

They shall enjoy without contradiction, the right of suffrage in all deliberations touching the affairs of the empire; but above all, when the business in hand shall be the making or interpreting of laws, the declaring of wars, imposing of taxes, levying or quartering of soldiers, erecting new fortifications in the territories of the states, or reinforcing the old garrisons. As also when a peace of alliance is to be concluded, and treated about, or the like, none of these, or the like things shall be acted for the future, without the suffrage and consent of the free assembly of all the states of the empire. Above all, it shall be free perpetually to each of the states of the Empire, to make alliances with strangers for their preservation and safety.[228]

Modern nations take such rights for granted. The states of Germany had never possessed them, and they had never been articulated with such force before. The Holy Roman Empire, a polity that had been in decline for centuries, was forced to abandon the fiction that it was, in any sense, the inheritor of the authority of the Caesars. Official dissolution would not arrive until 1806, but for all intents and purposes, it perished in 1648. From now on, Europe was conceived as a community of autonomous polities. The rights granted to Germany were quickly assumed by every one of the continent's rulers. There would be wars, border disputes, alliances, and enmities, but they would be pursued by sovereign nation-states. It was something of a revolution.

14

THE PHYSICS OF DIPLOMACY

Jus Gentium

THE PEACEMAKERS AT WESTPHALIA were not concerned
with establishing a system or framework of international
relations that would endure for centuries. They simply
wanted to put an end to a futile war that had emptied their coffers and decimated the population of central Europe. Nor would
the course of European politics run exactly as those peacemakers
had envisaged. The undue influence of the pope and the emperor—
conceived as relics of medievalism—were indeed done away with,
but by the end of the century Louis XIV's France had achieved a
position of dominance that was, if anything, even more damaging
to the political equilibrium of the continent.

What Westphalia did do, however, was to stoke the fires of a
debate that had been growing in intensity since the middle decades
of the sixteenth century. Europe and, at least by theoretical extension, the rest of the world was now envisaged as being made up of
sovereign, autonomous states. What remained undecided was how
those states ought to behave toward one another. Thus far, this has
not been a book of theory, but the greatest contribution the seventeenth and eighteenth centuries made to the history of the ambassadors was surely their musings on jus gentium, the Law of

Nations, or, in essence, the ambassador's rule book. Such musings, quite properly, sometimes descended into scholastic, dust-dry theorizing. For the most part they did not. In fact, they had novel, sometimes ebullient things to say about the human condition.

There were as many law codes as there were city-states and empires. These codes were of human manufacture—sometimes inspired, sometimes egregious, but always contingent, mutable, and suited to particular eras and places. They served for a time, but eventually they grew stale and had to be tinkered with or replaced. But as medieval theologians had long since argued, there was a grander, older, inevitable law—the law of nature. Its author, by most (though by no means all) accounts, was God. He looked at his creation, man, saw into his ragged soul, determined what would allow him to flourish, and established fundamental, immutable legal rubrics. This Natural Law was self-evident. It consisted of those things which we all know, by natural inclination, to be just. It was unchanging and, crucially, it could be fully discerned by the pure exercise of reason. Its legitimacy (unlike that of man-made laws) did not rest on the evidence of history or current conventions.

How, though, did this eternal, simple Natural Law relate to the complex, written laws of man, in particular, to the Law of Nations—the law that dealt with issues like when and how states should go to war or how they should make peace? Was the Law of Nations its derivative, something that was still being codified? Or were the Law of Nations and Natural Law one and the same? The great Dutch philosopher Hugo Grotius (1583–1645) insisted that the two laws were not identical. Natural Law, by his account, was rooted in the basic aspirations that all human beings shared— to prevent others from taking what belongs to us; to have such things given back if they are taken; to keep promises (or else the whole system falls apart); and to punish wrongdoing. That is what human nature demanded, and that was what made human society function efficiently.

Clearly, very similar principles might seem to suit the world of international relations. And so they did, Grotius agreed. But the specific tenets of the Law of Nations were manifestly in flux. Natural Law provided a model from which a changeable Law of Nations derived its rules. And while the rubrics of Grotius's Natural Law could simply be grasped by thinking about them—almost as an act of intuition—the Law of Nations could only be understood by looking to the real world. It was made up of those tenets, treaties, and regulations that the community of nations had jointly agreed on.

This was not a negative vision, however. On the contrary, Grotius believed that states realized the importance of creating an equitable Law of Nations and, just as importantly, abiding by it. Returning to that ancient debate between the idealists and the realists, Grotius—conscious and respectful as he was of things such as reason of state and self-interest—clearly believed in the moral content, the possibility of a moral order, in the dealings between nations.

So, too, did his disciple Samuel Pufendorf (1623–1694). Pufendorf was a Saxon-born law professor, who held tenure at the universities of Heidelberg, and Lund, in Sweden, before serving as the royal historiographer at both Stockholm and Berlin. The son of a Lutheran minister, he would retain his faith throughout his life, and his great mission was to reconcile his religious beliefs with the fashionable rationalist philosophy of the late seventeenth century. Pufendorf also had a very concise, elegant definition of Natural Law. It was derived from the two fundamental human attributes—the desire for self-preservation and the realization that, to survive, mankind must be sociable and peaceable. In his spare, 1673 masterpiece, *On the Duty of Man and Citizen*, he explained that "man shares with all the animals that have consciousness the fact that he holds nothing dearer than himself, and is eager in every way to preserve himself." He strives for those things that do him good, and rejects those things that do him harm. "This feeling is regularly so strong that all the others give way," and "if any man make an attack upon one's life," such an attack is deeply resented: "so much so that, even after the threatened danger has been averted, hatred usually still remains, and a desire for vengeance."

"But in one respect," Pufendorf suggested, "man seems to be in a worse state even than the brutes." In a natural setting, beasts were powerful and resourceful. Man, by comparison, was pitifully weak. He could not survive on his own.

> Let us imagine a man brought to maturity without any care and training bestowed upon him by others, having no knowledge except what sprang up of itself in his own mind, and in a desert, deprived of all help and society of other men. Certainly a more miserable animal it will be hard to find. Speechless and naked, he has nothing left him but to pluck herbs and roots, or gather wild fruits, to slake his thirst from spring or river, or the first marsh he encountered, to seek shelter in a cave from the violence of the weather, or to cover his body somehow with moss or grass, to pass his time most tediously in idleness, to shudder at any noise or the encounter with another creature, finally to perish by hunger or cold or some wild beast.

It was, therefore, the instinct for self-preservation that impelled men to gather together: "Whatever advantages now attend human life have flowed entirely from the mutual help of men."

Unfortunately, man was also a creature riddled with baser instincts. He was "an animal at no time disinclined to lust" with a belly that "desires not merely to be satisfied, but also to be tickled."

> Many more passions and desires unknown to the brutes are found in man, men are driven to mutual injury by want and the fact that their present resources are insufficient for their desires or their need. Moreover, men have in them great power for the infliction of mutual injuries. For though not formidable because of teeth or claws or horns, as are many of the brutes, still manual dexterity can prove a most effective means of injury; and shrewdness gives a man the opportunity to attack by cunning.

The saving grace was that all men realized this to be the case. If they were to survive, ways must be found to rein in their unsavory characteristics. The simple, ideal solution was to make every effort to live in harmony with one another. Man was "malicious, insolent and easily provoked...whence it follows that, in order to be safe, he must be sociable, that is, must be united with men like himself, and so conduct himself toward them that they may have no good cause to injure him, but rather may be ready to maintain and promote his interests." The laws of this sociability, "or those which teach how a man should conduct himself, to become a good member of human society" was the basis of Natural Law.

Of course, even with their newfound allies, men were still puny individuals in a hostile world. It made great sense, therefore, to unite together into human societies, out of which the great civilizations emerged. This leap—which Pufendorf only posited hypothetically (there was no historical moment when it actually occurred)—involved leaving the state of nature (a place governed solely by Natural Law) and entering societies that would be governed by any number of man-made, imperfect legal codes.

For the individual, Pufendorf believed, this was a wise and necessary development. But what about entire nations? Here Pufendorf departed radically from Hugo Grotius. Nations were powerful and resilient enough to, in effect, remain in a state of nature. Their behavior could, therefore, be governed by the fundamental Natural Law—the desire for self-preservation and the need to live peaceably together.

The Law of Nations—the ambassadors' bible—was therefore identical to Natural Law. Yes, there were endless customs and conventions, but it was theoretically and morally possible for a ruler to disregard or contravene them if they breached Natural Law. Ultimately, there were only three basic principles that a state should follow: to avoid doing injury to others (and to heal such injuries if they were ever inflicted); to treat all other states as one's equals; and to actively promote the advantage of other states. This bred sociability and peace, which in a convoluted way was the best way to make sure of one's own preservation.

Needless to say, the role of the ambassador in such a world was to avoid conflict at all costs. There were to be no wars aimed at securing more territory, to win prestige, or to square off against nations whose beliefs one detested. But there were still moments, if palpable harm was being done to oneself and the community, when the resources of diplomacy were exhausted.

> It accords most closely with the natural law, if men are at peace with one another, voluntarily performing their obligations; in fact peace itself is a state peculiar to man, as distinguished from the brutes. Yet at times, even for man himself, war is permitted,

and sometimes necessary; when, namely, owing to another's malice, we are unable to preserve our possessions, or gain our rights, without employing force.

At such moments,

> there must be no instant recourse to arms, especially when there is still some doubt about the right or the fact. But we must try to see whether the matter can be settled in a friendly way, for example, by arranging a conference of the parties, by appealing to arbitrators, or intrusting the case to the decision of the lot.

When all such efforts failed, however, war could justly be embarked on, and perhaps surprisingly, Pufendorf suggested fighting it as brutally and efficiently as possible. Respond to attacks with disproportionate retaliation. Harass the enemy unwaveringly. The point being that wars fought in such a way would reach their conclusion far more quickly.[229]

The theorizing of men like Grotius and Pufendorf did not go uncontested, of course. There were always ranks of more pessimistic or more hawkish philosophers. But as naïve as some commentators found Natural Law theorizing to be, it did, ultimately, triumph. Not by changing the political landscape, which remained as self-serving as it had ever been, but by imposing idealistic assumptions about the nature of international relations that, to a large extent, remain entrenched today.

Vattel

> The maxims laid down in this chapter—those sacred precepts of nature—were for a long time unknown to nations. The ancients had no notion of any duty they owed to nations with whom they were not united by treaties of friendship. The Jews especially placed a great part of their zeal in hating all nations;

and, as a natural consequence, they were detested and despised
by them in turn. At length the voice of nature came to be heard
among civilized nations; they perceived that all men are
brethren. When will the happy time come that they shall behave
as such?
    —Vattel, *The Law of Nations*[230]

This whistle-stop tour of Natural Law theory concludes with
the ideas of Emmerich de Vattel (1714–67), who spilled an unusually large amount of ink discussing the role of ambassadors in
the brave new community of nations. Vattel, a native of Neuchâ-
tel in Switzerland, published his first philosophical work at the age
of twenty-seven. His political career saw him serving as the ambassador of the elector of Saxony in Bern and later, in a series of min-
isterial posts in Dresden. His great contribution was to produce a
work of international theory—his 1758 *The Law of Nations*—that
not only consolidated the thinking of earlier writers, but was also
widely read, especially in the philosophical crucible of the early
American republic. Vattel travelled a middle road between the ideas
of Grotius and Pufendorf. Natural Law was, ultimately, concerned
with the moral universe of individuals. States, patently, were not
the same as individuals, because they usually reached their decisions after lengthy debate and deliberation. Pufendorf's image of
nations being in something equivalent to a state of nature was almost accurate, Vattel believed, but it had to be slightly adjusted to
accommodate the unique character of sovereign polities. The Law
of Nations was to be seen, therefore, as a slight adjustment of
Natural Law.
    At the heart of this Law of Nations was a credo, very similar
to Pufendorf's, of sociability and interdependence—again, to be
pursued because they ultimately served the nation's own best inter-

ests and allowed it to flourish. Each individual nation was bound to contribute everything in its power to the happiness and perfection of the others. Naturally, "the duties that we owe to ourselves [are] unquestionably paramount...When, therefore, [the state] cannot contribute to the welfare of another nation without doing an essential injury to herself, her obligation ceases on that particular occasion, and she is considered as lying under a disability to perform the office in question." In happier times, however, a nation owed an impressive range of duties to its peers.

> Every nation ought, on occasion, to labour for the preservation of others, and for securing them from ruin and destruction, as far as it can do this without exposing itself too much. Thus, when a neighbouring nation is unjustly attacked by a powerful enemy who threatens to oppress it, if you can defend it, without exposing yourself to great danger, unquestionably it is your duty to do so. Let it not be said, in objection to this, that a sovereign is not to expose the lives of his soldiers for the safety of a foreign nation with which he has not contracted a defensive alliance. It may be his own case to stand in need of assistance; and, consequently, he is acting for the safety of his own nation in giving energy to the spirit and disposition to afford mutual aid. Accordingly, policy here coincides with, and enforces, obligation and duty. It is the interest of princes to stop the progress of an ambitious monarch, who aims at aggrandizing himself by subjugating his neighbours.

Similarly, if a nation was afflicted with famine, "all those who have provisions to spare ought to relieve her distress, without, however, exposing themselves to want." Nor should a nation confine itself to the preservation of other states: "It should likewise, according to its power and their want of its assistance, contribute to their perfection." A learned nation, for instance, "if applied to for masters and teachers in the sciences, by another nation desirous of shaking off its native barbarism, ought not to refuse such a request."

Timing was everything in such dealings, and no nation was entitled "forcibly to obtrude these good offices" on its neighbors. "Such an attempt would be a violation of their natural liberty. In order to compel anyone to receive a kindness, we must have an authority over him; but nations are absolutely free and independent." For an example of misguided philanthropy, Vattel suggested, one need only think of "those ambitious Europeans who attacked the American nations, and subjected them to their greedy dominion, in order, as they pretended, to civilize them, and cause them to be instructed in the true religion... Those usurpers, I say, grounded themselves on a pretext equally unjust and ridiculous."[231]

For such a world to function, there could be no discrimination on the grounds of faith: "No nation can refuse [offers of help] to another, under pretence of its professing a different religion. To be entitled to them, it is sufficient that the claimant is our fellow-creature." It was also vital to retain a polite and friendly demeanor. "It is impossible that nations should mutually discharge all these several duties if they do not love each other...Every nation is obliged to cultivate the friendship of other nations, and carefully to avoid whatever might kindle their enmity against her."

With all such provisos in place, the prospect was truly inspiring:

How happy would mankind be, were these amiable precepts of nature everywhere observed! Nations would communicate to each other their products and their knowledge; a profound peace would prevail all over the earth, and enrich it with its invaluable fruits; industry, the sciences and the arts would be employed in promoting our happiness, no less than in relieving our wants; violent methods of deciding contests would be no more heard of; all differences would be terminated by moderation, justice, and equity; the world would have the appearance of a large republic; men would live everywhere like brothers, and each individual be a citizen of the universe. That this idea should be but a delightful dream! Yet it flows from the nature and essence of man.

Sadly, it might well be imagined that "disorderly passions, and private and mistaken interest, will forever prevent its being realized." The world was made up of ambitious, grasping political rivals, and as Vattel insisted, "the law of nature cannot condemn the good to become the dupes and prey of the wicked, and the victims of their injustice and ingratitude." "Melancholy experience shows that most nations aim only to strengthen and enrich themselves at the expense of others." Largesse, therefore, had to be tempered with realism. If a nation had a trading monopoly or had made some significant industrial breakthrough, it was quite entitled to keep it to itself. No nation was obliged to sell arms to a potential enemy.[232]

Such caveats aside, however, Vattel genuinely believed in the possibility of a harmonious world order, and many of the tenets he established in constructing his vision are still held sacred today. Aid was to be given, but only when expressly requested: There were to be no unprovoked interventions in the affairs of a sovereign nation. All states, at a moral level, were to be seen as equals. They might have larger or smaller armies, healthier or weaker economies, but they all shared the same rights and duties.

There were two fundamental laws of foreign relations. First, that nations, "being free and independent of each other, in the same manner as men are naturally free and independent...should be left in the peaceable enjoyment of that liberty which she inherits from nature." Second, that

> since men are naturally equal, and a perfect equality prevails in their rights and obligations, as equally proceeding from nature—nations composed of men, and considered as so many

free persons living together in a state of nature, are naturally
equal, and inherit from nature the same obligations and rights.
Power or weakness does not in this respect produce any difference. A dwarf is as much a man as a giant; a small republic is
no less a sovereign state than the most powerful kingdom.

How, though, were nations to go about creating this enlightened community of nations? It fell to the ambassadors—the
much-respected lynchpins of Vattel's theory. "It is necessary," Vattel began, "that nations should treat and hold intercourse together,
in order to promote their interests,—to avoid injuring each
other—and to adjust and terminate their disputes." The sending
of embassies was a right shared by all nations (and even by some
nonsovereign territories and cities), and they were "bound by reciprocal obligation to consent to such communication as far as the
situation of [their] affairs will permit [them]."

Naturally, kings and rulers were only rarely able to meet in person. "Such interviews would often be impracticable" and likely to
suffer from endless delays, troubles and expenses. "The only expe-
dient, therefore, which remains for nations and sovereigns, is to
communicate and treat with each other by the agency of procura-
tors or mandatories,—of delegates charged with their commands,
and vested with their powers—that is to say, public ministers."
Such men were "necessary instruments in the management of
those affairs which sovereigns have to transact with each other, and
the channels of that correspondence which they have a right to
carry on."

In peacetime, at least, the sovereign who sought to hinder the
sending of ambassadors "is attacking a nation in one of her most
valuable rights, and disputing her title to that which nature herself
gives to every independent society: it is offering an insult to na-

tions in general, and tearing asunder the ties by which they are united." War, Vattel admitted, "introduces other rights."

Such obligations did not mean that a ruler was forced to endure "at all times the residence of perpetual ministers, who are desirous of remaining at the sovereign's court, although they have no business to transact with him." There were many good reasons to avoid allowing too many resident embassies in one's dominions. History told many tales of ambassadors spreading dissent and corrupting citizens.

Such caution notwithstanding, ambassadors were at the very heart of the diplomatic system. "The representative character constitutes the minister of the first rank the ambassador. It places him above all other ministers who are not invested with the same character, and precludes their entering into competition with [him]." As such, the workings of the entire political world depended on their rights being jealously guarded. We have visited the issue of diplomatic immunity already, but in Vattel it was interrogated down to the last detail—a trend that would continue to the present day. Indeed, many of the orthodoxies of today's diplomatic immunity are contained within Vattel's exhaustive survey of the issue.[233]

———

"The respect which is due to sovereigns," Vattel began, "should redound to their representatives, and especially their ambassadors as representing their master's person in the first degree."

> Whoever offends and insults a public minister commits a crime the more deserving of severe punishment, as he might thereby involve his country and his sovereign in very serious difficulties

and trouble. It is just that he should be punished for his fault, and that the state should, at the expense of the delinquent, give full satisfaction to the sovereign who has been offended in the person of his minister.

Without such guarantees, the "right of embassy becomes precarious, and the success very uncertain." The person who attacked an ambassador was not only insulting a particular sovereign, but "also the common safety and well-being of nations: he becomes guilty of an atrocious crime against mankind in general."

All foreign visitors in a country were, in some measure, the responsibility of their hosts. They were to be protected from violence, for instance, but while the sovereign was free to pardon one of his citizens who attacked an ordinary tourist, he enjoyed far fewer privileges when an ambassador became involved. "The power of pardoning, in such cases, does not rest with the prince in whose dominions the crime has been committed, but with him who has been offended in the person of his representative."

Of course, there was a difference between wilfully attacking someone one knew to be an accredited envoy and mistakenly causing some offense that "is wholly unconnected with the law of nations, and falls within the class of ordinary transgressions."

> A company of young rakes, in a town of Switzerland, having, in the night-time, insulted the British minister's house, without knowing who lived in it, the magistracy sent a message to the minister to know what satisfaction he required. He prudently answered, that it was the magistrates' concern to provide for the public safety by such means as they thought best; but that, as to his own part, he required nothing, not thinking himself affronted by persons who could have had no design against him, as not knowing his house.

Officially, an ambassador did not begin his duties until he had presented his credentials to his host sovereign. That said, his im-

munity was deemed to be in effect as soon as he crossed the nation's border. Similarly, the passports he habitually carried were
seen as protecting him in all the countries he passed through while
travelling to his posting.

Even in time of war, certain immunities remained valid. If
anything, ambassadors were more vital when conflict broke out:
"The necessity and indispensable duty of preserving some resource
by which the minds of the belligerent parties may be brought to a
mutual understanding, and peace be restored, is a fresh reason why
the persons of ministers, as instruments in the preliminary conferences and final reconciliation, should be still more sacred and
inviolable."

Crucially, such immunities were not to be seen as matters of
mere convention or convenience. They were sacred because they
were demanded by Natural Law. Immunity was one of those
things "without which it would be impossible for nations to cultivate the society that nature has established among them, to keep
up a mutual correspondence, to treat of their affairs, or to adjust
their differences."

Ambassadors were often charged with unpalatable missions—
to do or say things that might be deemed offensive. Clearly, if they
lived in fear of persecution, they would be less willing and able to
fulfil their duties. "In a word, if an ambassador may be indicted
for ordinary offences, be criminally prosecuted, taken into custody,
punished—if he may be sued in civil cases—the consequence will
often be, that he will neither possess the power, the leisure, nor the
freedom of mind which his master's affairs require."

Of course, "this independency of the foreign minister is not
to be converted into licentiousness. It does not excuse him from
conforming to the customs and laws of the country in all his external actions, so far as they are unconnected with the object of his

mission and character—he is independent; but he has not a right to do whatever he pleases." If a local law prohibited investigating local fortifications or passing over a particular bridge, then the ambassador was to scrupulously avoid both the fortifications and the bridge.

When an ambassador failed to abide by such rules of conduct—or if he committed even more serious offenses—he could not be directly punished, but a sovereign did have some strategies available to him.

An ambassador might fail to show a prince due respect. In such instances, the prince was entitled to ask the ambassador's ruler to recall him, perhaps asking the ambassador to stay away from court until a decision was reached. In cases of gross discourtesy, an ambassador could be bodily ejected from the country. If an ambassador was suspected of any unwholesome activities, the prince's right to be master in his own dominions overrode his duty to maintain relations with other nations.

> Though sovereigns are generally obliged to listen to the overtures of foreign powers, and to admit their ministers, this obligation entirely ceases with regard to a minister, who, being himself deficient in the duties attached to this station, becomes dangerous to, or justly suspected by the sovereign, to whom he can come in no other character than that of a minister of peace. Can a prince be obliged to suffer that a secret enemy, who is raising disturbances in the state and plotting its ruin, shall remain in his dominions and appear at his court?

Such a strategy was "directly repugnant to all the rules of virtue and probity, and a flagrant violation of the law of nature... The corruptor is undoubtedly guilty of a crime against the wretch whom he seduces; and as to the sovereign whose secrets are thus treacherously explored, is it not both an offence and an injury committed against him, to abuse the friendly reception given at his court, and to take advantage of it for the purpose of corrupting the fidelity of his servants?" In such circumstances, a prince had every right to banish the ambassador and "demand justice of his employer."

But was that really the offended ruler's only sanction? "Shall an ambassador be suffered with impunity to cabal against the state where he resides, to plot its ruin, to stir up the subjects to revolt, and boldly to foment the most dangerous conspiracies, under the assurance of being supported by his master? If he behaves as an enemy, shall it not be allowable to treat him as such?" If he physically took up arms against the ruler then, yes, Vattel admitted, the law of self-defense permitted the ruler to respond in kind.

"The question," Vattel calculated, "is more difficult with respect to an ambassador who, without proceeding to overt acts, broaches plots of a dangerous tendency." On the face of things, the ambassador himself was effectively breaching the Law of Nations, and surely the prince—just like the ambassador—was to be afforded the protections that the law provided. What about the ruler's right not to be plotted against? Vattel conceded the point, but worried that its logic might lead to an outbreak of diplomatic incidents and the whole system of embassy being undermined. "If we allow the offended prince a right to punish a foreign minister in such cases, the subjects of contest and rupture between sovereigns will become very frequent; and it is much to be feared that the ambassadorial character will cease to enjoy that protection and inviolability which are so essential to it."

It was also excruciatingly difficult to be sure of the facts in such instances. "How shall we, in every case, be able to ascertain the precise boundaries of those different degrees of transgression?" Was the offense premeditated? Was the ambassador really guilty, or were his enemies conspiring against him? On balance, Vattel suggested that it was prudent for the ruler to forgo his right to prosecute an errant ambassador in the wider interests of the international community.

In more overt cases of open hostility, of course, the ambassador made himself into a public enemy, and at such times a ruler's right to self-defense could be invoked. For the most part, of course, ambassadors did not indulge in such unworthy behavior. They continued to be protected by both Natural Law and the endless codes of human legislation around the globe. Vattel noticed that the Aztecs (whose ideas had been fascinating Europeans since the sixteenth century), the Chinese, and the Indians had all cherished the immunities of envoys and ambassadors. Even the Quran "enjoins the Moslems to respect public ministers: and if the Turks have not in all instances uniformly observed that precept, their violations of it are rather imputable to the ferocity of particular princes than to the principles of the nation at large."[234]

—⚬—

What precise immunities did the ambassador enjoy in Vattel's scheme? At the time of writing, ministers across Europe were entitled to practice their various religions within embassy chapels. Vattel applauded this as a "privilege founded on reason," but argued that such a dispensation was not strictly necessary for an ambassador to carry out his duties. As such, it was protected by local laws rather than the Law of Nations. If any sovereign "should, for substantial reasons, refuse [an ambassador] permission to practise his religion in any manner which might render it an object of public notice, we must not presume to condemn the conduct of that sovereign." It would be regrettable but, ultimately, it was the sovereign's business.

As for the common practice of exempting ambassadors from the payment of customs duties, again, this was simply a convention, and had nothing to do with an ambassador's ability to carry out his sacred mission of allowing communication between nations. "If the sovereign is pleased to exempt him from them, it is an instance of civility which the minister could not claim as matter of right, any more than that his baggage, or any chests or packages which he imports from abroad, shall not be searched at the custom-house." The famed immunities of the diplomatic bag would continue to be something of a bugbear for governments. In 1865, Lord Elgin used it to export 35,000 antiquities out of Cyprus without molestation. A century later, the Soviet Union would use it to try to avoid the payment of customs duties on a nine-ton Mercedes tractor-trailer it was importing into Switzerland.[235]

Vattel's logic was becoming clear: For important immunities and privileges to be preserved, frivolous or dispensable ones ought not to be insisted on. This is a message that ambassadors, down to the present day, have sometimes been reluctant to heed. Vattel realized that he was entering controversial waters. Was it really appropriate for a nation to abolish "what general custom has established with respect to foreign ministers"? Such conventions were certainly important, and were to be honored by those who had agreed to abide by them. "Nevertheless, if, in process of time, any nation perceives that such custom is attended with inconveniences, she is at liberty to declare that she no longer chooses to conform to it: and when once she has made this explicit declaration, no cause of complaint lies against her for refusing thenceforward to observe the custom in question." Of course, the rest of the community of nations should be warned against this change of policy, and any ambassadors already in the country should continue to enjoy the privileges they had been granted upon their first arrival. Ultimately, though, in indifferent matters the independent state had total freedom to adjust its position.

Some immunities were sacred, however, because they were crucial to the success of an embassy. Ambassadors were always to be exempt from the civil jurisdiction of a country and were never to be forced into the civil courts—they were not its citizens, after all. That said, it was legitimate for ambassadors to come voluntarily before such courts. If he "chooses to renounce a part of his independency, and to subject himself in civil affairs to the jurisdiction of the country, he is undoubtedly at liberty to do so, provided it be done with his master's consent." Indeed, such gestures were apt to foster goodwill between nations.

But did an ambassador's personal immunity extend to his property? Vattel contended that "everything...which directly belongs to his person in the character of a public minister—everything which is intended for his use, or which serves for his own maintenance and that of his household,—everything of that kind, I say, partakes of the minister's independency, and is absolutely exempt from all jurisdiction in the country. Those things, together with the person to whom they belong, are considered as being out of the country." Here was the cumbersome notion of extraterritoriality.

This dispensation did not extend to personal possessions that were not directly related to the business of embassy. If an ambassador involved himself with private business ventures, then any profits, debts, or subsequent legal actions came under the purview of the host government. Similarly, if the ambassador bought private property, it, too, remained as much under the government's jurisdiction as any other property in the country.

Different rules applied to the buildings in which an ambassador conducted his official business.

> The independency of the ambassador would be very imperfect, and his security very precarious, if the house in which he lives were not to enjoy a perfect immunity, and to be inaccessible to the ordinary officers of justice. The ambassador might be molested under a thousand pretexts; his secrets might be discovered by searching his papers, and his person exposed to insults. Thus, all the reasons which establish his independence and inviolability, concur likewise in securing the freedom of his house. In all civilized nations, this right is acknowledged as annexed to the ambassadorial character; and an ambassador's house, at least in all the ordinary affairs of life, is, equally with his person, considered as being out of the country.

Vattel recalled a recent incident during which this privilege had been violated. On April 3, 1752, thirty soldiers entered the house of Baron Greiffenheim, the Swedish minister in St. Petersburg, "and carried off two of his domestics, whom they conducted to prison, under a pretence that those two men had clandestinely sold liquors, which the imperial farm alone has the privilege of selling." A furious Russian court ordered the immediate arrest of the officers in charge of this outrage. It sent an abject apology to the Swedish minister and a promise to the whole diplomatic community that there would be no repetition of such an incident.

Not that the ne'er-do-wells of society were to see an ambassador's house as some variety of refuge. The building's immunity only extended to the ambassador and his immediate household. An ambassador was not entitled to offer sanctuary to criminals or enemies of the state. Of course, a wise ruler would show discretion: Minor misdemeanors, such as the harboring of disreputable, though not strictly felonious persons might be overlooked.

An ambassador's carriages were also included in his personal immunity, and were not subject to stop or search. That said, as in the case of his house, this did not entitle the ambassador to use his carriages for discreditable purposes. "It would be absurd that a foreign minister should have the power of conveying off in his coach a criminal of consequence—a man, in the seizure of whose person the state was highly interested." This, Vattel reported, is what the French ambassador in Rome had recently tried to accomplish. He had sheltered Neapolitan rebels in his home and then tried to convey some of them out of the city. With absolute justification, the pope's guard had stopped the carriages at the city's gates and taken the rebels into custody.

Unlike Neapolitan rebels, members of a diplomatic retinue did share an ambassador's immunity. His wife, his secretary, and his couriers could not be prosecuted, or even arrested, without the ambassador's express consent. However, an ambassador was to remember that "it would nevertheless be highly improper that they should enjoy an absolute independence, and be at liberty to indulge in every kind of licentious disorder, without control or apprehension. The ambassador must necessarily be supposed to possess whatever degree of authority is requisite for keeping them in order, and some writers will have that authority to include even a power over life and death."

Thus ended Vattel's examination of diplomatic immunity, and with it his overarching treatise on international relations:

> I do not flatter myself with the idea of having given a perfect, full, and complete treatise of the law of nations; nor was that, indeed, my design; for it would have been too great a degree of confidence in my own abilities to have made such an attempt on a subject so extensive and so copious. I shall think I have done a great deal, if my principles are approved as solid, luminous,

and sufficient to enable intelligent persons to give a proper solution on any minute questions that may arise in particular
cases; and shall be happy if the result of my labours proves in
anywise serviceable to those men in power who love mankind
and respect justice.

His conclusions would not be uncontroversial, and the world
he dreamed of had not the slightest hope of becoming a reality.
Reason of state, rather than idealism, would continue to dictate
the nature of European politics. One imagines that (optimistic
supranational organizations notwithstanding) it always will, and
that it probably should. But Vattel's contribution to the theory of
diplomacy was still one of the landmarks of eighteenth-century
intellectual history.

Some of his obsessions—extraterritoriality, for instance—
would be abandoned, but many would endure. Perhaps his greatest achievement was the way he allowed the relations between
polities to be conceptualized. The state was to be thought of as an
autonomous individual: "She deliberates and takes resolutions in
common; thus becoming a moral person, who possesses an understanding and a will peculiar to herself, and is susceptible of obligations and rights." Those of us who live in an era when nations
(likened to errant schoolchildren or upstanding policemen) are
praised or pilloried for their ethical triumphs and shortcomings
are well aware that the state as a moral actor was a conceit that
would endure. All that remained to be seen was how such theorizing would play out in practice.[236]

A Tsar and a Scientist

The diplomatic world of eighteenth century Europe was as regimented as it was extensive. To Louis XIV, successful statecraft rested
on "keeping an eye on the whole earth and constantly learning the

news of all the provinces and all of the nations, the secrets of all courts, the dispositions and weakness of all the foreign powers and of all their ministers." Specialized foreign affairs departments began springing up—the Foreign Office in London, established in 1782; and the College of Foreign Affairs in St. Petersburg, founded in 1719—and the number of resident ambassadors spiralled. Britain had nine permanent ministers overseas in 1648, and thirty by the middle of the next century. Russia had none in 1695, but twenty-one only thirty years later.

Some aspects of diplomacy remained somewhat chaotic. The permanent embassy building was still to be invented, and this forced ambassadors to waste inordinate amounts of time on mundane chores. In 1762, the fourth duke of Bedford took up his posting in Paris. The fifty-five-year-old ambassador, "fat, round and merry" by one account, spent much of his first weeks in the capital hunting for furniture. After purchasing a rosewood desk for 136 livres, toilet mirrors, night tables, and a walnut chest of drawers, he next set about finding somewhere to put them. He finally settled on a house in the Rue St. Dominique, although it was in somewhat dilapidated condition, and Bedford next had to arrange for surveyors and decorators to be employed as well as fitting out his new home with toilets, beds, and bookcases.[237]

When Sir William Trumbull travelled to the French court during the reign of James II, he could not count on finding a fully stocked establishment when he arrived. His travelling household of forty servants thus carried to Paris

a coach, a chaise and twenty horses...two trunks full of plate, nine boxes full of copper and pewter vessels, fifty boxes filled with pictures, mirrors, beds, tapestries, linen, cloth for liveries, and kitchen utensils...seven or eight dozen chairs and armchairs, twenty boxes containing tea, coffee, chocolate, wine, ale and other provisions; four large and three small cabinets; six trunks and six boxes with Sir William and Lady Trumbull's apparel [and] forty boxes, trunks, bales, valises [and] portmanteaux containing the belongings of Sir William's suite.[238]

It was a kind of domestic management that modern-day embassies are usually spared.

For all that, diplomacy had undoubtedly become more professional. Whether it was morally pristine, as Emmerich de Vattel had hoped, was less clear. Old debates continued about the characteristics of the ideal ambassador. Some eternal truths remained in favor. It was always a boon if an ambassador was handsome, good at languages, or "a man of birth and breeding." As one seventeenth-century Spanish authority explained, he was also expected to be "suitable to the character and temper of the nation to which he is sent." "To send to the North a solemn, cautious recluse, or an enemy of the nation, is to ask that he should never leave his house or talk with anyone except his servants: if he never goes out, never sees visitors or hears anyone he will hardly be able to talk or discourse with any authority upon the business or news of the realm." The good ambassador "must try and accommodate himself to the character of the natives, though at the cost of doing violence to his own."[239]

These were attributes about which everyone could agree. A more sensitive question was whether an ambassador ought to be a moral paragon—as Vattel seemed to suggest—or a more worldly, even cynical, political operative. Abraham de Wicquefort (d. 1682) had enjoyed a turbulent diplomatic career. He had served as the elector of Brandenburg's minister in Paris but fell from grace when Louis XIII's chief minister, Cardinal Mazarin, found unflattering references to himself in Wicquefort's dispatches. After a spell in the Bastille, Wicquefort was shipped, via England, to his Dutch homeland. In Holland he took up his duties as the republic's official historiographer and also served as the resident envoy for the duke of Lüneburg. At the same time he secretly accepted a pension—in return for the provision of intelligence—from Louis XIV. This was a clear conflict of interests, as Wicquefort was essentially serving at least three masters.

He was arrested in 1675 on charges of espionage and sentenced to life imprisonment. After seven years incarceration he managed, with the help of his daughter, to escape and lived out the rest of his days in Hanover. While in prison, he had written what would become a classic text on diplomatic theory, *The Ambassador and His Functions*, first published in 1681. Along with works like François de Calliere's 1716 *The Art of Negotiating with Sovereign Princes*, Wicquefort's book abandoned an earlier paradigm of ambassadorial virtue. As might be expected from a man with Wicquefort's pedigree, he espoused an unabashedly realistic attitude toward the business of embassy. The ambassador was "an honourable spy" and on occasion vice served his interests far better than virtue.

Diplomacy had always been primarily about gathering intelligence. Sometimes this could be a morally neutral pursuit. In seventeenth century London it had even taken on something of a ritualistic character. "It was the fashion of the times, and did so continue to these," wrote Francis Osbourne, "for the principal gentry, lords, courtiers and men of all professions not merely mechanic, to meet in [St.] Paul's Church by eleven, and walk in the middle aisle until twelve, and after dinner from three until six, during which time some discoursed on business, others of news." Every issue of note was discussed during these bouts of "Paul's walking," providing an extraordinary source of news and intelligence or, as John Earle put it, "the whole world's map."[240] The realistic diplomat envisaged by writers like Wicquefort and de Callieres was expected to go to greater, less reputable lengths, even as far as espionage, to secure intelligence. It was ever thus. "The proper business of ambassadors and especially of residents," the Genoese lexicographer Andrea Spinola had declared in the fifteenth century, was "spying on the designs and secrets of princes," but it had rarely been so explicitly sanctioned.[241]

And if intelligence was useful, influence was vital; if it could be obtained in unorthodox ways, so be it. Louise-Renée de Penancoet de Kéroualle, later the duchess of Portsmouth, was a daughter of the Breton nobility. In 1670 she took up a position in the service of Catherine of Braganza, wife of Charles II of England. Access to the king was the key to diplomatic influence, and as the French ambassador at the English court well knew, Charles's mistresses were a tried and tested route to the king's ear. In October 1671 the ambassador arranged for de Kéroualle to be invited to a house party in Newmarket, at which the king would also be a guest. The plan worked. De Kéroualle caught Charles's eye, became his mistress and, as such, a figure of considerable influence. Her apartments were more luxurious than the queen's and she soon proved herself an able politician, regularly helping courtiers to gain favors and promotions. To the French ambassador she was invaluable. After Louis XIV sent her a fine pair of earrings in 1675, she began to arrange private meetings between the ambassador and the king in her apartments. Crucial matters of war and peace were discussed far more openly there than would ever have been possible in a public forum.[242]

By the middle of the eighteenth century diplomacy had become a profession. In England, a closely regulated hierarchy of public servants had been established. At the top were the men who

bore the actual title of ambassador—still a rare distinction, usually reserved for members of the nobility—who, in addition to the
usual raft of expenses, might expect a salary of £100 a week. Next
came the "envoys extraordinary and plenipotentiary," men sent on
specific missions (to negotiate a treaty, for instance) and vested
with full authority to act on the government's behalf. These diplomats received £8 a day, three pounds more than an envoy extraordinary, whose autonomy was circumscribed. "Residents" earned
£3 a day, and their secretaries £2. Diplomacy was now a career,
and it even offered the prospect of a pensioned old age. John Mur-
ray, after serving as a resident in Venice and Constantinople between 1754 and 1766, returned home in 1770 to a yearly pension
of £1000.[243]

One wonders, in such an organized diplomatic world, if there
was still room for the ambassadorial maverick. There was.

The relationship between Russia and western Europe that developed in the wake of embassies like Iosip Nepea's had always been
an uneasy one. The English, for instance, quickly adopted a snobbish attitude toward Russian visitors, regarding their standard gifts
of furs and tallow as a hallmark of their backwardness and barbarity. London society, rather than lavishing attention on Russia's
ambassadors, began to gossip about her diplomatic entourages getting hopelessly drunk and delousing one another.

From the sixteenth century onward, English ambassadors would
complain of bad roads, inferior lodgings, outbreaks of plague, and
the frosty reception they received in the Russian capital. They
would find themselves under constant surveillance and would

often be treated with gross discourtesy. In 1568 Thomas Randolph was made to wait a full seventeen weeks for an audience with the tsar.

Ivan IV, known to history as the Terrible, may have tried to reform Russia's legal and military systems, but he was also the man who cast away six wives (one drowned, two poisoned, three sent to nunneries) and blinded the architects who designed the bulbously beautiful St. Basil's Cathedral. His ruthlessness became legendary in the West, especially after he wreaked revenge on the rebellious city of Novgorod in 1570. Horrific stories were told of men being roasted alive, and of women and children being tied together and thrown into the freezing Volkhov River. He was, unsurprisingly, a temperamental diplomatic partner—not least because he despised Elizabeth I, a monarch who had once haughtily, if prudently, rebuffed his offer of marriage.

On occasion, suspicion and ill will gave way to outright squabbling. In 1583, the ambassador Jerome Bowes seemed to be having an amicable conversation with the tsar, toasting Elizabeth I with Rhenish wine laced with sugar. Suddenly, the tsar's mood soured and "with a stern and angry countenance" he announced that "he did not reckon the Queen of England to be his fellow, for there are those that are her betters." His monarch's honor insulted, Bowes replied "with like courage and countenance...that the queen his majesty was as great a prince as any that was in Christendom, equal to him that thought himself the greatest, and well able to defend herself against his malice." An incandescent tsar ordered Bowes out of his presence, remarking that "were he not an ambassador he would throw him out of doors."

Quite soon, however, the tsar regretted his outburst and ordered a generous increase in the daily allowance of food and drink allotted to the ambassador and his retinue. Every day they could now look forward to (among much else) two live geese, twenty hens, seven sheep, one side of pork, seventy eggs, ten pounds of butter, three ounces of saffron and cinnamon, two ounces of cloves, and one ounce each of mace and nutmeg.[244]

Moscow would never be regarded as a plum diplomatic posting. Even as late as the eighteenth century, an ambassador like Charles Whitworth only took up a position in Russia because he lacked adequate patronage to do any better for himself. He would spend his time in the capital grumbling about the four long months it had taken to get there; about the four weeks one had to wait for a letter home to reach its recipient; and about Moscow's abysmal food, weather, and utter lack of theatrical entertainment.[245] There was, at least, one thing for which Whitworth could be grateful—an enlightened, inquisitive, if imperious, tsar.

The grand embassy of Peter the Great, tsar since 1682, marked Russia's emergence as a world power. A dedicated believer in the westernization of his country, Peter modernized his armies, began to establish a formidable navy, and sought to eradicate traces of what he regarded as Russian medievalism—old calendars, traditional clothing, and long beards. Isolation gave way to engagement, and Peter proved that, on occasion, a career bureaucrat was not the best man for an ambassadorial job. Peter's aim was simple: to recruit allies against the Turks and to establish lasting friendships with the leaders of western Europe. He was also passionately curious about everything the West had to offer.

He did not travel in state. Along with a thousand sledges and three officials, he left Russia in March 1697 disguised as a commoner named Peter Mikhailov—one of thirty-five craftsmen destined for the shipyards of Holland. Upon reaching the port of

Riga (a Swedish possession at the time), this subterfuge began to seem like a foolish idea. While Peter was looking over the ships in the harbor, a group of Swedish officers, fearful that the Russians were engaged in maritime espionage, rudely ordered Peter and his entourage to move on. It was an insult to his dignity that Peter would long remember, though one for which he was entirely responsible. Had his clothing revealed him to be a tsar he would have received a very different reception.

Undeterred, Peter continued his clandestine diplomatic mission, although Europe's rumor mill had made the tsar's incognito travels across the continent something of an open secret. Having traversed Germany he finally arrived in Amsterdam dressed as a Dutch sailor and took up his lodgings in a blacksmith's tiny house. The next four and a half months were a bizarre mixture of nights filled with lavish diplomatic receptions and days spent in the Amsterdam shipyards studying at the feet of the master shipwright Claas Paul, learning a trade that had always fascinated him.

In January 1698 Peter crossed the channel to England. Here he talked with naval experts, enjoyed scientific experiments, and had his portrait painted by Sir Godfrey Kneller. Peter was astounded by the cultural and mercantile diversity of the country, avidly buying up watches, scientific instruments, and even a coffin for Russian coffin-makers to replicate. The British were rather taken with Peter, too. The old image of Russian barbarity had not faded, and the sight of an inquisitive tsar, desperate to learn from the technological genius of the West, was a gratifying sight.

After a visit to Vienna—where the disguise was once again temporarily discarded during important negotiations—rebellion at home forced Peter's return to Moscow. Little had been achieved on the diplomatic front, but the six-foot-seven-inch tsar had caused a sensation, and the cultural and intellectual links he had forged would yield enormous dividends. In the coming years, western shipwrights, doctors, and mathematicians flooded into Russia, and Peter's vision of a modern, forward-looking nation began to emerge.[246]

The lesson about unconventional ambassadors was one that the eighteenth century learned time and again. When the United States dispatched its first ambassador to Paris, at the height of military engagement with the British, it did not choose a polished, urbane career diplomat. It chose Benjamin Franklin, humble of attire, unaffected of manners, but a man the French took to their hearts. His scientific reputation preceded his arrival in Paris in December 1776—he had been elected to the French Academy of Science four years earlier—and his endearing blend of humility, candor, and prodigious intellect allowed him to score diplomatic triumph after diplomatic triumph. He was in no sense the textbook ambassador, but he secured financial aid and then a full treaty of alliance from the French government. It is entirely possible that without his exertions, the War of Independence would have taken a very different turn.

The boring niceties of modern diplomacy did sometimes intrude on Franklin's mission, and unseasoned as he was in such affairs, he did not always perform as might be expected. When a Russian count arrived in Paris, he sent cards to all of the resident ambassadors, with the name of the Russian envoy, Prince Bariatinski, written on them. At this stage, Russia had not recognized America's independence, and any diplomatic dialogue between the two powers was a legal impossibility. It was therefore inappropriate for the count to send a card to Franklin, but that, accidentally, is precisely what he did.

Franklin was at a loss as to how to react. Was he to visit the Russian count as the delivery of a calling card usually demanded? He sought the counsel of a more experienced diplomat at court, who told him that, in the unusual circumstances, he should take his carriage to the ambassador's house and, without leaving a card or requesting an audience, simply ask that his name be recorded in the porter's book. Franklin assumed that he had fastened on an elegant solution, but the matter was not so easily dispensed with.

First, the servant who had originally delivered the Russian count's card visited Franklin "in great affliction, saying that he was like to be ruined." Then one of Franklin's friends revealed that the Russian count was utterly mortified by his mistake. The prince wanted Franklin to know that he had "great personal regard for me and my character, but that, our independence not yet being acknowledged by the court of Russia, it was impossible for him to permit himself to make me a visit as minister." Something of an impasse had been reached, until Franklin dispensed with all of the absurd rules of diplomatic etiquette with an example of his fabled common sense. "I thought the remedy was easy; he had only to erase my name out of his book of visits received, and I would burn their card."[247]

Franklin had not only transcended the rules of diplomacy, he had also seen the Montgolfier brothers fly their balloon, he had conversed with Voltaire, and he returned to America in triumph.

⊷⊶

In fact, the diversity and adaptability embodied by men like Franklin and Peter the Great had always defined the history of the ambassadors. In the coming decades, it would be as valuable as it had ever been. Very soon, the charm and elegance Franklin had encountered in Paris would be shattered by revolution. "I am sorry," Earl Gower wrote on January 21, 1793, "it has fallen to my lot to be the messenger of the most disagreeable intelligence that I, or anyone else was ever obliged to communicate." The revolution that had begun in France in 1789 was entering its most radical phase, one that appalled the man who had recently completed his service as England's ambassador to the French court. The National Convention, after thirty-four hours' debate, had voted to execute King Louis XVI.

Gower was "much afraid [that] if his majesty is not already dead he can scarcely be saved. The day I left Paris there were some thousands of men parading in different parts of the city ready to commit any sort of riot and threatening destruction should the king not be put to death."[248] Once again, ambassadors were the privileged witnesses of history, and as well as living through the chaos of revolution they were also charged with legislating its aftermath.

The Congress of Vienna of 1814–1815 sought to redraw the map of Europe in the wake of the revolutionary and Napoleonic wars that had raged since the 1790s. The terms and compromises reached at Vienna need not detain us. What really matters is that the Congress has, with good reason, been seen as the beginning of a new era in European diplomacy. Men like Castlereagh, Talleyrand, and Metternich—the principal English, French, and Austrian representatives—have the air of modern diplomatists, fully formed: the models for the hundreds of ambassadors and ministers who would crowd the chancelleries and embassies of Europe for the next two hundred years. And so they were; but ultimately the events at Vienna were not so very different from the ambassadorial chores and adventures that had been unfolding for thousands of years.

The setting was grander and the stakes were higher than those to which Bronze Age tribes or Assyrian envoys were accustomed—but the purpose was the same: to meet, to talk, and, should things go well, to reach an accord. The posturing of the delegates was familiar, too. Every morning Talleyrand would hold a public audience, where people could watch his two barbers primping his extravagant wig. Like so many ambassadors before him he was showing off, asserting his, and his nation's style and cultural sophistication.

Diplomacy often conceals mistrust beneath a façade of civility. That was the case in ancient Greece, when Demosthenes visited Philip of Macedon; it was the case when thirteenth-century friars journeyed to the Mongol khans; and it was the case at Vienna. The entertainments devised for the delegates, the ritual grandeur of a Byzantium adjusted for a different age, were lavish— balls and banquets, sledging and hunting excursions, Beethoven conducting his Seventh Symphony—but the atmosphere of intrigue was palpable.

The Austrian emperor received daily accounts of the movements of important figures at the Congress, supplied by his chief of police, Baron Hager. Agents crisscrossed the city, recording every movement of every influential king, prince, or minister. Coachmen and porters, housemaids and even beggars were all pressed into service, gathering information about the great powers' intentions. "The British mission," Hager lamented one day, "owing to excessive caution, has engaged two housemaids of its own. Before I can get at the waste-paper which they throw into the baskets I must see whether I can count on these two women."[249]

It was not so very far from the Mauryan strategies of Kautilya's *Arthasastra*. The genius and value of diplomacy, however, had always been that nations could meet and parley despite such distractions. Duplicity and double-dealing only ever made the ancient game more interesting.

ACKNOWLEDGMENTS

I WOULD LIKE TO THANK my editors, Michael Fishwick, Richard Johnson and Andrea Schulz and my agents, George Lucas, Peter Robinson and John Saddler.

ENDNOTES

Place of publication is London unless otherwise indicated.

1. "A discourse of the honourable receiving into England of the first ambassador from the emperor of Russia, in the year of Christ 1556," in R. Hakluyt, *The Principal Navigations, Voyages, Traffiques and Discoveries of the English Nation* (12 volumes, Glasgow, 1903–5), II: 350–360.

2. "A copy of the first privileges granted by the emperor of Russia to the English Merchants in the year 1555," in Hakluyt, *Principal Navigations*, II: 297–304.

3. E. A Bond, ed., *Russia at the Close of the Sixteenth Century* (1856), 2–4, 5–6, 8–15, 146–152.

4. G. Glover, *The arrival and intertaiments of the embassador Alkaid Jaurar Ben Abdella* (1637), 2, 3, 8, 15.

5. C. M. Brand, ed./tr., *The Deeds of John and Manuel Comnenus by J. Kinnamos* (New York, 1976), 158–159.

6. Ibid., 156–157.

7. L. Macmahon, "Courtesy and Conflict: The Experience of English Diplomatic Personnel at the Court of Francis I," in D. Grummitt, ed., *The English Experience in France, c. 1450–1558: War, Diplomacy and Cultural Exchange* (Aldershot, 2002), 186.

8. W. L. Moran, ed., *The Amarna Letters* (Baltimore, MD, 1992), passim.

9. F. Thynne, *The Perfect Ambassadour, treating of the antiquitie, priviledges, and behaviour of men belonging to that function* (1652), 8.

10. F. Adcock and D. J. Mosley, *Diplomacy in Ancient Greece* (1975), 261–262.

11. P. J. H. Darton, ed., *The Golden Ass of Apuleius in the Translation of William Adlington* (1924), 194.

12. C. Brown, T. Nardin and N. Rengger, eds., *International Relations in Political Thought* (Cambridge, 2002), 17.

13. J. H. Vince, ed., *Demosthenes Orations I* (Cambridge, MA, 1930), 69–99.

14. B. B. Rogers, ed., *Aristophanes* (Cambridge, MA, 1924), 461–467.

15. C. D. Adams, ed., *Aeschines Orations* (1919), 158–301. See K. Dover, *Greek Homosexuality* (1978), 19–47.

16. C. A. Vince and J. H. Vince, eds., *Demosthenes Orations III* (Cambridge, MA, 1953), 247–478.

17. Adams, *Aeschines,* 1–156.

18. J. W. Thompson and S. K. Padover, *Secret Diplomacy: A Record of Espionage and Double-Dealing, 1500–1815* (1937), 121–122.

19. J. Chardin, *Travels in Persia* (1927), 88.

20. R. C. Majumdar, *The Classical Accounts of India* (Calcutta, 1960), 147–150.

21. J. W. McCrindle, *Ancient India as Described by Megasthenes and Arrian* (Calcutta, 1926), passim; G. Woodcock, *The Greeks in India* (1966), 49ff.

22. J. W. Rich, *Declaring War in the Roman Republic in the Period of Transmarine Expansion* (Brussels, 1976), 64.

23. R. Thapar, *Asoka and the Decline of the Mauryans* (Oxford, 1977), 262–263.

24. A. Seneviratna, *King Asoka and Buddhism* (Kandy, Sri Lanka, 1994).

25. Thapar, *Asoka,* 250–260.

26. Thapar, *Asoka,* 17.

27. R. Boesche, "Kautilya's *Arthasastra:* on War and Diplomacy in Ancient India," *Journal of Military History,* 67 (2003), 9–37.

28. D. Boucher, *Political Theories of International Relations* (Oxford, 1998), 34.

29. Brown, *International Relations*, 53–60.

30. Kautilya, *Arthashastra*, ed./tr., R. Shamasastry (Bangalore, 1915), passim.

31. J. Boardman, *The Greeks Overseas* (1980), 139.

32. H. Serrys, *Sino-Mongol Relations During the Ming*, Volume II (Brussels, 1967), 583.

33. P. Fleming, *The Siege at Peking* (Hong Kong, 1983), 125, 126–127.

34. W. A. P. Martin, *The Siege in Peking. China Against the World* (New York, 1900), 51.

35. P. Cohen, *History in Three Keys: The Boxers as Event, Experience and Myth* (New York, 1997), 55.

36. R. L. Walker, ed., *China and the West: Cultural Collision* (Yale, 1956), 33–35.

37. R. B. Merriman, *Suleiman the Magnificent 1520–1566* (Cambridge, MA, 1944), 129.

38. Serrys, *Sino-Mongol Relations*, II: 481–488.

39. J. W. Sadler, *India and the Greek World: A Study in the Transmission of Culture* (Totowa, NJ, 1980), 81.

40. E. M. Thomson, ed., *The Chamberlain Letters* (1966), 28–29.

41. Majumdar, *The Classical Accounts of India*, 474.

42. Y-S. Yu, *Trade and Expansion in Han China* (Berkeley, CA, 1967), 37.

43. L. Torday, *Mounted Archers: The Beginnings of Central Asian History* (Bishop Auckland, 1997), 1–4, 104–139; M. Loewe, *A Biographical Dictionary of the Qin, Former Han and Xin Periods* (Leiden, 2000), 687–688, 407–411; F. Wood, *The Silk Road: Two Thousand Years in the Heart of Asia* (2004), 50–59, 65; N. Di Cosmo, *Ancient China and its Enemies: The Rise of Nomadic Power in East Asian History* (Cambridge, 2002).

44. L. Auel, *Tokens and Treasures: Gifts to Twelve Presidents* (Washington, DC, 1996).

45. A. Cutler, "Gifts and Gift Exchange as Aspects of the Byzantine, Arab, and Related Economies," *Dumbarton Oaks Papers*, 55 (2001), 247.

46. Thomson, *Chamberlain Letters*, 142–143.

47. M. Brown, *Itinerant Ambassador: The Life of Sir Thomas Roe* (Lexington, KY, 1976), 31.

48. R. Barbour, "Power and Distant Display: Early English Ambassadors in Moghul India," *Huntington Library Quarterly*, 61 (2000), 363–364.

49. H. Bielenstein, *Diplomacy and Trade in the Chinese World, 598–1276* (Boston, 2005), 357.

50. Majumdar, *The Classical Accounts of India*, 228.

51. G. Wiet, *Baghdad: Metropolis of the Abbasid Caliphate* (Norman, OK, 1971), 8–9.

52. N. M. El Cheikh, *Byzantium Viewed by the Arabs* (Cambridge, MA, 2004), 91–97.

53. M. Becher, *Charlemagne* (New Haven, CT, 2003), 2–3.

54. Ibid., 7.

55. *Secret Memoirs of the Court of St. Cloud* (1904), letter x, Paris, August 1805.

56. *Song of Roland*, ed., G. Burgess (1990).

57. F. L. Ganshof, *The Carolingians and the Frankish Monarchy* (1971), 162–204.

58. L. Thorpe, ed., *Two Lives of Charlemagne* (1969), 141, 143.

59. H. Wace, ed., "Life of Constantine," in *Library of Nicene and Post-Nicene Fathers, Second Series, Volume I* (Grand Rapids, MI, 1890), 524.

60. E. A. Thomson, *A History of Attila and the Huns* (Oxford, 1948), 148–152.

61. J. K. Fairbank, *The Chinese World Order: Traditional China's Foreign Relations* (Cambridge, MA, 1968), 48.

62. F. L. Ganshof, *Histoire des Relations Internationales: Le Moyen Age* (Paris, 1953), 49.

63. F. Joannes, *The Age of Empires: Mesopotamia in the First Millennium B.C.* (Edinburgh, 2000), 71.

64. Ammianus Marcellinus, *History of Rome from Constantine to Valens*, ed./tr., C. D. Yonge (1885); O. J. Maenchen-Helfen, *The World of the Huns* (1973), 1–7.

65. Gordon, *The Age of Attila*, 57–111.

66. S. A. Meier, *The Messenger in the Ancient Semitic World* (Atlanta, GA, 1988), 68–69.

67. P. Chaplais, *English Diplomatic Practice in the Middle Ages* (2003), 1–2.

68. B. Behrens, "Treatises on the Ambassador Written in the Fifteenth and Early Sixteenth Centuries," *English Historical Review*, 51 (1936), 624.

69. P. de Bethune, *The counsellor of estate* (1634), 57.

70. A. Zannini, "Economic and Social Aspects of the Crisis of Venetian Diplomacy," in D. Frigo, ed., *Politics and Diplomacy in Early-Modern Italy: The Structure of Diplomatic Practice 1450–1800* (Cambridge, 2000), 115.

71. F. A. Wright, ed., *The Works of Liudprand of Cremona* (1930), 235–270.

72. M. Angold, *Byzantium: The Bridge From Antiquity to the Middle Ages* (2001), 1–15.

73. T. Widerman, "The Fetiales: A Reconsideration," *Classical Quarterly*, 36 (1986), 478–480.

74. Ostrogorsky, G., "The Byzantine Emperor and the Hierarchical World Order," *Byzantion*, 19 (1956–57), 12; E. Barker, *Social and Political Thought in Byzantium: From Justinian to the Last Palaeologus* (Oxford, 1957), 103–104.

75. A. Comnena, *The Alexiad of the Princess Anna Comnena*, tr. E. Dawes (1928), 264.

76. Ostrogorsky, "The Byzantine Emperor and the Hierarchical World Order," 1–14.

77. D. Obolensky, "The Principles and Methods of Byzantine Diplomacy," in *Byzantium and the Slavs: Collected Studies* (1971), 59–60; J. Martin, *Medieval Russia, 980–1584* (Cambridge, 1995), 5–11.

78. M. Twain, *The Innocents Abroad* (1906 ed.), 96.

79. D. Queller, *The Office of Ambassador in the Middle Ages* (Princeton, NJ, 1967), 13.

80. Nicol, *Byzantium and Venice*, 167–170.

81. D. Matthew, *The Norman Kingdom of Sicily* (Cambridge, 1992), 102.

82. J. Bentley, *Restless Bones: The Story of Relics* (1985), 50–52; G. Majeska, "Russian Pilgrims to Constantinople," *Dumbarton Oaks Papers*, 56 (2002), 93–108.

83. G. De Villehardouin, *Memoirs or Chronicle of the Fourth Crusade and the Conquest of Constantinople*, ed./tr., F. T. Marzials (1908), 1–9.

84. Brand, *The Deeds of John and Manuel Comnenus*, 210.

85. Nicol, *Byzantium and Venice*, 47.

86. C. M. Brand, *Byzantium Confronts the West, 1180–1204* (Cambridge, MA, 1968), 41–43, 195–196.

87. Villehardouin, *Memoirs*, 1–9.

88. Queller, *Office*, passim.

89. W. W. Rockhill, ed., *The Journey of William Rubruck...with Two Accounts of the Earlier Journey of John of Pian de Carpine* (Hakluyt Society, 1890), 40.

90. Hakluyt, *Principal Navigations*, I: 50–54.

91. Rockhill, *Rubruck*, 49.

92. J. Boyle, *The Mongol World Empire* (1977), 77.

93. Rockhill, *Rubruck*, 168, 103–104, 172–175.

94. Ibid., 2.

95. Ibid., 4.

96. Ibid., 4.

97. Ibid., 5.

98. Ibid., 5–6.

99. Ibid., 7.

100. Ibid., 9, 10.

101. Ibid., 11–12, 13, 17.

102. Ibid., 18–19, 120–121.

103. Ibid., 22–30.

104. Ibid., 29.

105. Hakluyt, *Principal Navigations*, I: 136.

106. Rockhill, *Rubruck*, 62–63, 67.

107. Ibid., 73–76.

108. Ibid., 207–211; Hakluyt, *Principal Navigations*, I: 137–138.

109. J. Giles, ed./tr., *Matthew Paris's English History* (3 vols., 1852–1854) I: 131–132.

110. E. A. Wallis Budge, *The Monks of Kublai Khan Emperor of China* (1928), 124–139, 161–197.

111. G. Le Strange, ed./tr., *Clavijo: Embassy to Tamerlane 1403–1406* (1928), 94–103.

112. Nicol, *Byzantium and Venice*, 338ff.

113. Le Strange, *Clavijo*, 177–180.

114. Ibid., 215–217.

115. Ibid., 228–230.

116. Ibid., 278–281.

117. Ibid., 288–300.

118. Ibid., 25–26.

119. Ibid., 219, 149–150.

120. S. Anglo, *Machiavelli* (1971), 188.

121. M. Rowdon, *Lorenzo the Magnificent* (1974), 71–72, 143–151.

122. G. Mattingly, *Renaissance Diplomacy* (1955), 55–105.

123. P. De Commines, *The Memoirs Containing the Histories of Louis XI and Charles VIII, Kings of France, and of Charles the Bold, Duke of Burgundy* (2 vols., 1882–1883) I: 180–187.

124. S. Nofke, *The Letters of Catherine of Siena* (Binghamton, NY, 1988), 207–215.

125. Ibid., 108–130.

126. Anglo, *Machiavelli*, 264–265.

127. T. Churchyard, *A Prayse and Reporte of Maister Martyne Frobisher's Voyage to Meta Incognita* (1578), 7.

128. D. Settle, *A True Reporte of the Laste Voyage into the West and Northwest Regions... Worthily Achieved by Capteine Frobisher* (1577), sig. CIv.

129. Ibid., sig. C5.

130. R. G. Thwaites, ed., *The Jesuit Relations and Allied Documents* (73 volumes, 1896–1901), XXVII: 247.

131. Ibid., 251.

132. Ibid., 257.

133. F. Parkman, *The Jesuits in North America in the Seventeenth Century* (1997 edition, Lincoln, NE), 388, 393.

134. M. Brown, *Itinerant Ambassador: The Life of Sir Thomas Roe* (Lexington, KY, 1976), 41.

135. R. P. Toby, *State and Diplomacy in Early Modern Japan* (Princeton, NJ, 1984), 188–194.

136. J. Brown, "Courtiers and Christians: The First Japanese Emissaries to Europe," *Renaissance Quarterly*, 47 (1994), 872–906.

137. J. G. Russell, *The Field of Cloth of Gold: Men and Manners in 1520* (1969).

138. R. Brown, ed., *Calendar of State Papers Venetian, 1527–1533* (1981), 285–289.

139. Ibid., 285–289.

140. Ibid., 292, 179–184.

141. Ibid., 2–3, 57–61.

142. Ibid., 204, 219.

143. Ibid., 250, 256.

144. G. Elton, *The Tudor Constitution* (Cambridge, 1960), 344–349.

145. Brown, *Calendar*, 551.

146. Ibid., 338, 357, 348.

147. J. S. Hansom, "Proceedings Against Catholics for Attending Mass at the Spanish Embassy on Palm Sunday, 1614," *Miscellanea VII* (Catholic Record Society Publications, 9, 1911), 122–126.

148. J. H. Pollen, "Relation of a Brawl Between the King's Officers and Servants of the French Ambassador Concerning the Catholics who Resorted to Mass at Durham House," *Miscellanea I* (Catholic Record Society Publications, I, 1905), 92–95.

149. Thynne, *Perfect Ambassador*, sigs. 71–72v.

150. W. C. Abbot, *The Writings and Speeches of Oliver Cromwell* (4 vols., Cambridge, MA, 1937–47), III: 98–101, 354–356.

151. L. S., *Letter from a Gentleman at Fez to a Person of Honour in London* (1670), 1.

152. M. Keen, *The Laws of War in the Late Middle Ages* (1965), 189–207.

153. M. Anderson, *The Rise of Modern Diplomacy, 1450–1919* (1993), 256.

154. David Morgan, *The Mongols* (Oxford, 1984), 67.

155. "A Relation of the Mutiny in the New Exchange," in J. Somers, ed., *A Third Collection of Scarce and Valuable Tracts* (1751), II: 65–81.

156. M. A. S. Hume, ed., *Calendar of State Papers Spanish, 1559–68* (1892), 69.

157. Ibid., 126.

158. Ibid., 232–233.

159. Ibid., 236.

160. Ibid., 238–247.

161. Ibid., 276–302, 315.

162. Ibid., 89, 119, 132, 270, 319; G. D. Ramsay, *The City of London in International Politics at the Accession of Elizabeth Tudor* (Manchester, 1975), 93–99.

163. M. Khadduri, *War and Peace in the Law of Islam* (Baltimore, MD, 1955), 239–250.

164. J. Chrysostomides, "Byzantine Concepts of War and Peace," in A. Hartmann and B. Heuser eds., *War, Peace and World Orders in European History* (2001), 98–99.

165. M. Vaiou, "The Diplomatic Relations Between the Abbasid Caliphate and the Byzantine Empire: Methods and Procedures," Unpublished D.Phil. Thesis (Oxford, 2001), 211–215; G. Le Strange, "A Greek Embassy to Baghdad in 917 A.D.," *Journal of the Royal Asiatic Society* 29 (1897), 35–485.

166. O. Grabar, "The Shared Culture of Objects," in H. Maguire, ed., *Byzantine Court Culture from 829–1204* (Washington, DC, 1997), 121.

167. B. Lewis, *The Muslim Discovery of Europe* (1982), 93–94.

168. E. Levi-Provençal, *Histoire de l'Espagne Musulmane* (Paris, 1950), II: 143–153.

169. Lewis, *Muslim Discovery*, 52.

170. B. F. Reilly, *The Medieval Spains* (Cambridge, 1993), 67.

171. A. Nixon, *The Three English Brothers* (1602), sig. H4v.

172. D. Blanks and M. Frassetto, eds., *Western Views of Islam in Medieval and Early Modern Europe* (New York, 1999), 226.

173. R. Knolles, *The Generall Historie of the Turkes* (1603), preface.

174. D. Goffman, *The Ottoman Empire and Early Modern Europe* (Cambridge, 2002), 139.

175. B. Ari, "Early Ottoman Diplomacy: Ad Hoc Period," in A. N. Yurdusev, ed., *Ottoman Diplomacy: Conventional or Unconventional?* (2004), 40–41.

176. H. G. Rawlinson, "The Embassy of William Harbourne to Constantinople, 1583–8," *Transactions of the Royal Historical Society*, 4th series, 5 (1922), 1–27.

177. Knolles, *Turkes*, 713.

178. R. Barbour, "Power and Distant Display: Early English Ambassadors in Moghul India," *Huntington Library Quarterly*, 61 (2000), 348–350.

179. Knolles, *Turkes*, preface.

180. O. G. de Busbecq, *The Four Epistles* (1694), epistle I, 10–30.

181. V. Carretta, ed., *The Letters of Ignatius Sancho* (1988), x.

182. C. Hibbert, *King Mob: The Story of Lord George Gordon and the Riots of 1780* (1958).

183. Carretta, *Letters*, x.

184. D. M. Jones, *The Image of China in Western Social and Political Thought* (Basingstoke, 2001), 38–43; J. Hevia, *Cherishing from Afar: Qing Guest Ritual and the Macartney Embassy of 1793* (Durham, NC, 1995).

185. J. Oliphant, "The Cherokee Embassy to London, 1762," *Journal of Imperial and Commonwealth History*, 27 (1999), 1–26.

186. J. Day, W. Rowley and G. Wilkins, *The Travels of the Three English Brothers*, in A. Parr, ed., *Three Renaissance Travel Plays* (Manchester, 1995), 63.

187. W. Parry, *A New and Large Discourse of the Travels of Sir Anthony Sherley* (1601), preface, 4.

188. A. Sherley, *His Relation of his Travels into Persia* (1613), 29.

189. Ibid., 109–112, 119.

190. P. Sykes, *A History of Persia* (2 vols., 1921), II: 176–177.

191. Parry, *Discourse*, 5, 24, 26, and passim.

192. "Anthony Sherley," *New Dictionary of National Biography*.

193. A. Nixon, *The Three English Brothers* (1602), sig. G1v.

194. J. Day, W. Rowley and G. Wilkins, *The Travels of the Three English Brothers*, in A. Parr, ed., *Three Renaissance Travel Plays* (Manchester, 1995), scene i, 105–27; ii, 45–53; iii, 5–6; vii, 1–25.

195. L. P. Smith, *The Life and Letters of Sir Henry Wotton* (2 vols., Oxford, 1907), I: 25.

196. Ibid., I: 215.

197. Ibid., I: 216–219.

198. C. Howard, *English Travellers of the Renaissance* (1923), 73.

199. R. Ascham, *The Schoolmaster*, ed. L. V. Ryan (Charlottesville, VA, 1974), 67.

200. J. Bruce, ed., *Calendar of State Papers Domestic, 1631–33* (1862), xiii.

201. *The traveiler of Jerome Turler* (1575), 66; M. C. Clarke, "British Travellers to Rome in Tudor and Stuart Times," *History Today*, 28 (1978), 747.

202. Smith, *Wotton*, I: 271–277.

203. Ibid., I: 40–41.

204. Ibid., I: 317.

205. Ibid., I: 46–53.

206. Ibid., I: 367.

207. Ibid., I: 330–336.

208. Ibid., I: 350.

209. Ibid., I: 398.

210. Ibid., I: 462–478.

211. Ibid., I: 478–479.

212. Ibid., I: 126–127.

213. Ibid., II: 143–145.

214. Ibid., II: 153–155.

215. Ibid., I: 478–479.

216. Nicol, *Byzantium and Venice*, 232.

217. Smith, *Wotton*, II: 55–56.

218. B. Luard, *The Balance of Power: The System of International Relations, 1648–1815* (1992), 134–135.

219. Luard, *Balance of Power*, 135–136.

220. Smith, *Wotton*, II: 248.

221. Ibid., II: 262.

222. Ibid., II: 232–234.

223. Ibid., II: 279.

224. P. Limm, *The Thirty Years War* (1984), 101–105.

225. Smith, *Wotton*, I: 243–245.

226. A. Almansa y Mendoza, *The ioyfull return of the most illustrious Charles, prince of Great Britain from the court of Spain* (1623), 13.

227. Smith, *Wotton*, II: 198.

228. R. G. Asch, *The Thirty Years War* (1997), 126–149.

229. S. Pufendorf, *On the Duty of Man and Citizen*, ed. H. Wright (New York, 1927), Book I, ch. 3, paras 2–13; Books II, ch. 16, paras 1–17.

230. E. Vattel, *The Law of Nations*, ed./tr., J. Chitty (Philadelphia, 1883) Book II, ch. 1, para 20.

231. Ibid., II. 1, 3–8.

232. Ibid., II. 1, 15–16.

233. Ibid., IV. 6, 69–79.

234. Ibid., IV. 7, 80–109.

235. G. McClanahan, *Diplomatic Immunity* (1989), 144.

236. Vattel, *Law of Nations*, IV. 7, 80–109; 8, 110–116; 9, 117–127.

237. J. Evans, "The Embassy of the 4th Duke of Bedford to Paris, 1762–3," *Archaeological Journal*, 113 (1956), 138–139.

238. D. B. Horn, *The British Diplomatic Service 1689–1789* (Oxford, 1961), 66–67.

239. H. J. Chaytor, ed./tr., "Embajada Española: The Spanish Embassy," *Camden Miscellany XIV* (1926), 5, 15.

240. C. Carter, *The Secret Diplomacy of the Habsburgs, 1598–1625* (New York, 1964), 287.

241. D. Frigo, ed., *Politics and Diplomacy in Early-Modern Italy: The Structure of Diplomatic Practice 1450–1800* (Cambridge, 2000), 10.

242. J. Delpech, *The Life and Times of the Duchess of Portsmouth* (1953); *Oxford Dictionary of National Biography*.

243. Horn, *Diplomatic Service*, 46–47.

244. "A letter sent from her highness to the said great duke of Russia, by Sir Jeremy Bowes aforesaid, her majesty's ambassador," in Hakluyt, *Principal Navigations*, III: 308–328.

245. J. Hartley, "'Losing My Best Days': Charles Whitworth, first British Ambassador to Russia," *History Today*, 50 (2000), 40–46.

246. L. Hughes, *Peter the Great* (Yale, 2002), 40–58.

247. J. Sparks, *Life of Benjamin Franklin* (1850), chapter 10.

248. O. Browning, ed., *The Despatches of Earl Gower* (Cambridge, 1885), 279–280, 211.

249. H. Nicolson, *The Congress of Vienna: A Study in Allied Unity: 1812–1822* (1946), 204–205.

SELECT BIBLIOGRAPHY

The history of diplomacy has generated an enormous body of scholarly literature, one that cannot hope to be reflected in this bibliography. All that follows is, with a handful of important additions, a list of books cited. Place of publication is London unless otherwise indicated.

Abbot, W. C., *The Writings and Speeches of Oliver Cromwell* (4 vols., Cambridge, MA, 1937–47).

Adair, E., *The Extraterritoriality of Ambassadors in the Sixteenth and Seventeenth Centuries* (New York, 1929).

Adams, C. D., *Aeschines* (Cambridge, MA, 1919).

Adcock, F. E. and Mosley, D. J., *Diplomacy in Ancient Greece* (New York, 1975).

Almansa y Mendoza, A., *The ioyfull return of the most illustrious Charles, prince of Great Britain from the court of Spain* (1623).

Anderson, M., *Britain's Discovery of Russia, 1553–1815* (1958).

Anderson, M., *The Rise of Modern Diplomacy, 1450–1919* (1993).

Anglo, S., *Machiavelli* (1971).

Angold, M., *Byzantium: The Bridge From Antiquity to the Middle Ages* (2001).

Anon, "A Relation of the Mutiny in the New Exchange," in *A Third Collection of Scarce and Valuable Tracts* (1751), II: 65–81.

Armitage, D., ed., *Theories of Empire, 1450–1800: An Expanding World* (Aldershot, 1998).

Ascham, R., *The Schoolmaster*, ed. L. V. Ryan (Charlottesville, VA, 1974).

Auel, L., *Tokens and Treasures: Gifts to Twelve Presidents* (Washington DC, 1996).

Aylmer, G. E., *The State's Servants: The Civil Service of the English Republic, 1649–1660* (1973).

Barbour, R., "Power and Distant Display: Early English Ambassadors in Moghul India," *Huntington Library Quarterly*, 61 (2000), 343–368.

Barker, E., *Social and Political Thought in Byzantium: From Justinian to the Last Palaeologus* (Oxford, 1957).

Beauvoir, O de, *The Indian Travels of Apollonius of Tyana and the Indian Embassies to Rome from the Reign of Augustus to the death of Justinian* (1873).

Becher, M., *Charlemagne* (New Haven, CT, 2003).

Behrens, B., "Treatises on the Ambassador Written in the Fifteenth and Early Sixteenth Centuries," *English Historical Review*, 51 (1936), 616–629.

Bell, G. M., "Elizabethan Diplomatic Compensation: Its Nature and Variety," *Journal of British Studies*, 20 (1981), 1–25.

Bell, G. M., "John Man: The Last Elizabethan Resident Ambassador in Spain," *Sixteenth Century Journal*, 7 (1976), 75–93.

Bentley, J., *Restless Bones: The Story of Relics* (1985).

Béthune, P. de, *The Counsellor of Estate* (1634).

Bielenstein, H., *Diplomacy and Trade in the Chinese World, 598–1276* (Boston, 2005).

Blanks, D. and Frassetto, M., eds., *Western Views of Islam in Medieval and Early Modern Europe* (New York, 1999).

Boardman, J., *The Greeks Overseas* (1980).

Boesche, R., "Kautilya's *Arthasastra*: on War and Diplomacy in Ancient India," *Journal of Military History*, 67 (2003), 9–37.

Bond, E., ed., *Russia at the Close of the Sixteenth Century* (1856).

Boucher, D., *Political Theories of International Relations* (Oxford, 1988).

Boyle, J. A., "The Il-khans of Persia and the Princes of Europe," *Central Asiatic Journal*, 20 (1976), 25–40.

Braddock, R. C., "The Rewards of Office-Holding in Tudor England," *Journal of British Studies*, 14 (1975), 29–47.

Brand, C. M., *Byzantium Confronts the West, 1180–1204* (Cambridge, MA, 1968).

Brand, C. M., ed./tr., *The Deeds of John and Manuel Comnenus by J. Cinnamus* (New York, 1976).

Brett, G., "The Automata in the Byzantine Throne of Solomon," *Speculum*, 29 (1954), 477–487.

Brown, C., Nardin, T., and Rengger, N., eds., *International Relations in Political Theory* (Cambridge, 2002).

Brown, J., "Courtiers and Christians: The First Japanese Emissaries to Europe," *Renaissance Quarterly*, 47 (1994), 872–906.

Brown, M., *Itinerant Ambassador: The Life of Sir Thomas Roe* (Lexington, KY, 1976).

Brown, N., *Hermes the Thief: The Evolution of a Myth* (2nd edition, New York, 1969).

Bull, H. et al., eds., *Hugo Grotius and International Relations* (Oxford, 1990).

Bury, J. P., "The Ceremonial Book of Constantine Porphyrogenetos," *English Historical Review*, 22 (1907), 209–227, 417–439.

Bury, J. P., "The Embassy of John the Grammarian," *English Historical Review*, 24 (1909), 296–299.

Busbecq, O. G. de, *The Four Epistles* (1694).

Butler, G. and Maccoby, S., *The Development of International Law* (1928).

Cameron, A., "The Construction of Court Ritual: the Byzantine Book of Ceremonies," in D. Cannadine amd S. Price, eds., *Rituals of Royalty: Power and Ceremonial in Traditional Societies* (Cambridge, 1987).

Carter, C., *The Secret Diplomacy of the Habsburgs, 1598–1625* (New York, 1964).

Chaplais, P., *English Diplomatic Practice in the Middle Ages* (2003).

Chaplin, J. E., *Subject Matter: Technology, the Body, and Science on the Anglo-American Frontier, 1500–1676* (Cambridge, MA, 2001).

Chardin, J., *Travels in Persia* (1927).

Chaytor, H. J., ed./tr., "Embajada Española: The Spanish Embassy," *Camden Miscellany XIV* (1926).

Chrysostomides, J., "Byzantine Concepts of War and Peace," in A. Hartmann and B. Heuser, eds., *War, Peace and World Orders in European History* (2001), 98–99.

Churchyard, T., *A Prayse and Reporte of Master Martin Frobisher's Voyage to Meta Incognita* (1578).

Clarke, T. B., *Omai, First Polynesian Ambassador to England* (Honolulu, HI, 1940).

Cleaves, F. W., *The Secret History of the Mongols* (1982).

Clot, A., *Harun al-Rashid and the World of the Thousand and One Nights* (New York, 1986).

Cohen, P., *History in Three Keys: The Boxers as Event, Experience and Myth* (New York, 1997).

Cohen, R., ed., *Amarna Diplomacy: The Beginnings of Diplomacy* (Baltimore, MD, 2000).

Collinson, R., ed., *The three voyages of Martin Frobisher in search of a passage to Cathay and India by the north-west, A.D. 1576–8* (Hakluyt Society, 1st series, 38, 1867).

Commines, P. de, *The Memoirs Containing the Histories of Louis XI and Charles VIII, Kings of France, and of Charles the Bold, Duke of Burgundy* (2 vols., 1882–1883).

Comnena, A., *The Alexiad of the Princess Anna Comnena*, tr. E. Dawes (1928).

Cosmo, N. Di, *Ancient China and its Enemies: The Rise of Nomadic Power in East Asian History* (Cambridge, 2002).

Cranmer-Byng, J. L. and Levere, T. E., "A Case Study in Cultural Collision: Scientific Apparatus in the Macartney Embassy to China, 1793," *Annals of Science*, 38 (1981), 503–525.

Curtin, P. D., *Cross-Cultural Trade in World History* (Cambridge, 1984).

Cutler, A., "Gifts and Gift Exchange as Aspects of the Byzantine, Arab, and Related Economies," *Dumbarton Oaks Papers* 55 (2001).

Dalton, P. J. H., ed., *The Golden Ass of Apuleius in the Translation of William Adlington* (1924).

Davies, C. S. L., *Peace, Print and Protestantism, 1450–1558* (1977).

Davies, D., *Elizabethans Errant: The Strange Fortunes of Sir Thomas Sherley and His Three Sons* (1967).

Day, J., Rowley, W., and Wilkins, G., *The Travels of the Three English Brothers*, in A. Parr, ed., *Three Renaissance Travel Plays* (Manchester, 1995).

Delpech, J., *The Life and Times of the Duchess of Portsmouth* (1953).

Dover, K., *Greek Homosexuality* (1978).

Eaves, R. G., and Simmons, R. E., "Anglo-Russian Relations in the European Diplomatic Setting, 1572–84," *New Review of East-European History*, 14 (1974), 117–130.

El Cheikh, N. M., *Byzantium Viewed by the Arabs* (Cambridge, MA, 2004).

Evans, J., "The Embassy of the 4th Duke of Bedford to Paris, 1762–3," *Archaeological Journal*, 113 (1956), 137–156.

Evans, N. E., "The Meeting of the Russian and Scottish Ambassadors in London in 1601," *Slavonic and East European Review*, 55 (1977), 517–528.

Fairbank, J., "Tributary Trade and China's Relations with the West," *The Far-Eastern Quarterly*, 1 (1941), 129–149.

Fairbank, J., ed., *The Chinese World Order: Traditional China's Foreign Relations* (Cambridge, MA, 1968).

Fleming, P., *The Siege at Peking* (Hong Kong, 1983).

Fletcher, R., *Moorish Spain* (1992).

Folz, R., *The Concept of Empire in Western Europe from the Fifth to the Fourteenth Century* (1969).

Foster, W., ed., *The Embassy of Sir Thomas Roe to the Court of the Great Mogul, 1614–1619* (Hakluyt Society Publications, 2nd Series, 1–2, 1899).

Frigo, D., ed., *Politics and Diplomacy in Early-Modern Italy: The Structure of Diplomatic Practice 1450–1800* (Cambridge, 2000).

Ganshof, F. L., *Histoire des relations internationales: le moyen age* (Paris, 1953).

Ganshof, F. L., *The Carolingians and the Frankish Monarchy* (1971).

Gellinek, C., *Hugo Grotius* (Boston, MA, 1983).

Giles, G., ed./tr., *Matthew Paris's English History* (3 vols., 1852–1854).

Gillingham, P., "The Macartney Embassy to China, 1792–94," *History Today*, 43 (1993), 28–34.

Glover, G., *The arrival and intertaiments of the embbassador Alkaid Jaurar Ben Abdella* (1637).

Goffman, D., *The Ottoman Empire and Early Modern Europe* (Cambridge, 2002).

Gordon, C., *The Age of Attila: Fifth Century Byzantium and the Barbarians* (Ann Arbor, MI, 1960).

Grabar, O., "The Shared Culture of Objects," in H. Maguire, ed., *Byzantine Court Culture from 829–1204* (Washington DC, 1997), 115–129.

Greenblatt, S., *Marvellous Possessions* (Chicago, 1991).

Hakluyt, R., *The Principal Navigations, Voyages, Traffiques and Discoveries of the English Nation* (12 volumes, Glasgow, 1903–5).

Hall, E., *Inventing the Barbarian* (Oxford, 1989).

Hansom, J. S., "Proceedings Against Catholics for Attending Mass at the Spanish Embassy on Palm Sunday, 1614," *Miscellanea VII* (Catholic Record Society Publications, 9, 1911).

Harris, J., *Byzantium and the Crusades* (2003).

Hartley, J., "'Losing My Best Days': Charles Whitworth, first British Ambassador to Russia," *History Today*, 50 (2000), 40–46.

Hartman, A. and Heuser, B., eds., *War, Peace and World Orders in European History* (2001).

Hevia, J., *Cherishing from Afar: Qing Guest Ritual and the Macartney Embassy of 1793* (Durham, NC, 1995).

Hibbert, C., *King Mob: The Story of Lord George Gordon and the Riots of 1780* (1958).

Holt, T. G., "The Embassy Chapels in Eighteenth-Century London," *London Recusant*, 2 (1972), 19–37.

Horn, D. B., *The British Diplomatic Service 1689–1789* (Oxford, 1961).

Houbon, H., *Roger II of Sicily: A Ruler Between East and West* (Cambridge, 2002).

Howard, C., *English Travellers of the Renaissance* (1923).

Huges, L., *Peter the Great* (Yale, 2002).

Jones, D. M., *The Image of China in Western Social and Political Thought* (Basingstoke, 2001).

Jones, C. P., *Kinship Diplomacy in the Ancient World* (Cambridge, MA, 1999).

Joannes, F., *The Age of Empires: Mesopotamia in the First Millennium B.C.* (Edinburgh, 2000).

Kaplan, B., "Diplomacy and Devotion: Embassy Chapels and the Toleration of Religious Dissent in Early Modern Europe," *Journal of Early Modern History*, 6 (2002), 341–361.

Kautilya, *Arthashastra*, ed./tr., R. Shamasastry (Bangalore, 1915).

Keen, M., *The Laws of War in the Late Middle Ages* (1965).

Kendall, P., and Ilardi, V., *Dispatches with Related Documents of Milanese Ambassadors in France and Burgundy 1450–1483* (Athens, OH, 1970).

Kennedy, H., *The Early Abbasid Caliphate* (1981).

Khadduri, W., *War and Peace in the Law of Islam* (Baltimore, MD, 1955).

King, P. D., *Charlemagne: Translated Sources* (1987).

Knolles, R., *The Generall Historie of the Turkes* (1603).

Kruger, H. C., "The Italian Cities and the Arabs before 1095," in K. Seton, ed., *History of the Crusades, I* (1969), 40–53.

Larson, A., "English Embassies During the Hundred Years War," *English Historical Review,* 55 (1940), 423–31.

Le Strange, G., ed./tr., *Clavijo: Embassy to Tamerlane 1403–1406* (1928).

Le Strange, G., "A Greek Embassy to Baghdad in 917 AD," *Journal of the Royal Asiatic Society,* 29 (1897), 35–485.

Lewis, B., *The Muslim Discovery of Europe* (1982).

Liverani, M., *Prestige and Interest: International Relations in the Near-East, c. 1600—1100 B.C.* (Padua, 1990).

Loades, D. M., *Charles V and the Ottomans* (Witney, 1998).

Lockhart, L., "The Relations Between Edward I and Edward II of England and the Mongol Il-khans of Persia," *Iran,* 6 (1968), 21–31.

Loewe, M., *A Biographical Dictionary of the Qin, Former Han and Xin Periods* (Leiden, 2000).

Luard, B., *The Balance of Power: The System of International Relations, 1648–1815* (1992).

Macmahon, L., "Courtesy and Conflict: The Experience of English Diplomatic Personnel at the Court of Francis I," in D. Grummitt, ed., *The English Experience in France, c. 1450–1558: War, Diplomacy and Cultural Exchange* (Aldershot, 2002), 182–199.

Maencken-Helfen, O. J., *The World of the Huns* (1973).

Majeska, G., "Russian Pilgrims to Constantinople," *Dumbarton Oaks Papers,* 56 (2002), 93–108.

Majumdar, R. C., *The Classical Accounts of India* (Calcutta, 1960).

Manz, B. F., *The Rise and Rule of Tamerlane* (Cambridge, 1989).

Martin, J., *Medieval Russia, 980–1584* (Cambridge, 1995).

Martin, W. A. P., *The Siege in Peking: China Against the World* (New York, 1900).

Matthew, D., *The Norman Kingdom of Sicily* (Cambridge, 1992).

Mattingly, G., *Renaissance Diplomacy* (1955).

Maulde-La-Clavijere, R., *La diplomatie au temps du Machiavel* (3 vols., Paris, 1892–1893).

Mauromatis, L., *La foundation de l'empire Serbe* (Thessaloniki, 1978).

Mauss, M., *The Gift: Forms and Functions of Exchange in Archaic Societies* (1966).

McClanahan, G., *Diplomatic Immunity: Principles, Practises, Problems* (1989).

McCormick, M., "Analyzing Imperial Ceremonies," *Jahrbuch der österrichischen Byzantinistik,* 35 (1985), 1–20.

McCrindle, J. W., *Ancient India as Described by Megasthenes and Arrian* (Calcutta, 1926).

Meier, S. A., *The Messenger in the Ancient Semitic World* (Atlanta, GA, 1988).

Mergiali-Sahas, S., "A Byzantine Ambassador to the West and His Office During the Fourteenth and Fifteenth Centuries," *Byzantinische Zeitschrift,* 94 (2001), 588–604.

Merriman, R. B., *Suleiman the Magnificent 1520–1566* (Cambridge, MA, 1944).

Michell, R. and Forbes, N., ed./tr., *The Chronicle of Novgorod* (1914).

Millar, F., "Government and Diplomacy in the Roman Empire during the First Three Centuries," *International Historical Review,* 10 (1988), 345–377.

Miller, D. A., "The Logothete of the Drome in the Middle Byzantine Period," *Byzantion,* 36 (1966), 438–470.

Morgan, D., *The Mongols* (Oxford, 1986).

Morton, W. L., ed., *The Amarna Letters* (Cambridge, MA, 1992).

Muir, E., *Civic Ritual in Renaissance Venice* (Princeton, NJ, 1981).

Muldoon, J., *Popes, Lawyers and Infidels* (Philadelphia, 1979).

Nicol, D. M., *Byzantium and Venice: A Study in Diplomatic and Cultural Relations* (Cambridge, 1988).

Nicolson, H., *The Congress of Vienna: A Study in Allied Unity: 1812–1822* (1946).

Nicolson, H., *The Evolution of Diplomatic Method* (1954).

Nixon, A., *The Three English Brothers* (1602).

Obolensky, D., "The Principles and Methods of Byzantine Diplomacy," in *Byzantium and the Slavs: Collected Studies* (1971), 43–61.

Oliphant, J., "The Cherokee Embassy to London, 1762," *Journal of Imperial and Commonwealth History*, 27 (1999), 1–26.

Ostrogorsky, G., "The Byzantine Emperor and the Hierarchical World Order," *Byzantion*, 19 (1956–57), 1–14.

Ostrogorsky, G., *History of the Byzantine State* (rev. ed., 1969).

Parkman, F., *The Jesuits in North America in the Seventeenth Century* (1997 edition, Lincoln, NE).

Parry, W., *A New and Large Discourse of the Travels of Sir Anthony Sherley* (1601).

Pollen, J. H., "Relation of a Brawl Between the King's Officers and Servants of the French Ambassador Concerning the Catholics who Restored to Mass at Durham House," *Miscellanea I* (Catholic Record Society Publications, I, 1905), 92–95.

Postgage, J. N., *Taxation and Conscription in the Assyrian Empire* (Rome, 1974).

Pufendorf, S., *On the Duty of Man and Citizen*, tr./ed. by H. Wright (New York, 1927).

Queller, D., *The Office of the Ambassador in the Middle Ages* (Princeton, NJ, 1967).

Queller, D., *The Fourth Crusade: The Conquest of Constantinople, 1201–1204* (1977).

Rachewiltz, I. de, "Some Remarks on the Ideological Foundations of Chinggis Khan's Empire," *Papers in Far-Eastern History*, 7 (1973), 21–36.

Ramsay, G. D., *The City of London in International Politics at the Accession of Elizabeth Tudor* (Manchester, 1975).

Rawlinson, H. G., "The Embassy of William Harborne to Constantinople, 1583–8," *Transactions of the Royal Historical Society*, 4th series, 5 (1922), 1–27.

Reilly, B. F., *The Medieval Spains* (Cambridge, 1993).

Rich, J. W., *Declaring War in the Roman Republic in the Period of Transmarine Expansion* (Brussels, 1976).

Richard, J, "The Mongols and the Franks," *Journal of Asian History*, 3 (1969), 45–57.

Richardi, J., *The Mughal Empire* (Cambridge, 1993).

Rockhill, W. W., ed./tr., *The Journey of William Rubruck to the Eastern Parts of the World, 1253–55, as Narrated by Himself, with Two Accounts of the Earlier Journey of John Pian de Carpine* (Hakluyt Society, 1900).

Rogers, B., ed., *Aristophanes* (Cambridge, MA, 1924).

Roosen, W., *The Age of Louis XIV: The Rise of Modern Diplomacy* (Cambridge, MA, 1976).

Roosen, W., "Early Modern Diplomatic Ceremonial: A Systems Approach," *Journal of Modern History*, 52 (1980), 452–476.

Ross, E. D., *Sir Anthony Sherley and his Persian Adventure* (1933).

Rowdon, M., *Lorenzo the Magnificent* (1974).

Runciman, S., *Byzantine Civilisation* (1933).

Russell, J. G., *The Field of Cloth of Gold: Men and Manners in 1520* (1969).

Sadler, J. W., *India and the Greek World: A Study in the Transmission of Culture* (Totowa, NJ, 1980).

Sarasin, V., *Tribute and Profit: Sino-Siamese Trade, 1652–1853* (Cambridge, MA, 1977).

Saunders, J. J., "Matthew Paris and the Mongols," in T. A. Sandquist and M. R. Powicke, eds., *Essays in Medieval History Presented to Bertie Wilkinson* (1969), 116–132.

Savory, R., *Studies in the History of Safawid Iran* (1987).

Schwoebl, R., *The Shadow of the Crescent: The Renaissance Image of the Turk (1453–1517)* (Niewkoop, 1967).

Seneviratna, A., ed., *King Asoka and Buddhism: Historical and Literary Studies* (Kandy, Sri Lanka, 1994).

Serrys, H., *Sino-Mongol Relations During the Ming* (Brussels, 1967).

Settle, D., *A True Reporte of the Laste Voyage into the West and Northwest Regions... Worthily Achieved by Capteine Frobisher* (1577).

Shaw, I., ed., *The Oxford History of Ancient Egypt* (Oxford, 2000).

Shennan, J. H., *International Relations in Europe 1689–1789* (1995).

Shepard, J. and Franklin, S., eds., *Byzantine Diplomacy* (Cambridge, 1990).

Sherley, A., *His Relation of his Travels into Persia* (1613).

Sinar, D., *Inner Asia and its Contacts with Medieval Europe* (1977).

Smith, L. P., *The Life and Letters of Sir Henry Wotton* (2 vols., Oxford, 1907).

Smith, V., *Asoka* (Oxford, 1901).

Southern, R.W., *Western Views of Islam in the Middle Ages* (1962).

Sparks, J., *Life of Benjamin Franklin* (1850).

Strachan, M., *Sir Thomas Roe, 1581–1644: A Life* (1989).

Strohmaier, G., "Umara ibn Hamza, Constantine V and the Invention of the Elxir," *Graeco-Arabica*, 14 (1991), 21–24.

Thapar, R., *Asoka and the Decline of the Mauryans* (Oxford, 1977).

Thompson, J. W., and Padover, S. K., *Secret Diplomacy: A Record of Espionage and Double-Dealing: 1500–1815* (1937).

Thomson, E. M., ed., *The Chamberlain Letters* (1966).

Thorpe, L., ed., *Two Lives of Charlemagne* (1969).

Thwaites, R. G., ed., *The Jesuit Relations and Allied Documents* (73 volumes, Cleveland, 1896–1901).

Thynne, F., *The Perfect Ambassador* (1652).

Tinnefield, F., "Ceremonies for Foreign Ambassadors at the Court of Byzantium," *Byzantinische Forschungen*, 19 (1993), 193–213.

Toby, R. P., *State and Diplomacy in Early Modern Japan* (Princeton, NJ, 1984).

Tongas, G., *L'Ambassadeur Louis Deshayes de Cormenin* (Paris, 1937).

Torday, L., *Mounted Archers: The Beginnings of Central Asian History* (Bishop Auckland, 1997).

Toynbee, A., *Constantine Porphyrogenitus and His World* (Oxford, 1973).

Trimble, W. R., "The Embassy Chapel Question, 1625–60," *Journal of Modern History*, 18 (1946), 97–107.

Vaiou, M., "The Diplomatic Relations Between the Abbasid Caliphate and the Byzantine Empire: Methods and Procedures," Unpublished D.Phil. Thesis (Oxford, 2001).

Vattel, E., *The Law of Nations or the Principles of Natural Law*, ed./tr. by J. Chitty (Philadelphia, 1883).

Villehardouin, G. De, *Memoirs or Chronicle of the Fourth Crusade and the Conquest of Constantinople*, tr./ed., F. T. Marzials (1908).

Vogt, A., *Le livre de ceremonies* (Paris, 1935).

Wace, H., ed., "Life of Constantine," in *Library of Nicene and Post-Nicene Fathers, Second Series, Volume I* (Grand Rapids, MI, 1890).

Wallace, M. B., "Early Greek *Proxenoi*," *Phoenix*, 24 (1970), 189–208.

Wallis Budge, E. A., *The Monks of Kublai Khan* (1928).

Watson, A., *The Evolution of International Society* (1992).

Widerman, T., "The Fetiales: A Reconsideration," *Classical Quarterly*, 36 (1986), 478–480.

Wiet, G., *Baghdad: Metropolis of the Abbasid Caliphate* (Norman, OK, 1971).

Wood, A., *The History of the Levant Company* (Cambridge, 1935).

Wood, F., *The Silk Road: Two Thousand Years in the Heart of Asia* (2004).

Woodcock, *The Greeks in India* (1966).

Woodrow, Z., "Imperial Ideology in Middle Byzantine Court Culture," Unpublished PhD Thesis, University of Durham, 2001.

Wright, F. A., ed., *The Works of Liudprand of Cremona* (1930).

Yu, Y-S., *Trade and Expansion in Han China* (Berkeley, CA, 1967).

Yurdusev, A. N., ed., *Ottoman Diplomacy: Conventional or Unconventional?* (2004).

INDEX